Amma's Daughters

Our Lives: Diary, Memoir, and Letters

Social history contests the construction of the past as the story of elites—a grand narrative dedicated to the actions of those in power. Our Lives seeks instead to make available voices from the past that might otherwise remain unheard. By foregrounding the experience of ordinary individuals, the series aims to demonstrate that history is ultimately the story of our lives, lives constituted in part by our response to the issues and events of the era into which we are born. Many of the voices in the series thus speak in the context of political and social events of the sort about which historians have traditionally written. What they have to say fills in the details, creating a richly varied portrait that celebrates the concrete, allowing broader historical settings to emerge between the lines. The series invites materials that are engagingly written and that contribute in some way to our understanding of the relationship between the individual and the collective. Manuscripts that include an introduction or epilogue that contextualizes the primary materials and reflects on their significance will be preferred.

Series Titles

Amma's
Daughters

Meenal
Shrivastava

a memoir

AU PRESS

Copyright © 2018 Meenal Shrivastava
Published by AU Press, Athabasca University
1200, 10011 – 109 Street, Edmonton, AB T5J 3S8
ISBN 978-1-77199-195-7 (pbk.)   ISBN 978-1-77199-196-4 (PDF)
ISBN 978-1-77199-197-1 (epub)   doi: 10.15215/aupress/9781771991957.01

www.ammasdaughters.com

Cover image © Jessica Sharmin and Jovana Milanko / Stocksy.com
Cover design by Natalie Olsen, kisscutdesign.com
Interior design by Sergiy Kozakov
Promotional website design by Darren Johnston, Grit Multimedia
Printed and bound in Canada by Marquis Book Printers

Library and Archives Canada Cataloguing in Publication

Shrivastava, Meenal, 1971-, author
    Amma's daughters : a memoir / Meenal Shrivastava.

(Our lives: diary, memoir, and letters)
Includes bibliographical references.
Issued in print and electronic formats.

    1. Shrivastava, Meenal, 1971- —Family. 2. Gandhi, Mahatma, 1869-1948. 3.
India—Politics and government—1919-1947. 4. India—History—Autonomy and
independence movements. I. Title. II. Series: Our lives (Edmonton, Alta.)

DS480.45.S57 2018   954.03'5   C2018-900965-9
                                         C2018-900966-7

We acknowledge the financial support of the Government of Canada for our
publishing activities and the Canada Council for the Arts, which last year invested
$153 million to bring the arts to Canadians throughout the country. Assistance is
also provided by the Government of Alberta through the Alberta Media Fund.

For Amma's great-granddaughters, Aditi, Adya, and Ananya— may you lead your lives with courage, compassion, and conviction.

And for Zoleka V. Ndayi, my willful goddaughter—may you rest in power.

We live by stories, we also live in them. One way or another we are living the stories planted in us early or along the way, or we are also living the stories we planted—knowingly or unknowingly—in ourselves. We live stories that either give our lives meaning or negate it with meaninglessness.

Ben Okri, *A Way of Being Free*

Contents

Preface

In the early 1990s, when I was a student of modern Indian history, women were seldom mentioned in connection with the events that shaped the new nation. The relatively few who appeared in the historical literature were for the most part the wives or sisters or daughters or nieces of prominent independence activists—women who found themselves in the middle of massive social and political upheaval and were sometimes thrust into positions of leadership, often when their more famous male relative happened to be in jail. Only many years later did I discover, to my surprise, that of the more than eighty thousand people arrested during the civil disobedience of 1930–31, some seventeen thousand, or better than one in five, were women. And yet, for the most part, the stories of these women—women who had the courage of their convictions and went to prison for it—are lost to memory.

In the quest for social justice, a story can be a powerful tool of intellectual and emotional persuasion, in its ability to move from one perspective to another, to render history immediate and personal, and to immerse us in the experience of oppression. Stories can also reclaim what standard histories have conspired to erase, as well as shedding light on the mechanisms of this erasure. In the process, such stories do more than fill in empty pages in the historical record. They alter the lens through which we view the past, while they also provide a solid historical grounding that can help us better understand the persistence of inequality and injustices in a society.

Among the seventeen thousand women arrested in 1930 and 1931 was a twelve-year-old girl. At the time, she was known as Shanti, although she was later given the name Prakashwati. This girl was my mother's mother—her Amma. I never really knew my grandmother: she died when I was still an infant. But, from the time she was only eight, she kept diaries, and she also wrote an autobiography, published when she was in her mid-forties. My mother, Surekha Sinha, the younger of Amma's two daughters, long intended to write her own account of her mother's life, as seen from the perspective of a daughter. But she also wanted to complete the story—to write about family relationships, about her father, who was hardly mentioned in her mother's autobiography, and her older sister and about how their lives unfolded up to the time of Amma's death. Sadly, that book remained unwritten.

Amma's Daughters is that book, the one my late mother never found an opportunity to write. I wrote it in her voice because it is her account, not my own. As one of Amma's daughters, she came to know some of the women whom history has largely forgotten—her mother's friends from the days of the freedom struggle. And, through her mother's recollections, she met some of the men whose names have most certainly not been forgotten—Dr. Rajendra Prasad, Jawaharlal Nehru, and, above all, Mahatma Gandhi, in whose ashram at Sevagram she spent the better part of a decade. Through her eyes, we also witness the sometimes futile struggle of women to escape confinement within their families, first as daughters and then as wives, and to overcome countless centuries of oppression.

This, then, is not merely a narrative account of my grandmother's life: it is a story about a family. Beyond that, it is the story of some of the many otherwise ordinary women who were quietly extraordinary—women who insisted on opening up space in which their children could continue to redefine the boundaries of freedom, for themselves and for others.

Meenal Shrivastava (née Sinha)
North Saanich, June 2018

A Note on Forms of Address

In India, kinship terms are generally placed after a person's name, rather than before. Thus, "Shankar chacha" is the Hindi equivalent of "Uncle Shankar." As the list below indicates, however, kinship terms frequently distinguish younger from older and paternal from maternal relatives. A *chacha,* for example, is a father's younger brother—so "Shankar chacha" would not be used for an uncle who is older than one's father. To complicate matters further, kinship terms can also used be to address people who are not, in fact, kin, as a sign of respect or endearment. Although this tradition has weakened somewhat in modern urban India, it is still quite common to refer to friends of one's parents by appending a generic term for "uncle" or "aunt" to their name. Amma's daughters thus refer to their mother's friend Kamala as "Kamala mausi," Auntie Kamala.

As one would expect, Surekha and her sister refer to their parents as "Mummy" and "Daddy"—Amma and Babu. But, in India, the use of a kinship term in place of a family member's given name extends well beyond the familiar "mother" and "father." For example, Surekha calls her sister Didi, "older sister," while their uncle addresses their mother as Bhabhi, "brother's wife."

Here, then, are the kinship terms that appear in the book:

bahuria	daughter-in-law
bapu	father
behen	sister
bitiya	daughter

bhabhi	brother's wife
bhai	brother
bhaiya	elder brother
bua	father's sister
chacha	father's younger brother
chachi	father's younger brother's wife
dada	paternal grandfather
dadi	paternal grandmother
didi	elder sister
jija	sister's husband
kaka	uncle
mama	mother's brother
mami	mother's brother's wife
mausi	mother's sister

India also abounds with honorific forms of address, such as *saheb* ("sir") or *bai* ("miss") in Rajasthan. Perhaps the most universal of these honorifics is the suffix *-ji,* which can be added to the names of both men and women. Like many people of her generation who were influenced by Gandhian ideals, Amma taught her daughters to use *-ji* even when referring to people of humble status, as a reminder that everyone, regardless of their social position, deserves to be honoured.

Amma's Daughters

1

Dislocations

JAIPUR, 1953

Babu is attacking the side of a mountain with a heavy mace. He swings the long wooden club in a wide arc and smashes it down on the rock, shattering it into large pieces the same silver-grey colour as his hair. They cascade down the jagged slope, like thunder rolling across the sky. The next swing brings the head of the mace close to my face, and on it I now see Amma's features. I wake up with a scream stuck in my throat.

I opened my eyes to discover a high ceiling, stretching like a bone-white canopy above my mother's single bed, so cool and soft. A brown and black cotton rug, woven by inmates of Jaipur's central jail, where Amma taught classes in the evenings, was all that separated her overstuffed mattress from the sandstone floor. From where I lay I could see the stern, straight-backed wooden chair that sat before her teak writing desk, piled high as usual with papers and files. No mountain—only the two floor-to-ceiling bookshelves, jammed with books, that flanked her desk, and the stout wrought-iron trunk in the corner, where Amma stored her clothes. On the window above the desk, the familiar batik curtains framed the world beyond in azure folds. But something felt different.

I craned my neck toward the open double doors, straining to hear any sound from the courtyard. Nothing—except the stillness of a summer afternoon when the breath of the earth shimmers in a hot haze. This almost eerie silence forced away the last traces of sleep, and with wakefulness came a vague recollection of last night—Babu's muffled anger barely audible through the wooden panels of the door to Amma's room, Didi and me hovering anxiously on the other side. Babu's outbursts, especially when directed at Amma, always terrified us. Fully awake now, I wondered if my father had left us again.

I sat up, brushed the hair out of my eyes, and emerged from Amma's cool room into the silent white heat of the courtyard. My steps took me across the courtyard and into Babu's room at the other end. It was bigger than Amma's but felt emptier, despite the infinitely larger number of books, overflowing more bookshelves than I could count, and his beloved harmonium. Unlike Amma, whose capacious desk always bore signs of activity, Babu wrote at a narrow wooden school desk with nothing more than an unused inkwell on it. The simple desk was paired with an equally plain wooden chair.

It was impossible to tell whether my father's bare wooden bed had been slept in. It had only a square block of granite for a pillow and no mattress. The white khadi-cotton sheet, all that was allowed to cover the planks in the warmer months, was neatly folded at the foot. But then I noticed Babu's indoor footwear, a pair of wooden *khadau,* tucked under the bed, while his shoes were missing. This was the only clue that he was not at home.

I turned away just in time to see Mangi bai hurry out of the kitchen from the other side of the courtyard. Her lined face stretched into a toothy smile as she approached, and I could tell that she had been looking for me. "You are up, my little one!" Amma's trusty cook—or, as Amma liked to put it, our "home minister"—crouched down in front of me.

The arrested scream, the one that had lingered after my nightmare, now escaped my throat as a strangled cry, and the sound as it echoed in the empty courtyard startled me. I stumbled forward into Mangi bai's wiry frame, almost knocking her over, but she stood up and steadied us both.

"What's wrong?" she asked. She smelled of freshly cooked rotis and *beedi,* the aroma of wood smoke and dough blending with that of the tobacco. "Are you hungry?"

I swallowed, determined to find speech. The rotis could wait. Unformed questions spat out, in a confused mixture of Marwari and Hindi. "Where is Didi? Did Babu take her for a walk without me? Why didn't anyone wake me up?" But Mangi bai didn't understand my verbal barrage, and I got no answers. I wanted to head next door, to Bai ki ma's house, to find someone else, anyone else. But I knew I could not leave until Mangi bai had given me a wash, so I allowed her to lead me to the nearby brass mug and bucket and to soak me from head to toe. The water was unpleasantly warm, despite having been stored in a cement tank in the shade.

I didn't cooperate. Secretly, I enjoyed this battle of wills with Mangi bai, only possible when Amma was not around to put me in line with a stern look and a reminder to act like a "big girl." After the wash, Mangi bai had to hold me by one arm in order to dress me. She loosened her grip to reach for the jasmine hair oil and the wide-toothed comb, and I broke free, darting away, my wet hair snaking around my shoulders. I could hear her cursing as I darted out of our courtyard to head next door, but she did not chase me.

Bai ki ma's courtyard was enclosed behind a wall that had massive double doors. The brass knockers and heavy wooden bolts jangled and creaked whenever the doors turned on their hinges. I leaned hard to push them open and then entered, only to discover Amma, who was sitting in a chair under an awning. Jain saheb, the head of the family, stood a few feet away from her. They had obviously been talking but had probably stopped when they heard the noise of the doors.

Wet grass curtains enclosed the halls that bordered the courtyard, keeping the inner rooms cool. I inhaled the sweet vetiver fragrance—like earth after a monsoon. On the other side of those certains, Jain saheb's wife, Bai ki ma, and their oldest daughter, Bai, were probably busy as usual. I imagined them at work, tending to their endless housekeeping and child-rearing chores, their broad foreheads gently furrowed, the bangles on their wrists jingling melodiously, their petite frames bent, burdened by layers of clothing, children, and jewellery.

Bai already had a younger sister, Poorna, as well as two younger brothers, and Bai ki ma had recently given birth to another daughter, Nisha. The two sons, Ravi and Uday were enrolled at an all-boys school that served the business community of Jaipur, and they were already learning to help their father with the family jewellery business. My mother had managed to persuade Jain saheb that his daughters also needed an education, and so Bai, who was a few years older than my sister, Didi, was learning to read and write from a young man who visited their home several evenings a week. The two had to be separated by a curtain at all times, and the younger children helped by passing notebooks between them. Luckily for me, Jain saheb had decided to let his second daughter attend the girls' school that my mother ran—the Shri Veer Balika Vidyalaya. Poorna was in my class, and she was my best friend.

I ran over to Amma and dived into her cozy lap. She didn't push me off, but she chided me gently for being too big, seven-year-old that I was. Babu could still swing me onto his shoulders with one arm, I protested.

Amma responded with a frown: "Aren't you forgetting something? What about greeting your elders?" There was no point arguing, so I slid down her lap and stepped over toward Jain saheb, then bowed low with my hands folded. He chuckled and bent down equally low, bringing his face level with my own.

The ritual complete, I turned again to Amma, who looked at me with the same sad smile I'd seen the night before. And then, suddenly, my world fell apart.

"We will be moving away soon," she told me, "to a city called Lucknow. It's a beautiful place, much like Jaipur, and you'll like our new home there."

"But we have a home here!" My voice was louder than I expected. I glared at her in disblief. "Where is this Lucknow?" The reply came: about 350 miles east of Jaipur.

"But what about Poorna?" I cried. "And Bai ki ma, and Anita, and Pramila, and ..." Desperately, I listed all of the friends and aunties I could not live without. But Amma was unmoved. Didi had been told the news earlier in the day, she explained, and I would need to help with packing. Didi and Babu had already begun, she added.

I wanted to shout at her that neither of them was even at home, that they were probably out on a walk without me. I was angry with her for never going on these walks with us. And now she wanted to drag us hundreds of miles away from our home, our neighbours, our friends, and our school. Away from the secret grove of sandalwood trees in the Ram Niwas Garden, Babu's favourite place to rest after our walks, and the sprawling lawns surrounding the majestic Albert Hall Museum.

I folded my arms across my chest and inhaled deeply, reaching for my most grown-up voice, but all that emerged were a few inarticulate sounds of protest. My mother remained still, patient, as I struggled for words. Finally, some part of what had been building up inside me burst out: "And who is going to run the school? Have you thought about that?" The one thing clear in my mind was that a new home in another city would also mean an entirely new school. My school was the centre of my world. "And is Mangi bai coming to this Lucknow with us? Is that why Babu was so angry last night?"

"This was *his* decision," Amma said. "He has accepted a teaching position in Shillong, and I have taken a government job in Lucknow. So we have to move soon." Her tone was firm.

"Rekha." Bai ki ma's voice startled me. From behind the curtains she called out once more: "Rekha, come here."

When Amma was not around, Bai ki ma became our mother, spoiling Didi and me with stories, hugs, and our favourite foods. Invisible to the outside world, she was the one person who made Amma's occasional absences bearable to me. I was taken aback now by her voice, which carried through the vetiver curtain. Obedient to her command, I removed my sandals and then climbed the one step up onto the cool marble floor of the hall.

It took a moment for my eyes to adjust to the darkness of the hall behind the curtains. Once they did, I was surprised to discover Didi sitting on the big swing there. She was leaning against Bai ki ma, whose face, as I could now see, glistened with tears. I watched them, perplexed, until Bai ki ma held out her arms to draw me into the circle of warmth.

Nearly two weeks later, Didi and I were on the railway platform in Jaipur with Amma, waiting to board the overnight train to Lucknow, our luggage already safely stowed in our compartment by porters. Several of the school trustees and members of the board of education had come to the station to bid us farewell. Amma acknowledged kind words, good wishes, and sad faces with folded hands but few words. The red dot of *kumkum* on her forehead, applied in farewell blessings by the tearful aunties who had gathered earlier at Bai ki ma's house, had cracked in many places under the strain of Amma's worried frown. Poorna and I had exchanged our favourite dolls when I last saw her, and now her soft, fabric doll, neatly dressed in a *salwar-kamiz,* felt reassuringly solid in the crook of my arm. I had fought with both Mangi bai and Amma, who wanted to pack away the small figure. I kept thinking I could hear Babu call my name. Every now and then I even thought I could see his big head of closely cropped silver hair bobbing in the crowd. But it was never him.

Finally, the three of us climbed onto the train and settled into our compartment. The two large holdalls occupied most of one of the two upper berths, and the trunks were pushed under our two lower berths. Didi and Amma sat down next to each other on the lower berth, and I sat on the one opposite them, turned away from the receding faces in the window, studying the embroidered face of my new favourite doll. I looked up and out of the window only when the air changed from heavy and metallic to gusty and light as Jaipur's densely crowded buildings gave way to a broad sandy landscape occasionally broken by green fields. Now that our journey was underway, I tried repeatedly to draw Amma and Didi's attention to the many interesting things in our compartment. I checked out the mechanics of the folding table and then climbed into the empty upper berth and made faces at Didi, hoping to provoke a reaction. When she refused to rise to the bait, I ran out into the passage to count the number of compartments. I counted eight in a row. At either end of the passage, there were two toilets with sinks and two outside sinks with mirrors that were both too high for me to reach. Finally, Didi interrupted my running around and noisy chatter by coming out into the passage and grabbing my wrist. She pointed to the rather humourless-looking men who were trying to read newspapers in their quiet compartments as she dragged me back to our own. I reluctantly returned to my seat and then resumed my excited commentary, this time focused on the landscape speeding by outside the window. But even my love of train rides couldn't draw Amma and Didi out of their silence. Soon the gathering dusk enveloped the vanishing countryside, which added to the general gloom in our little compartment.

Didi was only three and a half years older than I was, but she was often more serious-minded than some of the adults in my life. Although she was a little young, she insisted on always wearing a sari. She received many compliments, some wanted and some unwanted, for her large almond-shaped eyes, beautifully accented by heavy lids, her light skin and glowing complexion, and her elegant demeanour. She tamed her long wavy dark-brown hair into two dainty braids, the ends of which she twisted between her fingers when she was agitated. She was doing this now.

Didi's saris weren't as long and wide Amma's, but they were in the same simple style, a white expanse of cotton bordered by colourful threads woven into a geometric or floral design. Amma threw the *pallu* of her sari carelessly over her head, but Didi pinned the long end of hers fashionably over her left shoulder.

I liked the idea of wearing a sari, but it got in the way of riding my bike. When I wasn't wearing my school uniform of skirt and blouse, I preferred the loose trousers and long shirt of the *salwar-kamiz*. Normally, Didi laughed at my failed attempts to pin and knot the long dupatta out of my way. She said there wasn't enough flesh on my body to hold my clothes in place.

I caught myself swinging my legs and cast a quick look at Amma, braced for disapproval. But behind her glasses with their pointed corners, Amma's eyes were fixed on the fat book she'd been holding since the train left the station. Her long black hair, streaked with grey, tied as usual into a tight bun, was partially hidden under the *pallu* of her sari. Beside her on the seat was her khadi-cloth shoulder bag—her portable repository of books, writing pads, pencils and pens, change purse, handkerchief, and packet of salted and roasted nuts "just in case." When she was not reading, as now, or writing, Amma was always hurrying somewhere or talking to someone in her firm, even voice. I felt Amma's presence even when she was somewhere else, busy dealing with the needs of the hundreds of other people who also called her "Amma," but sometimes I was not sure I knew her.

What a contrast she made with Babu! Clad in homespun dhoti and kurta, his six-foot-tall former body-builder frame exuded an air of superiority and authority. I was sure of his love when he was with us, but every one of his frequent, inexplicable absences from our lives still made me apprehensive while it lasted. When he was at home, Babu would sit poring over books for long periods of time, entirely quiet, until he suddenly decided to use his booming voice to dramatic effect. Perhaps he was compensating for his nearly deaf left ear. His sonorous oration made the folktales stories of the *Panchatantra* and the legends of the *Mahabharata* come alive. I could almost hear him now, reciting and then explaining a Sanskrit *shloka*:

> *sarve bhavantu sukhinaḥ sarve santu nirāmayāḥ |*
> *sarve bhadrāṇi paśyantu mā kaścid duḥkhabhāg bhavet ||*

> May all be happy, all be without disease;
> May all behold the good, and none be sorrowful.

Babu's resounding voice always made me wonder which god would ever dare ignore his invocation.

The surest way to make Babu read aloud was to sit in his lap when he was reading at his desk. Some evenings, when he was home, he would take up his harmonium, which he loved as much as his books. He played it ever so softly to accompany the words of Meera Bai's devotional poems, written five hundred years before. When he sang, Babu closed his eyes and tilted his head to one side, his good ear slightly bent toward the harmonium. His deep bass voice became a murmur like a breeze haunting a deep valley, so unlike the clickety-clack of the train I was now on, passing through darkness that seemed like an unending tunnel. I missed Babu and his music now more than ever, and I wondered when we would see him again.

Amma read my mind better than the book in her lap. She looked up from it now to remind us of the many times that Babu hadn't returned from work or his morning walk. Of how he would disappear for days on end, only to reappear with total nonchalance. Of the excuses she would make for his absences to his colleagues and our neighbours. Didi and I had always known better than to ask Amma for more than whatever excuse she was prepared to provide.

Amma also reminded us of the elation we always felt when he returned. She told us to hold on to that feeling until we saw him again. Unlike his work at the newspaper, which had allowed him little time off, his new job at the government college in Shillong came with regular holidays that he could spend with us if he chose. Babu was on another train at this very moment, also heading east, but he would go much farther than Lucknow. He would travel to the northeastern reaches of the Himalayas, to the abode of clouds.

Amma's assurances about holidays made me feel better. She explained that Babu had been unhappy about the changes at the newspaper where he'd been working. It was losing sight of the ideals it once supported and becoming more and more commercial, which made him angry. They both thought that he might be happier teaching at a college, and Shillong was a lovely, quiet spot, nestled among rolling hills. But it was not a large city, and she hadn't been able to find a suitable job there for herself. So, in the end, she had decided to accept a position in Lucknow—a long way from Shillong, but closer than Jaipur. Amma's new job was with the government of Uttar Pradesh, in its Social Welfare Department, she said, and it would give her an opportunity for public service. It would also include lots of travelling to different parts of UP, and, in the summers, we would have a chance to travel with her and see all sorts of new places.

"Will Babu come with us?" I tried to read her face.

"I hope so."

Amma fell silent again. I could see that her thoughts were elsewhere, as she gazed out the window into the darkness. So I asked her to tell us the story of our names, which always made me feel special. Amma dutifully repeated the familiar history, about how Didi was born on 14 November 1942, Nehruji's birthday, in Mahatma Gandhi's community at Wardha, almost five years before the struggle for independence finally bore fruit. When Gandhiji first saw her, he commented on her divine aura—*ābhā* in Sanskrit—which became her name.

My family moved to Jaipur three years later, and I was born soon after that, on 25 April 1946. Amma had accepted someone's suggestion to call me Rekha—a *rekhā* is a line or a boundary—since it is customary to give names to girls that signify an ending, symbolically expressing that the parents do not want any more daughters. But when Babu learned of my name, he was very angry and immediately wanted to change it. Amma had pleaded with him, saying that I already recognized Rekha as my name. "In that case," he had declared, "her name will be Surekha." In Sanskrit, the prefix *su-* means "beautiful."

This story usually made me feel special, but this time I realized that Babu had not been there when I was born—and perhaps not for a long time after. Amma read my thoughts again. "But we do manage well without him, don't we, my little soldiers?"

Didi responded by leaning her head heavily against Amma's shoulder. I left the doll on my seat and crossed the short distance between us to climb into my mother's lap. The joy I felt in the rocking movement of the lumbering train was double now, as I inhaled the smell of jasmine, soap, and old furniture that always emanated from Amma.

I loved it when Amma called us her little soldiers. One day I had scraped my knee badly while at school. I had cried, not so much from the pain, but at the sight of the blood, and I had sobbed, "Amma, Amma," as Verma Teacher cleaned the wound. She offered to take me to Amma's office, but I shook my head vigorously. So Verma Teacher allowed me to sit with Didi in her class for the rest of the day. Then, in the evening, once we were all at home together, Amma touched my knee. In that moment she showed more pain on her face than I had felt when I got hurt. She left her hand on my knee, and it seemed to radiate a soothing heat that warmed and soothed me, and she called me her brave little soldier. Her comforting touch now was as calming as ever.

My eyelids drooping, I murmured, "Yes, we will be all right. Babu will be fine. The school will be fine, and Mangi bai will be all right, too."

Mangi bai had wept when Amma told her we were moving to Lucknow. As far back as I could remember, Mangi bai had been a constant presence in our lives, efficiently bridging the gaps caused by Amma and Babu's periodic absences. Amma had invited Mangi bai to come with us to Lucknow, but she had refused, insisting that her home was in Jaipur. I thought now of my visits to the dark little room in the farthest corner of her brother's house that Mangi bai called her own. Sometimes Amma would scold Mangi bai for not standing up to her abusive relatives, who considered her inauspicious—a childless woman abandoned by her husband. Amma would grumble at Mangi bai's "false sense of social decorum," which forced her to return to that callous hearth at the end of each day, even when she could have stayed with us.

She had told Mangi bai that Lucknow could be a new beginning for her, as it would take her far from her family, who kept dipping into her savings. But Mangi bai had shaken her head and said she could not leave her home. Instead, she had helped us pack up our household, tears streaming down her cheeks.

As I snuggled into Amma's shoulder, I thought of all the people and places this train was rushing away from. I already missed my school—my second home, and the centre of our daily routine. I remembered how we used to arrive at school before anyone else each morning, how we would greet the gardener, Maliji, as he tended the grounds. Then Didi and I would play or read in Amma's office, while she marked the latest pile of assignments. I loved that time of day, when Amma's sari was still crisp and the breeze still cool. I sighed and took another deep breath.

The train rocked me into sleep's welcoming embrace, although the farewells of the day and the anxieties of our venture into the unknown soon leached into my dreams.

LUCKNOW, 1953

Amma looked and sounded right at home when we arrived in Lucknow just before noon. We had had a delicious breakfast of crisp vegetable bread cutlets and hot milky tea, after Amma and Didi had spent several minutes lifting me up to the sink in the passage to brush my teeth and wash my face. Even as we stepped down from the train, she was responding to greetings in a dialect that neither Didi nor I had ever heard. We were met by a small band of porters, led by a bespectacled man who introduced himself in Hindi as Deen Dayal Verma, Amma's personal assistant. Somehow, amid all the confusion, the porters had managed to fetch our luggage, the contents of which would keep us going until the rest of our household belongings arrived. As we emerged from the station, another man rushed up to greet us. This turned out to be our driver, who directed us toward a large white car, simultaneously shouting orders at the porters to be careful with the luggage. Deen Dayalji declined Amma's invitation to ride in the car with us; he said he would follow us on his bicycle.

I was mesmerized by the sight of the broad Gomti River, which flowed through this city of stately buildings, and by the magnificent walls and gateways enclosing lush gardens. The stonework on the buildings was as fine as exquisite embroidery. I pointed this stone embroidery out to Amma and then bit my tongue. But it was too late. Her history lesson began as the burly car rumbled through ancient cobbled avenues, turned down narrow streets, emerged abruptly into wide new roads.

Amma always said that if we treated history like a good friend, then it did not have to be a stern teacher. If any building sported a plaque, Amma and Babu made us read it. We were not allowed to forget what we read, and we were expected to ask questions to find out more. I had learned a long time ago that the surest way to please them was to collect historical information on our visits to Jaipur's public library. Now Amma reeled off the lengthy history of this city and its exquisite buildings, explaining that Lucknow, now the capital of Uttar Pradesh, was once ruled by the Delhi Sultanate but had been absorbed into the Mughal Empire in the mid-sixteenth century, a legacy still visible in the poetic lines of the city's Persian architecture. As Mughal power waned, Lucknow had become the capital of the princely state of Awadh and the home of a series of wealthy nawabs, under whom the city flourished.

I was distracted by the new sights and sounds, but I tried at first to force myself to listen carefully—I knew there could be questions later, especially about Lucknow's recent history. The city was one of the sites of the Indian Rebellion of 1857, when sepoys rose up against the British East India Company, and had continued to play a prominent role in the independence movement. I could tell from the shift in Amma's tone of voice how important this story was to her. Thankfully, Amma did not seem to be paying attention to Didi and me, delivering her monologue as though she were lecturing to a class. Didi had long since stopped listening; she was too enthralled by the view from the car windows. I followed her lead and ignored Amma's lecture in favour of the chaotic but captivating scenes unfolding along our route.

Finally we arrived at a tree-lined avenue of neatly kept gardens punctuated by white bungalows, and the history lesson was over, for the time being. "Here we are in Civil Lines," Amma declared. She stressed the word "Civil" as though she were trying to blow out a small anise seed stuck in her teeth. It was clear in that moment that she found the name of our new community distasteful, although we did not then know the history of these enclaves built and named by the English, who seemed to consider themselves more "civil" than their Indian neighbours.

The car stopped in front of one of the bungalows, where an old man bowed deeply before opening the low wrought-iron gate for us to drive through. Despite his salt and pepper hair, Deen Dayalji managed to arrive just after us. He had ridden his bicycle with great agility, often darting into narrow lanes and re-emerging onto the main street just behind the car. Now leaning his bike against an enormous *ashok* tree, he caught sight of a man who was standing on the veranda with a tray of sherbet glasses. Deen Dayalji rushed toward the veranda, shouting instructions. We later learned that the wiry sherbet-man, clad in a dhoti-kurta and turban and, at this moment, perspiring in the humid heat of midsummer, was Ramu kaka, the cook. He had worked for many of the previous occupants of this government bungalow and hoped to be retained by Amma.

I took the glass of aromatic rose-syrup drink that Ramu kaka offered me and finished it in a few big gulps. Then I checked hastily to make sure that neither Amma nor Didi had witnessed my uncouth behaviour. Fortunately, Amma was busy talking to Deen Dayalji, who kept addressing her as "Sir" or "Saheb," even though she told him to call her either Behenji or Mrs. Sinha. Babu's name was Rajeshwar Narayan Sinha, but, back home, we'd never heard anyone call our mother "Mrs. Sinha." Deen Dayalji looked very nervous, avoiding eye contact with my mother, choosing instead to look down at his bush shirt or his leather sandals. He smiled openly, though, when he caught my eye.

Didi, meanwhile, assumed ladylike airs, emptying her glass in dainty sips, not casting a single glance in my direction. Even though Didi's sari was somewhat limp from the long train ride, she looked very elegant. Didi had spent several minutes in front of the little sink and mirror on the train, washing the sleep from her face, fixing her hair, and straightening the creases of her sari with a wet kerchief. Despite her many instructions, I had not cared to do anything beyond brushing my teeth and washing my face. I had even tussled with Didi a bit when she tried to tame my hair into a braid.

Now, however, I was acutely aware of my coarse, crumpled kurta. I wondered if Amma would find new "sewing ladies" in Lucknow. In Jaipur, Amma had sought out young widows, who were typically hidden away in the darkest corners of large family homes, often raising a couple of very young children. Whenever a sewing machine arrived—usually a donation coaxed from one of the many wealthy patrons of our school— Amma made sure that both Didi and I went along on her visit to the latest recipient. Amma would buy lengths of khadi fabric and teach each woman a few basic sewing skills, and sometimes Didi and I would have the honour of showing off how the machine worked. By way of a trial run, Amma would place an order for a kurta for me, reassuring the fledgling seamstress that it would fit as long as she made it loose and long. Then Amma would take me back to the sewing lady's home to try on my new clothes, and, as often as not, I would discover myself clad in a shapeless sack with crooked seams that could have accommodated me and a couple of friends. While she helped me change, Amma would look at me sternly and pinch me if I squirmed. Her earnest-sounding praise of the garment drowned out my complaints.

I considered the kurta I was wearing now, one of my dwindling stock of "sewing-lady" garments. Perhaps the seamstresses in Lucknow would be more gifted.

The veranda swing was the size of a bed, with decorative wooden barriers on three sides. I sat down, idly swinging my legs. This unseemly behaviour caught Amma's eye, but all she did was sit down next to me and take my hand. Then she called Didi over and instructed us both to follow Deen Dayalji because he was about to show all three of us the rest of the bungalow.

The bungalow was painted chalky-white inside and out. The large hall in the centre had two doors on each side and was big enough to serve as a living and dining room. There was even enough space for Amma's writing desk under one of the windows that looked out onto the veranda. The house had wide windows with metal bars, too large for me to open or close on my own. It was all very different from Jaipur, where houses had small outer windows and doors, designed to keep the desert heat and sandstorms out. In Jaipur, buildings stood close to each other, not separated by fences and gardens, and each one was home to many families who shared the various courtyards and terraces. They were full of people and noise. Rooms faced inward, onto bustling courtyards, whereas our new house was an outward-facing, rectangular island.

Amma explained to us that bungalows like these had been built for colonial administrators on the outskirts of most major cities in India. I gathered from the tone of her voice that Amma did not care much for the austere seclusion of the bungalow. But this was where we were to live, so Amma asked Didi and me to choose one of the three bedrooms each, without fighting.

"But if Didi and I have our own rooms, then what about Babu?" I asked.

Amma looked strangely sad. "The two of you will just have to share a room when Babu comes to visit us."

Ramu kaka was standing patiently at the far door that led to the small kitchen, waiting to ask about dinner. Amma told him to make whatever he had bought from the market that morning, as long as it was vegetarian. There was another building behind the bungalow, separated by a thicket of trees. "Servant quarters," explained Deen Dayalji when he found me looking at it from the kitchen window. Amma said it would remain locked and empty, since Ramu kaka preferred to return at the end of each day to his family, who lived on a farm nearby.

Outside the bungalow, flowerbeds full of jasmine and hibiscus bordered the lawn, and the thick hedge that surrounded the grass in front of the house was broken up by flamboyant *gulmohar* trees. In the back garden, mango and guava trees separated the servant's quarters from the bungalow.

I was happy to see that there were many nooks and crannies to explore but very aware that there was no Poorna to play with. Didi had already coldly declined my offer to play hide-and-seek. Instead she had grumpily asked Amma to find her a sitar tutor as soon as our belongings arrived from Jaipur, so she would not fall out of practice. Our new house was only sparsely furnished, and the rest of our belongings weren't due to arrive for several weeks. Without Amma's and Babu's books, Babu's harmonium, and Didi's sitar, the sombre bungalow was far from feeling like home.

Soon the periwinkle sky turned inky black. Nightfall was quieter and darker in this house. In Jaipur, our ground-floor rooms off the courtyard had had the soothing company of light and activity from the stairwell that connected the upper two floors. I missed the ceaseless sound of the movement of strange and familiar people, of baby gurgles and wails, children's games and fights, prayer songs and mantras, occasional theatrical outbursts both mock and earnest, water splashing from bucket baths, and kitchen noises of cutting, grinding, frying, stirring, and eating. The bungalow in Lucknow was almost eerie in its emptiness.

After dinner was served, Ramu kaka left for home, as did the *chowkidar,* Ram Bahadurji, who had been manning the gate, now locked for the night. Amma double-checked the heavy padlock and then asked Didi and me to join her on the swing in the veranda: she needed, she said, to meet with her cabinet. Babu, the president of our cabinet, was missing; however, Amma, the prime minister, had some things to discuss with her council of ministers. The three of us sat together in the dark, not moving, listening to the quiet.

Just as I began to wonder whether Amma and Didi were waiting for me to break the silence, which I considered my duty from time to time, a chorus of crickets started to chirp in the nearby hedges, and they were soon joined by the gleeful, throaty croaking of a frog in the farthest part of the garden. I liked frogs and had already noticed a couple of large green ones. The only frogs we had seen in Jaipur were the small brown toads that lived near lakes and reservoirs and sometimes strayed into our courtyard in the city during the monsoon season, so I decided to walk over to the boundary hedge to check on the source of the croaking. Amma anticipated and thwarted my movement with a firm hand on my wrist. "There might be a snake in the bushes."

"But I like snakes too," I protested, pouting.

Amma laughed, despite herself. "Instead of disturbing the creatures of night going about their business, sit down and pay attention. Tomorrow morning you will meet Kamala behenji, one of my freedom-fighter sisters. You have to call her Kamala mausi and be on your best behaviour. Her family home is here in Lucknow, and she has generously agreed to take care of the two of you in my absence."

Didi and I were not happy to hear this mention of absence. "We just got here," Didi pointed out. "And you are already planning to leave?"

Amma sighed. "This is why I was reluctant to take this position, but now that we are here, we will make it work, won't we?"

I nodded automatically, as I always did in response to Amma's orders, and Amma launched into a familiar account of Gandhiji's dream that women would be able to live as respected members of society and of Nehruji's recent welfare programs for women.

I had heard Amma explain to Jain saheb about the role of the newly constituted Social Welfare Departments in several of India's larger states and about Nehruji's vision for transforming the feudal elements of Indian society. I had long known that Amma admired Nehruji as much as Babu detested him. Babu thought he was a selfish man who couldn't see beyond his personal political ambitions. I had heard Amma defend Nehruji's plans to build factories and modernize India's economy, and I had seen Babu storm out of the room in response.

So I knew most of the lecture that was to follow: two hundred years of colonization, the extensive drain of India's wealth, and the ongoing battle for *swaraj*—the self-rule that Gandhiji had envisioned. But I dared not turn off my ears as Amma's volume rose. "What has the country's independence done for its women?" she asked, as if to demand an answer from the silent night. "We did all we could for the freedom of our country. We went to jail just like the men did." Amma was seldom angry for long, except when she started talking about social injustices.

But now a note of hope smoothed the edge of outrage in her voice. "In my new job," she explained, "I will design programs to train women in rural areas. These programs will give women another opportunity for *swaraj,* true independence, especially to women who are too poor even to have the stifling walls of a family home as a refuge." She paused for a moment to look from Didi to me. We were listening. "But I need the help of my cabinet to do this difficult task."

Amma had already warned us that her new job would involve setting up new offices and facilities in the Lucknow, Kanpur, and Jhansi divisions, which would require travel. Now she told us that every month she would be expected to spend three weeks in the regional training centres and touring the field, with only one week in the office in Lucknow.

"Only a week at home," I mumbled.

"Yes, but during school holidays we can travel together. In the summer months, I will have to be at the training centre at Jeolikot, up in the mountains near Nainital. Won't that be fun?" Amma drew us closer to her, but there was no sense of anticipation in her voice.

Despite the frogs' best efforts to disturb it, silence crept over our cabinet meeting again. I wondered if Babu had left us because Amma now worked for Nehruji's government. But I wasn't sure how to ask her.

Babu would curse any Congress Party leader whom Amma referred to as her freedom-fighter brother or whose public work she tried to tell him about. His vehement dislike of Nehruji, our prime minister, extended to our president, Dr. Rajendra Prasad, and his wife, with whom Amma was acquainted. Whenever Amma mentioned Dr. Prasadji, Babu would launch into a diatribe about a good man allowing himself to sit at the head of a table of thieves. Whenever Amma was summoned to Delhi to help the president's wife host an event or celebrate a festival, Babu would tell her that she could do as she pleased, while denouncing her association with the couple, calling her another blind loyalist who had forgotten the reasons for the fight for freedom, a fight that was far from over.

Babu's fiery pronouncements were always followed by a sullen, silent phase, during which Amma would make her case for attending a particular event or speaking engagement. Her lengthy explanations often ended in a measure of grudging reconciliation, with Babu helping her polish a speech or draw up an itinerary. But his outbursts of anger could be terrifying. In Jaipur, his powerful voice had resonated effortlessly through the walls and courtyards of our home, sometimes startling our neighbours even when he was speaking in normal tones. But when he raised his voice in anger, it was like a thunderclap. Although he mostly kept it contained, I knew that Babu's anger ran deep. I had seen it whenever he read the newspaper or discussed politics and social issues with Amma. Sometimes I saw it even when it was invisible—when he didn't come home for days on end.

I thought about this now. "Why is Babu so angry, Amma?"

"Your Babu wanted something different—not just independence but a total revolution. Now he has to work through his disillusionment after a lifetime of sacrifices, his own and those of the people he looked up to. But you must remember that your Babu loves both of you more than anything in this world."

"He has a strange way of showing it," Didi muttered.

Amma tried to placate her. "You know how he is—his anger is like a burst of camphor fire, hot but short, no ash left behind."

But we all knew that fire burns, however brief it may be.

The next morning, it was evident that Amma had not slept much. After unpacking the luggage that had come with us from Jaipur, she had worked most of the night to prepare for the first day of her new job. Before leaving, she also prepared us for Kamala mausi's arrival, with a lecture on how even educated, middle-class women often struggled under the burden of oppressive customs and traditions.

As a young girl, Amma told us, Kamala mausi had been home-schooled to read and write both Hindi and English, and she had taken a special interest in literature from an early age. But her keen mind and her talent for writing poetry had not prevented her father from marrying her off at the age of twelve to a man in his early twenties, also from Lucknow, who was studying law.

By the time Kamala mausi was old enough to live with her husband in his family home, he had become very involved in the freedom struggle, abandoning his law practice. Her in-laws taunted her for her dark skin and stout body and made it clear that the only reason she had the privilege of being their daughter-in-law was the hefty dowry that her father had provided. But Kamala mausi managed to win the respect of her husband by helping him with his nationalist writings.

Then misfortune struck. Her husband was imprisoned for sedition and, while he was in jail, he developed pleurisy. When the news came that he had died, Kamala mausi was at her parents' house delivering their first child. Her brothers went to her in-laws with gifts and news of a daughter's arrival, only to be told that the young widow and her baby were no longer welcome in her husband's family home. She had no choice but to remain in the household of her birth, but her brothers and their wives were not at all pleased to have a widow in their midst. She knew that they would not let her stay with them forever.

Amma had no time to waste on reminiscences—she had to report for her first day at work and then leave for Kanpur, which was two hours away by train. She had woken Didi and me up at dawn, with instructions to shower and get dressed. Nevertheless, we could tell that this personal history was urgently important, for, as Amma organized paperwork and finished packing for her trip, she talked incessantly about her freedom-fighter sister.

At the age of only twenty, Kamala mausi had found herself facing the prospect of moving all the way to Vrindavan, which had become something of a dumping ground for widows from the upper castes. There, she and her young daughter could look forward to living in a home where she would be given one meal a day and expected to earn the rest by singing on the streets. Empty of hope, she had considered killing herself. This was when she and Amma first met. At the time, Amma was living in the Mahila Ashram at Wardha, not far from the village of Sevagram, where Gandhiji had relocated his headquarters in 1936. Didi and I had often heard the story of the Mahila Ashram, which was officially founded early in 1933, just a few years before Amma arrived. It had evolved from the Mahila Seva Mandal, a centre dedicated to the social uplift of women, in part through education and vocational training, that one of Gandhi's steadfast supporters, Jamnalalji Bajaj, had established at Wardha in 1924. It was through the network of freedom fighters, Amma now told us, that she had learned of Kamala mausi's situation and had subsequently arranged for her to be invited to the Mahila Ashram.

Amma went on to explain that young women raised with middle-class values found it hard to leave the protection of their family home, however precarious that safety. But Kamala mausi had been brave enough to travel more than six hundred miles south, from Lucknow to Wardha, in order to start a new life for herself and her child. At Wardha, she continued her education, eventually taking teacher's training and then working in a local school.

Now, fifteen years later, Kamala mausi's daughter, Kanti, whom Amma remembered as a bright and sensitive girl who, like her mother, wrote moving poetry, had finished high school, and was now studying in Amravati, a city not far west of Wardha, at the HVP Mandal Degree College for Physical Education. Kamala mausi had recently returned to Lucknow to care for her father, who had had a stroke. Her family found her help useful, and they said they admired her perseverance.

In the long letters she had recently written to Amma, Kamala mausi had revealed that she was under tremendous pressure from her family to stay on in Lucknow, and she was considering using her savings to buy a small place near her family or perhaps to build a floor on the terrace of the family home. Her brothers were now insisting that she live with them, but Amma suspected that this insistence was driven more by worry about the propriety of a woman living alone than by any real fondness for their sister. Amma worried that Kamala mausi might be overwhelmed by her family's acceptance: "I know the heady pull of home and the feeling of belonging," she said. "But I do not trust people for whom kindness and respect are a matter of convenience."

In any case, Kamala mausi was presently in Lucknow and, delighted to find out about Amma's new job in the same city, she had offered to help set up our new household. Amma was grateful for the offer, she told us, but she also hoped that the distance from her family would allow Kamala mausi the chance to think carefully about her decision.

Kamala mausi arrived early, just as Ramu kaka finished making a breakfast of *upma*—a savoury semolina porridge made with cashews, ginger, cumin, mustard, and lemon juice—which he served with sweet milky chai, for Amma, and glasses of sweetened hot milk for Didi and me. But we rose from the table to greet the new arrival.

Wrapped in a white khadi sari, Kamala mausi's large, dark caramel body loomed over Amma as she embraced her. Several inches taller than Amma, Kamala mausi looked down at the world with mirthful generosity. She wore an oblong streak of sandalwood on her forehead that matched the colour of the frames of her thick elliptical glasses. With an affectionate smile on her smooth, round face, she addressed Amma as her older sister, her *badi behenji,* even though Amma was actually a few months younger.

When Amma protested the undeserved honorific, Kamala mausi clasped her hands. "How can I call you anything other than my elder? You saved me and my daughter."

Amma shook her head. "Nonsense," she said. "You saved yourself, with your courage and hard work."

Kamala mausi joined us at the breakfast table and we returned to our meal, this time in her company. Before she started in on her *upma,* however, she showered Didi and me with blessings and immediately launched into a story about the infant Didi in Wardha, merrily eating an orange in Gandhiji's lap, dripping all over his pristine white dhoti.

To the relief of Didi, who had become quite a fastidious eater, Amma interrupted Kamala mausi's cheerful account. "The tour orders were waiting for me when I reached Lucknow. I don't know how long I will be gone. I will return home as soon as I have made sure that the girls can stay with me until their school starts."

Kamala mausi was clearly annoyed with Amma's superiors, who showed no concern for a woman with young children who had just moved from another city. But Amma dismissed her friend's verbal volleys with a shrug. "You remember Acharya Jugal Kishorji from our Wardha days? Now he's the Minister of Labour and Social Welfare for Uttar Pradesh. He wrote to congratulate me when he found out that I'd been offered this position. He also warned me that my performance would be watched closely by those who may be envious and will see me as a political appointment. There are many people who would like to see me fail. So I'm prepared for a rough start." Amma paused, glancing from Didi to me. "I have experience handling whatever life throws at me, but the girls are still so young."

Before any of us could say anything, however, Amma changed the mood with a proud smile. "Abha-Rekha are very self-sufficient and will not be any trouble. I wouldn't hesitate to leave them by themselves if they knew people nearby. But, as you know, we arrived only yesterday." She rose from the table to leave. "I'm very grateful that you can be here as we figure out our new life."

Kamala mausi pointed to her suitcase to indicate that she was there to stay. "Badi behenji, do what you must and take however long it takes. Show them what a woman can do."

Amma had a catch in her throat as she folded her hands together. "I will forever be in your debt."

Didi and I rose from our seats to encircle Amma in a hug, stifling our farewell sobs. We held each other, just for a moment. Then Amma started issuing instructions about our behaviour and routine in her absence, and she was gone. The long summer that had begun in joyful Jaipur was about to end in lonely Lucknow.

After Amma left, Kamala mausi introduced Didi and me to the Amir-ud-Daula public library. She had been quick to notice our interest in history, but she told us that literature came closer to the truth than most history books and steered us in a different direction at the library. She showed us *Nirmala,* by Munshi Premchand, a story about a young girl unhappily married to a much older man, and explained that modern poets and novelists often wrote about social issues and the struggle for independence. Real history was made up of the experiences of everyday people, she said, not just what kings, colonialists, and nationalist leaders thought and did, and she pointed us to *Mere bachpan ke din,* a childhood memoir by Mahadevi Verma, one of the foremost poets of the romanticist Chhayavaad movement in Hindi literature who also worked to promote women's education and uplift. Kamala mausi drew up a summer reading list for each of us, containing everything from Hindi classics to recent novels that brought India's independence movement to life, such as *Maila aanchal,* by Phanishwar Nath Renu, and *Godan,* also by Munshi Premchand. I particularly enjoyed the vivid, heroic poetry of Subhadra Kumari Chauhan and could recite from memory all eighteen stanzas of "Jhansi ki Rani," her poem about Lakshmibai, the queen of Jhansi, who fought to defend her kingdom against the British. Although she was too polite to say so, Didi was less interested in political themes. She was delighted by Devaki Nandan Khatri's magical romance *Chandrakanta,* written in the late nineteenth century, but she was also drawn to the idealism and humanism of poems by Suryakant Tripathi Nirala, one of the founders of the Chhayavaad movement.

Kamala mausi was, if anything, even more regimented than Amma in organizing our days, but the rhythm she enforced on our daily routine did help to calm our anxiety about the new place and all the new people. Long hours spent reading ended with evening walks to public parks surrounded by high ornate walls or with cool strolls by the snaking Gomti River.

In this way, and with the kind attention of Kamala mausi and Ramu kaka, we got through the first week of waiting. When Amma finally arrived back at the bungalow, her sari looked as worn as she did, and much of her greying hair had escaped her tight bun, but she seemed oblivious to her dishevelment. We hugged tightly. She smelled of sweat and a pungent herbal soap. Seeing my wrinkled nose, she pushed me away with a chuckle. "There's little time for a two-showers-per-day regimen when you're out in the field." And from that moment she could hardly stop smiling or talking.

The training centre where Amma worked was located in a small village called Narwal, some fifteen miles outside the city of Kanpur. There, nearly a hundred women from all over the state were receiving training as rural social workers. As UP's deputy director of women's welfare, Amma also supervised a total of fifteen district organizers, all women, who covered three of UP's districts: Lucknow, Kanpur, and Jhansi. Each district organizer was in charge of fifteen village workers, also women, and each of these *gram sevikas* ran a welfare centre that served three or four villages. At these welfare centres, village women were taught basic literacy, as well as practical skills such as sewing, vegetable gardening, and preserving fruits, and they also received some general education, including health information. Amma was responsible for arranging seminars and training programs for the *gram sevikas* in both Narwal and Jeolikot, as well as for overseeing the day-to-day operations of the welfare centres in the fifteen districts.

After a detailed description of her activities in the training centre, she smiled proudly at her old friend. "Kamala behenji, if you thought you and I had a hard life, you should meet some of the women at the training centre. Their stories of the callous cruelty shown to them by their own families filled my heart with anger and pain. But the real story is the fighting spirit of these women. They survived, and they will return to the communities they came from to help make a better future for everyone. I feel so privileged to be working with such women."

As Amma went on to describe what this better future would look like, Didi and I waited patiently to find out what lay ahead for us. Finally, Didi interrupted Amma's monologue. "So how long are you going to be home this time?"

Amma glanced briefly at Didi and me but then, with a look of sudden embarrassment, turned her attention to Kamala mausi. "*Arre haan!* I almost forgot. Kamala behenji, did you get a chance to visit your father, or were you too busy with these two?"

"I can go to see him now. I'll come back whenever you need me."

Amma compared dates from her diary and the calendar. "I've worked out a schedule for the next month—until the schools open. The girls can travel with me for the next two weeks. We'll return to Lucknow in time for our things to arrive from Jaipur and for the new school term for the girls. If you're still available and willing, we would really appreciate your presence when my travel starts up again. I've also written to some of my freedom-fighter family in Lucknow to ask if they know a trustworthy older woman who needs full-time employment and who can live with us in the house."

Amused by Amma's efficiency, Kamala mausi said that she would be more than happy to come back in a few weeks. Didi seemed mollified by this exchange, and I could not wait to board a train again.

Amma then asked Kamala mausi whether she was planning to return to Wardha, despite her brothers' insistence that she move back into the family home. "Don't let them rush you into anything," she advised her friend, with a wistful smile. "Take your time and use your clever mind, not your soft heart."

Kamala mausi laughed her full-throated laughter, shaking her head. "Badi behenji, you still think of me as a wild-eyed doe with a young fawn to raise. I know why I'm no longer just a widow whose shadow pollutes: right now, my family finds me useful. I've even heard my older brother boast to others about my being a teacher and living in Gandhiji's ashram— the same brother who was perfectly prepared to kick me out of my family home with an infant in my arms! Nor does it seem to matter to them that this infant is now in college, and her mother might not want to move to a city so very far away. Yet I have to admit—the idea of returning to Lucknow is very tempting. I've ached for home for a long time, and, even with all their traditional nonsense, the contentment I feel when I'm back with my family is hard to resist."

Amma's gaze lowered, her normally firm voice sounding like the whisper of a little girl. "I can only imagine."

Kamala mausi looked pained and gently put her hand on Amma's arm.

With almost visible effort, Amma pulled herself out of her thoughts and turned her attention to us. "Abha-Rekha, this isn't the first time I've had the chance to live in Lucknow."

Didi and I had gathered as much just from seeing Amma's familiarity with the local language, but now was our chance to learn more. Amma explained that she was last in Lucknow in the late 1920s, at the time when protests against the Simon Commission were erupting all over the country. She had been invited for a visit by Manoramadevi, the principal of her school in Mathura, whose family home was in Lucknow. They took part in marches after the death of Lala Lajpat Rai, who had been badly beaten by the police in Lahore during one of the protests. They had witnessed similar sights in Lucknow, Amma told us—unarmed protestors brutally assaulted by the police. It was also here that Manoramadevi had introduced Amma to a network of generous men and women who had been more than family to her over the years.

With past history lessons in mind, Didi interrupted Amma. "The Simon Commission was set up in 1928. How old were you then, Amma?" The strain of puzzlement was writ large on her face.

Amma looked evenly at Didi: "I was no older than you are now, around ten years old."

Didi was incredulous. "And your parents let you attend a protest march?"

Amma looked blankly at the wall. "I was no longer living at home."

"Why not?" I asked. This history was new to me.

But, once again, Amma redirected the conversation. "That's another story for another time. Anyway, I have written to many of these brothers and sisters, and they have offered to help us. Misraji and his wife, Lalitaji, were with me in the civil disobedience movement. Their home here in Lucknow is full of children and grandchildren. They offered to have you two stay with them when we cannot travel together."

"But Amma, we want to go where you go," I piped up for Didi and me.

Amma hesitated and then spoke, carefully choosing her words. "I would like that too. But be warned that it will not be easy. You will have to share a room with me, eat whatever they give you, wash your own clothes, perhaps draw water out of a well, and maybe even help out in the training programs. Are you prepared for that, my little soldiers?"

I sprang to attention. "*Ji haan!*" I expected to hear Didi's voice echo my own eager affirmation. I turned around to look at my sister, whose large almond eyes were fixed intently on Amma.

Amma put her hand on Didi's knee. "What say you, Madam Cabinet Minister?"

Amma's gesture softened Didi. She could not suppress the smile that accompanied her nod.

2

Many Homes

W e lived like nomads for over a year, spending every available school holiday with Amma, travelling all over the vast state of Uttar Pradesh to the welfare centres she now supervised. In all that year we saw nothing of Babu, despite the vacations that came with his new job. However, Amma knew people everywhere we went, and their homes opened to us as though we were long-lost limbs of an extended family tree.

As we kept meeting new family in new homes, we also kept discovering new stories about Amma's life—and Babu's too. This was how we learned that, at the age of only fifteen, Amma had stabbed a man.

We were in Agra, staying with two of Amma's old friends, Suman mami and her husband, Hari mama. An exacting man, with an angular jaw and a commanding presence, Hari mama had recently retired from teaching at the local college. As a follower of the Arya Samaj—a reform movement, founded in the 1870s, that blended Hindu nationalism with opposition to the hierarchies of caste—he began each day with ritual oblations to ancient Vedic dieties, accompanied by the sonorous recitation of verses from the *Rigveda,* privileges ordinarily reserved for Brahmans.

Although short in stature, he stood tall, his starched kurta hanging stiffly over his wide pajama pants and his broad shiny forehead, crowned by short-cropped hair, glistening from daily applications of coconut oil. He lowered his voice for no one—particularly not for his wife, whom he frequently scolded. The moment her husband entered a room, Suman mami's usual animated manner, punctuated by bouts of giggling, would abruptly dissolve into diffident mumbles.

We were seated on the back veranda, where Amma was helping Suman mami shell a large pile of peas, her face bent toward the big steel bowl that was filling rapidly from their joint effort. For no particular reason, Suman mami launched into an account of the time that Amma was accosted on her way back from a Congress Party meeting there in Agra. The man was drunk. Clad in an army uniform, he towered in her path, her head barely reaching his chest. Amma waited until his hands reached out to grab her and then, in an instant, pulled out the knife she carried in her shoulder belt and plunged it into his torso. His screams brought people running, some of whom rushed Amma to a safe house, while others took the blood-covered man to the military hospital. Hari mama was one of those who had helped Amma to escape arrest, Suman mami told us proudly. A few years later, when Amma was once again in Agra, a senior Congress Party leader, Revati Sharanji, had presented her with a beautiful *kataar*, or push-dagger, to replace the long Gurkha knife that she had left in the chest cavity of her assailant.

Didi and I listened incredulously to this story. I looked over at Amma—a strict vegetarian who refused to eat eggs because they are "seeds of life" and wouldn't even let us kill a cockroach. She was capable of pushing a blade *through someone's flesh*? My jaw was nearly in my lap. "My Amma killed a man?" I exclaimed.

At this, Amma looked up for the first time since Suman mami began telling the story. Her grim voice stood in stark contrast to Suman mami's lively tone. "No, he did not die. I did not aim for a kill." After a pause, she added, "When a woman is nobody's daughter, wife, or mother, she is absolutely alone. She's considered fair game."

"How dare you call yourself alone? Am I no longer your elder brother?" Hari mama, who had appeared on the veranda without our realizing it, interrupted our conversation in his familiar bombastic manner. As usual, Suman mami visibly shrank when she heard her husband's voice. But Amma only smiled at Hari mama's chiding.

Suman mami picked up the steel bowl and retreated toward the kitchen, Hari mama barking at her as she left, demanding his afternoon tea. Amma admonished Hari mama for the terror he invoked in his wife, but the rebuke flowed over him like water.

Returning her attention to Didi and me, Amma pointed to the small fenced garden at the back of the house and told us that it used to be a large orchard with an outhouse on its edge, before Hari mama's son renovated the property. Hari mama and his wife had saved not only her life, Amma said, but also our father's. Long before Amma knew Babu, he had hidden in their outhouse for three days to evade the police.

"But Babu wasn't afraid of being jailed," Didi protested. "I still remember him showing us the whipping marks on his back from his many trips to jail. And didn't he also lose the hearing in his left ear after he was beaten by guards?"

"Prison tortures, bomb blasts, and who knows what else his strong body had been through," Hari mama confirmed. "But you're right. Your Babu never avoided jail out of fear. He was badly hurt when he arrived here and needed to stay out of prison to carry on his work."

"How did he get hurt?" Didi asked.

"Some bomb that exploded at the wrong time. He didn't like to talk about it." Hari mama sounded more irritated than usual.

Amma continued the story. Babu was convalescing in this very house when a nosey neighbour tipped off the police that Hari mama might be sheltering a revolutionary. The police, who had long suspected this Arya Samaji of harbouring nationalist sympathies, arrived at the house, demanding to search the premises. But, as Hari mama argued loudly with the armed policemen at their door, Suman mami quickly led Babu into the little outhouse to hide.

Having finished with the house, the police began inspecting the grounds, moving toward the outhouse. At that point, Suman mami rushed into it ahead of them, pretending to be in great pain from diarrhea, letting out a barrage of curses that she kept up until the policemen left. For the next three days, Suman mami—who continued to pretend to be suffering from the runs—brought food to Babu several times a day, along with a small brass water pitcher of water infused with medicinal herbs. She was very brave, Amma said. Her foresight and courage kept Babu safely out of sight until he was finally able to escape under cover of darkness.

Hari mama did not conceal his pride at this reminder of his wife's actions, although he mocked Amma's use of the word "brave" to describe them.

I looked out at the yard. Where the outhouse had once stood there was now a neat little garden dominated by a velvety green drumstick tree, some showy coral trees, and a majestic *jamun* tree laden with ripening fruit. Beyond the garden, the rest of the orchard had been swallowed up by new construction, buildings sprouting as far as the eye could see. But, for a fleeting moment, my mind conjured up the image of a dense orchard with a narrow wooden outhouse sitting in a small clearing. I could see the door opening just enough to allow Babu's large frame to emerge silently and then slip into the thicket near the fence.

Our journeys that first summer took us to various parts of western Uttar Pradesh—Mathura, Kanpur, Agra, Nainital—but my favourite place was Jeolikot, a serene hill station nestled in the middle Himalayan range, nearly two miles closer to the clouds than we were in Lucknow. Amma told us that Jeolikot was one of many mountain villages to which the British retreated to escape the summer heat. But it was also a refuge for some of the spiritual leaders of the nationalist movement, such as Sri Aurobindo and Swami Vivekanand, who withdrew to the remote serenity of Jeolikot in order to meditate. There, our home was a government cottage set in the shadow of towering mountain peaks haloed in snow.

During the long summer days, we were never alone. We made friends with the trainees and the staff at the various welfare centres we visited and spent time with families of the *chowkidar*s of the bungalows and cottages where we stayed. Didi and I also joined the Girl Guides. My favourite camp activity was horse-riding, and Didi's was marksmanship. Best of all, we revelled in the love shown to us by members of the family of freedom fighters who greeted us in every new place. I hoped the summer would never end.

But it did.

The end of the summer in the plains and the mountains meant endless spells of heavy rain. When the clouds rolled in, the villagers beat a special drum to warn everyone to close windows and doors. If you missed the cue, a wet silver fog pushed through openings, drenching everything in its wake. These fogs were nothing like the sporadic drizzles in Jaipur, which were no more than an invitation for a picnic at Jal Mahal, the palace in the middle of the lake.

The end of summer also meant going back to school.

Our school was housed in a three-hundred-year-old red sandstone building, once the palace of a nawab. Legend had it that the nawab hid most of his treasure, which included the largest ruby ever known, beneath the stone floors or behind the walls of his mansion. Amma explained that our new school was the only one of its kind in Lucknow, with a full day of classes and then additional activities in the late afternoon and early evenings. But I did not like it.

Most girls arrived at school in chauffeur-driven cars or exquisitely decorated horse-drawn carriages, while Didi and I shared a simple tonga. Most mornings of the school term, I had trouble getting up and getting ready. The only tolerable parts of the long day were the dance and music classes in the evenings. I loved to practice my music lessons on Babu's harmonium—which had, eventually, arrived, along with the rest of our belongings. Sometimes I pretended that he was sitting in the room, swaying to the sound of his beloved instrument, his good ear slightly bent toward me.

The start of the school year also meant often coming home at the end of the day to a house without Amma. Every few months there was a different arrangement. Sometimes someone's female relative stayed at our house in Amma's absence, but often that arrangement ended just as we were getting to know our temporary companion. Amma told us that we must write a letter to her and Babu every day, detailing our activities. Whenever she returned from a trip, she would read each one of these letters aloud, and, every month, she helped us choose some of these letters to mail to Babu in Shillong, where he was teaching. Amma also gave us each a notebook in which to keep a daily diary. This diary, she said, would be our best friend in times of fear, loneliness, or confusion, as well as of joy. At first, I wasn't sure what to write about, so my diary quickly became a record of interesting experiences, such as trying a new dish or exploring a new place. Later on, though, I discovered that she was correct.

Although Kamala mausi had continued to stay with us when she could, she had finally decided to return to Wardha, despite her brothers' irritation at losing the household help. So several times each month, when Amma was on one of her tours, Didi and I would end our long school day at the house of the Misras, where four generations all lived under a single roof. Lalita mausi was a firm, hardworking matriarch who ran her large household with an iron fist, firmly in command of three sons, their wives, and several grandchildren. Her husband—gentle, bespectacled Misraji—spent nearly all his waking hours in the little clinic that he ran from the ground floor of their house. His elderly mother, who was very frail, had a room on the main floor with an extra bed that was used for overnight visitors. Dadi ma, as everyone called her, was nearly deaf and blind and muttered to herself all the time. Didi and I shared the extra bed in her room.

It was hard to reconcile Dadi ma's wispy shadow of a self with Lalita mausi's description of the tyrannical matriarch who had once publicly repudiated her daughter-in-law for taking part in the freedom movement. Lalita mausi's father had been a physician in nearby Bahraich, who took her to political marches and meetings from the time she was little. Nevertheless, as was customary, Lalita mausi was married at a very young age, in this case to her father's student. By the time she came of age and went to live in her marital home, her father-in-law had passed away, and her mother-in-law strictly forbade her to participate in political activities. But Lalita mausi was not the docile sort.

In March 1931, three young revolutionaries—Bhagat Singh, Shivaram Rajguru, and Sukhdev Thapar—had been executed in Lahore for their part in avenging the death of Lala Lajpat Rai. Public protests had erupted, even as the country's new viceroy, Lord Willingdon, adopted policies of repression. Arrests and the brutal suppression of disturbances intensified that fall, while Gandhiji was away in London. At the start of January 1932, shortly after he returned to India, Gandhiji called for renewed civil disobedience and was promptly arrested, as were numerous other Congress leaders, setting off yet another round of struggle.

Outraged by the events unfolding around her, Lalita mausi managed to persuade her husband to allow her to join a protest march in Bahraich, which she did, with her youngest son tied to her back, just like the heroic Lakshmibai, the Rani of Jhansi, is said to have done. The peaceful march was broken up by riot police who rained lathis down on all and sundry, even women and children. Along with her toddler son, Lalita mausi was thrown into the Bahraich jail for six months for violating laws against public assembly. Subsequently, she and scores of other women prisoners were transferred to the larger Lucknow jail. This is where she met Amma, then barely fourteen, who was serving a sentence for treason and sedition. As a political prisoner, Lalita mausi was allowed to keep her son with her in jail. She would have sent him home with her husband, but Misraji never appeared.

Lalita mausi's proud but worried father visited her in jail and showed her the announcement in the local newspaper in which her husband's family renounced any association with her. To cement the banishment, her mother-in-law was determined to arrange for her son to remarry, but her plans finally moved him to action: Misraji left Bahraich and set up practice in Lucknow, where he waited for his wife's prison term to be over. Although temperamentally a quiet man, in 1942, during the Quit India movement, Misraji joined the thousands who courted arrest to protest the imprisonment of Gandhi and other Congress Party leaders after the British outlawed the All India Congress Committee and brutally enforced the ban on public assemblies under the 1939 Defence of India Act.

Back in Bahraich, all four of Misraji's brothers took positions of various types in different parts of the state, eventually leaving Dadi ma alone in the ancestral home. When Dadi ma became ill a few years ago, Misraji decided to bring her to Lucknow. Since then, Lalita mausi had cared for Dadi ma, in her practical, no-nonsense way.

Our stay in this bustling household was generally marked by an intensity of noise, movement, and physical proximity that Didi and I had never experienced. In Jaipur, where we had shared a sprawling building with large families, I had sometimes felt sorry for Didi and me, wishing we could be part of those large clusters of people of all sizes who never appeared pensive. Those people who surrounded us in Jaipur, however, were always a floor or a courtyard away, except when we periodically lived in Bai ki ma's house, pretending to be one of her many children and feeling their closeness fill a hole in our hearts. In the soft-spoken household of Bai ki ma, though, the only voice loud enough to carry over the threshold of a room was that of Jain saheb in one of his storytelling moods. In Lalita mausi's household everyone talked loudly, except for Misraji and his muttering, bedridden mother.

By the time we arrived in Lucknow, Lalita mausi's two daughters had married (but only after finishing high school) and were now regular visitors to their parents' home, with their young ones in tow. What with the Misras' three sons and their burgeoning families, there were, at any given time, close to a dozen children in the house, all laughing, jostling, shoving, running, reading, and eating noisily. The adults were no less raucous, since they needed to be heard over the din created by the numerous miniature humans careening around them. The result was a cacophony of scolding, talking, crying, singing, and screaming that started in the early hours of the morning and ended late at night. In Lalita mausi's house, Didi's usual quietness was stunned into a dazed silence. Not even my initial elation at finding a gang to join could withstand the constant pushing and yelling.

When we could, Didi and I retreated gratefully into the relative quiet of Dadi ma's room, where we tried to bury our heads in our books. Unfortunately, this invited a lot of sniggering comments, especially from the girls, who would follow us into our retreat. "They think they are memsahebs." "Look at the fat books they read." "They will go blind if they read so much." The worst of their stings was aimed at my dark complexion: "O Kali, can you hear us, or does reading make you deaf too?" Kali may be the name of the most fearful form of the mother goddess, but in this case it was a reference to her coal-black skin. I had inherited Amma's complexion, and now, despite her advice, I was unable to muster the courage to remind my tormentors that Kali also rides a lion and wears a garland made of the skulls of those slain in a battle with her.

I wished I had my bike. I wished I could ride it all the way back to Jaipur.

Summer finally arrived again, heralding the end of our hated school-term routine. I was playing a game of catch with Ramu kaka in the yard when a man's form appeared at the gate of our bungalow.

"Babu is here!" I ran screaming toward the gate.

It was a Sunday afternoon, and Amma was poring over some fat files in the living-room-office under the window that overlooked the main gate. She looked up in alarm as I turned back to shout again, "Babu is here!" In doing so, I lost my balance and fell flat on my face, making painful contact with the gravel that had been loudly crunching under my sandals a moment ago.

The man at the gate pushed past Ram Bahadurji, the *chowkidar,* and picked me up. He was not Babu. I was inconsolable, not so much from the humiliation of falling in such an undignified manner but from the disappointment of my discovery. As he held me, I sobbed, tears mixing with the blood trickling down my face from a cut above my eyebrow.

As my stubborn sobs slowly subsided, I was able to take in Amma's words to the stranger. I gathered that he was Babu's younger brother and that Didi and I were to call him Shankar chacha. He was still holding me, with my head resting on his shoulder and my arms tightly wound around his neck. He was the same height as Babu, but leaner, and had a moustache on his gentle face. His kind eyes were the antithesis of Babu's sharp and penetrating gaze.

Shankar chacha spoke to Amma with a strange mix of mirth and affection. I had never heard anyone talk to Amma this way, but when I lifted my head slightly to steal a look at Amma's face, Shankar chacha asked me if I wanted to get down. In response, I tightened my grasp around his neck. There was a lot of strength in my bony little arms, he chuckled—I should be careful not to choke him. Suddenly I was deeply ashamed and slid down his long torso until I was on my feet, coming face to face with Didi's look of disdain at my childish behaviour.

Shankar chacha was there to invite us all to spend the remainder of the summer with him and his family in Bhagalpur, located about 450 miles southeast of Lucknow, on the banks of the holy Ganga. Amma was explaining how much harder it was to manage the household in Lucknow without the neighbourly support she had in Jaipur. She had been managing by working from home as much as possible and with the generous help of old friends. But her travelling for work was only likely to increase, as the Social Welfare Department was considering extension projects in remote areas of the state.

Didi and I listened intently with a sense of anticipation and some measure of dread, looking for clues to answer questions that we did not know how to ask. We loved our travels with Amma, but, so far, life in Lucknow had been a series of unfamiliar people, unknown houses, and unusual circumstances. The biggest void was, of course, the absence of Babu. His brief letters appeared sporadically for Didi and me, mostly filled with questions about our studies and various other activities. From Amma we heard only the refrain that he could visit us whenever he wanted. We were not sure what that meant.

We were initially cautious around Shankar chacha, but his easy smile and gentle way of talking won us over. He stayed with us for two days and taught me how to make a slingshot and use it to pick mangoes from the trees behind our house. Just like Babu, Didi and I never passed up an opportunity to eat a mango—*phalon ka raja,* the king of fruits, as Babu used to say. We would gather our loot from the bountiful trees and take the mangoes to Ramu kaka to put to good use. The nearly ripe ones were carefully wrapped in straw for a couple of days to ensure that they would be sweet and dripping with fragrant juice. The unripe ones were cut and boiled with jaggary and spices, then cooled to make the most delicious summer drink, *panaa*. Ramu kaka was very happy with the mango crop that year and promised to make a big jar of mango pickles to send with Amma when we went to visit Shankar chacha's family.

On the first afterrnoon of his visit, Shankar chacha salvaged a couple of big, unripe mangoes from Ramu kaka's eager hands, greener than any green I have seen. These were washed and cut into thick, long chunks, then smeared with rock salt, a pinch of turmeric, and chili powder. When Shankar chacha offered the result to Didi and me, we were startled by the sourness of the taste, which was enhanced by the seasoning. The tartness made me squeeze my eyes shut, and even Didi was unable to maintain her ladylike composure; she rocked from side to side with her lips all puckered up. We laughed at each other as we polished off the contents of the plate.

Later on, though, I didn't feel so good. My stomach was really hurting. Amma came back from the office just as Shankar chacha returned from an evening stroll. When he saw my discomfort, he guiltily explained to Amma about the mangoes, at which point she sent Ram Bahadurji to fetch the doctor. In Jaipur, the nearest clinic was only two streets away, since our house was in the heart of the city, but the bungalow in the Civil Lines was far from everything. If we wanted to go somewhere, Ramu kaka or Ram Bahadurji had to call a tonga. Amma had a government car, but she refused to use it except for going to and from her office. Her soft-spoken but efficient assistant, Deen Dayalji, had delicately hinted that many directors in government departments use these cars as their personal vehicles. In fact, some even had the driver and his wife and children move into the servant's quarters, which made it easier to use not only the car but the entire family. This suggestion merely earned Deen Dayalji a long lecture on the true nature of public service.

Shankar chacha made the same mistake now, suggesting that we use the car to go to the doctor. Amma gave him a sharp look. I was expecting her to launch into one of her rants about public funds and "public servants" who treat the public as servants. But she didn't. Instead, she clenched her teeth and then said that he should not have given us unripe mangoes without first finding out whether our stomachs could handle them. Didi and I squirmed at Shankar chacha's look of shame.

Didi tried to defend him. "But I don't feel sick," she pointed out. "It's just Rekha." Through my pain, I nodded vigorously, while Amma glowered at Didi. Ignoring her baleful look, Didi tried to build on her argument, at which point Amma simply told her to go to her room. By this time, Ram Bahadurji had arrived with a bottle of Ayurvedic medicine and the news that the doctor would visit soon. I fell asleep after taking the medicine, along with Amma's home remedy of a spoon of turmeric powder in hot milk, and the next morning I felt right as rain, not even remembering the doctor's visit. Shankar chacha left that same day, but only after having extracted a promise from Amma that we would visit the family home soon.

In fact, Amma decided to make this trip much sooner than we expected.

BHAGALPUR, 1955

To accompany her white khadi saris, Amma's only adornments were normally a pair of gold earrings with a circle of pearls surrounding a ruby, a single gold bangle on one wrist and a gold-plated Favre-Leuba wristwatch on the other, and a decorative *bindi* on her forehead, the red colour of the dot signifying marriage. This time, though, before we left the house to board the train, she added a pair of silver toe-rings, a gold chain around her neck, and a thin line of bright orange-red *sindoor* along the first section of the part in her hair, again announcing her married status.

I admired the brilliant line of vermillion, as it set off Amma's dark skin, so I asked Amma why she didn't always wear it. Didn't she like being married? Amma sighed and said I had much to learn about the connection between symbols of marriage and women's subjugation. Then she added gravely, "His family needs to know that Sinha saheb still has a wife." I noticed that she did not refer to him as "your Babu," as she usually did.

The train took us to Bhagalpur toward the end of the summer, just a few weeks before our school was to reopen for the new term. Shankar chacha received us at the train station in a beautifully decorated tonga, which did not simply drop us off at our destination and then leave, as I had expected. Instead, once Shankar chacha helped Amma out of the tonga and escorted her inside, the horse was untied from the tonga and retied to a long rope in a little clearing, in front of what looked like a stable, next to the indigo-tinted outer walls of a large single-storey house. When he returned, Shankar chacha smiled at our fascination with the horse and invited us to feed him carrots as the carriage was being detached. Didi and I were thrilled to feel the horse's moist, leathery lips graze our fingers.

After a few minutes, Shankar chacha said that we should go inside before they sent a search party for us and pointed toward an arched gateway with double doors. When we stepped through the wooden gate, we found ourselves in a square courtyard with a large neem tree in the middle and a border of carefully tended herbs and flowers all along the east and west wings. Amma was already sitting in a wicker chair with her back to us, facing a stone bench under the neem tree, surrounded by several women and children. Some of the women were wiping away tears.

Everyone's attention turned to us when Didi and I came through the gate. Now the oldest-looking woman was weeping openly and loudly, pointing from Amma to us. Didi and I stood glued to the spot, unprepared for this outpouring of emotion. But Shankar chacha clutched both of us by our wrists and strode toward the group, calling out, "Why such unholy cacophony? Bhaiya is away, not dead." His scolding had no effect on the wailing woman, who was now beating her chest and repeating, "My Raja, my Raja." I could understand what Shankar chacha had just said, but he spoke in a lilting language that I didn't recognize rather than in the standard Hindi that he'd used until now.

He pushed his way into the middle of this theatrical display and, raising his voice so that he could be heard, asked Amma to follow him. Instead, Amma turned her face toward us and gestured for us to come closer. We could see tears in her own eyes. She instructed us to touch the feet of the wailing woman to ask her blessing and told us to call her Buaji. As Didi and I dutifully bent down to touch Buaji's feet, she wrapped us up in a damp embrace. She had stopped calling out to "Raja"—our Babu—by this point and now reeled off sentences in a rapid-fire monologue, despite her still-heaving sobs. Between the speed and the sobs, Didi and I couldn't understand a word. We were just beginning to get used to the Awadhi spoken in Lucknow, which was quite distinct from the Marwari we knew from Jaipur, but this language was different yet again.

As Didi and I stood stiffly in Buaji's determined embrace, straining to catch anything familiar sounding, I could hear Shankar chacha's voice above the din. Then I felt his tug on my shoulder, which broke me out of the wailing woman's uncomfortable hold. In response to his call for tea and refreshments, one of the other women headed down a passage toward what looked like another open courtyard at the rear of the house.

Many rooms surrounded the courtyard in which we stood, each with a wooden double door, a smaller version of the main gate. Across the courtyard, facing the main gate, was a hall with stout pillars and low arches, topped with rolled-up bamboo curtains that looked like a row of startled eyebrows. Shankar chacha ordered one of the boys to get some chairs for us. The boy darted into one of the rooms off the courtyard and promptly emerged with two wicker stools. As Didi and I sat down, most of the women and children dispersed in various directions, leaving only four young faces peering at the strangers who had just arrived.

The oldest face was that of Shankar chacha's daughter Meera, who was probably about Didi's age and was holding a little boy in her arms, who turned out to be her inquisitive two-year-old brother, Indra. She offered to take us into the inner courtyard, where the rest of the women were, but Shankar chacha suggested that we stay in the outer courtyard for now. Then he proudly introduced his older son, Suresh, a polite but eager boy who had recently turned eleven. Their younger sister, Rambha, stood shyly behind her older siblings, stealing unsure glances at the strangers. Didi and I were relieved that Suresh and Meera didi spoke to us in Hindi, rather than in the local language, which we later learned was Maithili. They elongated their vowels in a way characteristic of the region, which broke up the clatter of consonants and made their Hindi seem strangely melodious, but at least we could understand what they were saying.

First, Shankar chacha said, we needed to have something to eat, and then we could see the house and the grounds. As if on cue, one of the women reappeared, holding a large tray with tea and an array of sweet and savoury snacks, with a little girl of about four or five, whose name was Bala, clinging to her side. In the humid monsoon heat, the woman's petite frame looked weighted down by her silk sari. She laid her burden on the bench, the heavy bangles on her wrists clinking softly, and, without a word, offered the first cup of tea to Shankar chacha. He gestured for her to offer it to Amma instead, who took her wrist affectionately, asking Shankar chacha whether this was his wife. Shankar chacha grunted an affirmation. I noticed how haughty his demeanour suddenly was. The easy, affable disposition that we had known in Lucknow seemed to have vanished.

Turning to us, Amma indicated that we should seek our aunt's blessings. As we bent down to touch her feet, Chachi grabbed hold of us, her long face stretching into a sweet smile, and blessed us with a warm hug.

We enjoyed our refreshments, but Didi and I were excited when it finally came time for a tour of the house. It had so many rooms, of all different sizes, that we lost track of their number. Only some of the rooms were connected to others, but all of them had doors facing one of the courtyards. The large windows in each room were protected at the bottom with metal bars but crowned at the top with stone screens carved in elaborate floral designs. Some of the rooms contained tall bureaus, while others had enormous wooden storage chests, and in one of them was a large wooden bed so high that our uncle had to hoist us up one by one to sit on it. I suppressed an urge to swing my legs once we got up there.

"How did they get such big things in through such small doors?" I asked.

Shankar chacha laughed and said, "All this was made right here in this very room. That is why it fits so perfectly." And then, one by one, he lowered the two of us to the ground.

Didi, Amma, and I then followed him down the narrow passage that led to the inner courtyard. There we entered a different world, inhabited by women, children, and servants. The inner courtyard was the same size as the outer one, and, as with all courtyards, the central area was open to the sky. But the inner courtyard was shabby, enclosed by crumbling walls in various stages of disrepair. It, too, was surrounded by doorways, and on one side was another pillared hall with arches. Instead of having wooden doors, though, the openings in the walls were simply hung with bamboo curtains. The yard and hall were crowded with piles of fresh vegetables, fruits, and grains, different types of mortars and pestles, rows of large earthenware pots of varying sizes, and two wood-burning stoves, which were surrounded by a wide assortment of utensils used for seasoning, roasting, pickling, and other ways of making food memorable. Many familiar and unfamiliar aromas permeated the air, despite the large wooden lids on the cooking pots.

A portly man whom we had not yet met sat on a low stool, stirring one of the pots and giving orders to two thin women. They squatted on their haunches to perform each of their tasks. Buaji was there too, sitting on a wicker chair in the hall to the side. She wore a heavy silk sari and a great deal of jewellery around her neck and wrists, as well as a long, thick, gold ornament that belted her ample waist in frilly waves. One hand rested on top of the curved handle of her ornate walking stick; with the other, she vigorously fanned herself with a colourfully decorated palm-leaf *pankha*. Despite the breeze, I noticed, the talcum powder she had dusted around her neck was already showing signs of cakey defeat in its battle with the humidity.

I was relieved to see her smile at us as she issued a command in the general direction of the women. In response, one of them lifted the wooden lid of one of the clay pots and scooped out a creamy dollop of cool yogurt with a big wooden ladle. As I wondered how we would eat it, Shankar chacha bellowed, "Does this household have no plates and spoons?"

This prompted sudden movement from behind one of the hanging bamboo curtains, and a petite figure draped in silk appeared with a small stack of bowls and spoons. She had drawn the long end of her sari up, so that it covered her face, and then across her head. She hurried toward Buaji, her shoulders hunched forward. Buaji gestured for Amma to come closer. I thought Buaji was introducing the faceless woman to Amma, but I wasn't sure. My curiosity got the better of me, so as they spoke I sidled up to Amma, hoping to take a peek under the shrouded woman's veil. She noticed my stealthy approach, however, and startled me by loosening her veil just enough to show me her big almond eyes and then the rest of her face. She smiled quickly and playfully stuck out her tongue. Too late I realized that Didi was right behind me and had witnessed my humiliation.

I found some comfort in the creamiest yogurt I had ever tasted, so thick that I could make my spoon stand up in it. Buaji was talking again about something, but Shankar chacha interrupted this latest monologue of hers and told us to finish up the yogurt since he wanted us to see all of the grounds before nightfall. Instead of rushing, though, I let the yogurt melt sweetly in my mouth, while he explained to us what made it taste so good. It wasn't that sugar had been added to it. Its pinkish hue and sweet taste were produced by simmering milk for hours in an earthenware pot before it was finally allowed to cool and then mixed with a touch of starter. The yogurt stayed fresh for more than a week in there, he said, pointing to the wide-mouthed clay pot, which looked big enough for me to hide in.

I suppressed an urge to smack my lips, but at that news I blurted out, "If I have my way, we'll never find out how long it stays fresh. I could eat that whole pot in a day!" Shankar chacha just laughed and said that I had better keep my word. I was thankful that the shaking of Amma's head was delivered with a slight smile. Didi's look was less forgiving, but she did not resist when I linked my arm with hers as we all headed off for the next stage of our tour, an enthusiastic Suresh leading the charge.

The rooms lining this courtyard had small windows near the ceiling. Two of the rooms held large metal containers and piles of burlap sacks containing grain, though some rooms were not for food storage but for sleeping. We first walked toward a door at the farthest end of the pillared hall that led to an open space. This was the rear of the house, where a thin man was drawing pails of water from the well and filling troughs with it. Two thatched shacks were attached to the back wall of the house, and we learned that some of the servants lived in them. Untidy but bountiful rows of herbs and grapevines grew near the well, and shady fruit trees stretched as far as the eye could see—which wasn't far, what with the dense foliage of the orchard and the buildings on either side of it.

The mango trees, laden with fruit ripe for the picking, caught my eye. Remembering our love of mangoes, Shankar chacha took the time to identify some of the varieties that grew in this region—the sweet yellow *chausa,* the succulent green *dushehri,* the rosy *gulab khas,* the firm and fibrous *kishenbhog,* the fleshy and tart *langra,* the crisp, tangy *totapuri,* and the sweetest of all—the *malda* mango. He pointed to the buildings visible through the thicket of trees and asked us to imagine the whole area as an uninterrupted orchard of mango, plum, guava and other fruit-bearing trees.

As Shankar chacha led us down the crooked path that led through the trees, he became his familiar self again. His gruffness evaporated, and he went back to talking in crisp Hindi, sounding just like Amma and Babu. He told us that his job with the Indian Railways kept him busy with travelling but that he preferred to keep his family in Bhagalpur. He added, rather shyly, that it was a growing family.

Since the death of his parents, he explained, he'd had little choice but to remain involved with the ancestral house, whether he liked it or not. So many people depended for their livelihood on the house and the land, and the extended family expected him to maintain the household, he said, particularly his only sister, our Buaji. She visited the family house a few times every year, and it was important for her to find, when she came, all the trappings of a well-run home. On this visit, Buaji was accompanied by her two grandsons, two maids, and her youngest daughter-in-law. When we realized he was referring to the faceless woman we had met earlier, Didi whispered to Amma, "She's not much older than me!" Amma widened her eyes in an expression that meant *keep quiet*.

At the sound of their whispering, Shankar chacha turned to look at us. "So how did you like the house?" he asked, smiling.

Didi and I replied in unison. "Very nice!"

"I'm so glad that Amma brought us to see your house, Shankar chacha," I added, pleased at myself for sounding so polite.

Instead of replying, Shankar chacha stopped in his tracks and looked reproachfully at Amma. Then he crouched in front of Didi and me and stared into our eyes. "I'm sorry," he said, his voice tender. "I forgot to tell you—this is not just *my* house." Placing a hand on each of our shoulders, he added, "This is also *your* home."

I wasn't sure how to respond, and neither was Didi. Seeing our hesitation, Shankar chacha stood up, seeming a bit sad. "Bhabhi," he said to Amma, "you cannot deny them their heritage. They will need more than the idealism of their parents. They need to know where they come from."

Her face inscrutable, Amma merely reminded our uncle that he had wanted to finish the tour before dusk. Suresh, I realized, was well ahead of us.

We resumed our walk, but now Shankar chacha was holding my hand and Didi's while he shared more information about our home and family. Shankar chacha told us his youngest brother and his wife were on their way from Dhanbad, and we would meet them very soon. This was exciting! I asked him whether our youngest uncle had any children, but he said no. Didi asked, "Who else do we have in our family?"

With a mixture of pride and amusement, he replied: "A small battalion." Apart from our Babu, Shankar chacha had four other brothers—three older and one younger. Our late grandfather had encouraged all six of his sons to develop their minds and bodies, so they had been trained in traditional martial arts such as stick fighting and wrestling. Shankar chacha went on to explain that Bhagalpur had once been part of the British province of West Bengal, a region known for its history of political agitation that became a hotbed of revolutionary activities during the lengthy struggle for independence. Our grandfather, Babu Biharilalji, had often opened the doors of his home for political meetings, which were attended by many prominent local figures in the freedom struggle, including Anand Mohan Sahay and Dr. Rajendra Prasad.

During the 1920s, Shankar chacha said, the independence movement began to splinter, and his four elder brothers—Kumud Narayan, Shyam Narayan, Keshav Narayan, and our father, Rajeshwar Narayan—found themselves pulled in various political directions. He reminded us that, in February 1922, Gandhiji had suspended the satyagraha campaign, after a violent riot broke out in Chauri Chaura, a town we'd passed not far from on the train to Bhagalpur from Lucknow. But not all members of the Indian National Congress agreed with his decision: some felt that a single incident of violence wasn't sufficient reason to call a halt to the campaign. Some were also opposed to Congress's refusal to participate in elections to British legislative councils, arguing that it would be better to infiltrate these councils and undermine British rule from within. So, around the end of 1922, this group, led by Chittaranjan Das and Motilal

Nehru, broke away from Congress to form the Swaraj Party in order to continue the fight for independence.

Didi and I were listening intently, waiting to find out more about Babu's family history, when suddenly I felt confused. "But didn't Gandhiji also want *swaraj*?" I asked.

Shankar chacha smiled, but it was Amma who answered. "Of course he did," she said, "but he could not condone violence." Instead, Gandhiji and those who supported him focused on other ways of gaining independence, such as the khadi movement, which promoted the use of homespun cloth in place of British textiles. They also recognized the need to improve social conditions, and so they worked hard to eliminate the class of untouchables and raise the status of women, as well as to foster Hindu-Muslim unity. "Gandhiji wanted everyone to feel a sense of self-respect and to live peacefully with each other," she said. "That was the independent country he wanted to create."

Shankar chacha nodded and resumed his story. He explained that socialism was becoming popular at the time, and the independence movement developed a radical contingent, many of whom were influenced not only by Marxist theory but also by the Bolshevik revolution in Russia. In 1920, a Bengali, M. N. Roy, was instrumental in issuing a manifesto from Tashkent calling for the formation of a Communist Party in India. Other workers' parties soon sprang up, peasants rebelled against tenancy laws that kept them eternally in debt, and radical groups began to recruit young men and women with the goal of revolutionary action. Although Shankar chacha and his younger brother were still a little too young to become directly engaged in political struggle, his four older brothers were courted by all three of these very different groups—Gandhi loyalists, Swaraj Party supporters, and revolutionaries.

Despite his own commitment to independence, their father was conscious of his traditional duties as a patriarch and somewhat embarrassed that his oldest son, now over thirty, was still unmarried. So he persuaded Kumud Narayanji to accept a position at a civil court in Katihar, a town about fifty miles northeast of Bhagalpur, and soon after arranged his marriage. My grandfather's next task was to put an end to Shyam Narayanji's days of courting arrest for political actions by tying him down in marriage as well, something quickly followed by the birth of the first of several sons. To support his expanding responsibilities, Shyam Narayanji accepted a teaching position at a college in Afghanistan, leaving his wife and young children at the family home for a time—although, after returning from Afghanistan, he chose to move his family to the more modern section of Bhagalpur.

Even before Shyam Narayanji left India, the third brother, Keshav Narayanji, had begun to display signs of mental illness, which had gradually grown worse. He had retreated into a solitary shell and refused to interact with anyone in the family or in the outside world. He never married, and he still lived in the family home, where he remained disconnected from his surroundings. Shankar chacha, who was not yet twenty at the time that Keshav Narayanji became ill, did not know what had caused the complete emotional withdrawal of a young man who had been as active and vibrant as his two older brothers. But he did remember that Babu had left home without warning as soon as it became clear that, as son number four, he was next in line to be tied to the anvil of marriage and family responsibilities.

When Babu was still living at home, attending TNB College for his degree in mathematics, Rajendra Prasadji, a Gandhi loyalist, had briefly come to practice law in Bhagalpur and had taken him under his wing. After Babu abruptly departed, the family learned that he was studying at the law college in Patna for another degree. Word was that he continued to build his physical strength by swimming across the mighty Ganga, which flows through Patna. Such news always travelled home through others, though, since Babu had chosen to sever all links with his family.

Some time later, they heard that he was working for Dr. Rajendra Prasadji's English-language political weekly, *Searchlight,* based in Patna. Then, in 1929, they learned that he had joined the revolutionary group Yuvak Sangh. After that, he essentially disappeared.

For years, the family received no news about him except for rumours that he was working with an underground revolutionary network connected to Subhash Chandra Bose. "We also heard that Raja bhaiya was in jail for his role in some violent conspiracy," Shankar chacha told us. "But we had no way to contact him, even when our father lay dying.

Many in the family labelled him irresponsible for abandoning his family, but I know my brother. Raja bhaiya must have had his reasons." Shankar chacha sighed.

In the end, then, it fell to Shankar chacha to take charge of the house and the assorted pieces of the family remaining in Bhagalpur. "It is not easy to manage my responsibilities with a job that requires me to travel so much," he admitted. "But we make do." During the Second World War, he said, his youngest brother, Ridheshwar Narayan, had wanted to join the army. But he suffered from asthma, and the family was very relieved when he failed the physical exam. He was now the manager of a glass factory in Dhanbad, about 150 miles south, and he visited the family home frequently with his wife. "You'll love your youngest *chachi*. She adores children, especially clever little girls like you two."

Shankar chacha's storytelling paused for a moment as he glanced back to make sure that Amma was following us on the path, which meandered around dense bushes and lush trees. Then his thoughts returned to our Babu. "For nearly ten years," he said, "we received no word from Raja bhaiya. But we kept hoping to see him one day."

"How did you know if he was even still alive?" Didi asked. This was a question that often entered my head when Babu would go off to work or head out for a walk and simply not return, and it scared me to hear it spoken.

"We didn't," Shankar chacha replied. "Not until the Ramgarh session of the Indian National Congress in March 1940." By that time, the Second World War was well underway, and Gandhiji had learned from his experience after the First World War. He had refrained from political agitation during that war and had even toured western India to recruit soldiers for the British Indian army. More than one million Indian troops were deployed in Europe during the First World War, and some 74,000 of them were dead by the war's end. But Gandhiji's unswerving support of Britain was repaid with the Rowlatt Act of 1919—the so-called Anarchical and Revolutionary Crimes Act, which gave British administrators in India the power to arrest without warrant and detain without trial. So when the Second World War broke out, Gandhiji vowed to resist British attempts to once again force their war on India.

"I was one of the scores of volunteers at the Congress meeting in Ramgarh," Shankar chacha revealed. "I was posted near the stage to manage the crowds and to run errands. On the stage sat the leaders of the Congress—Mahatma Gandhi, Maulana Azad, Sarojini Naidu, Jawaharlal Nehru, Dr. Rajendra Prasad, and many others."

Emotion crept into Shankar chacha's voice as he recounted his surprise at being summoned by Dr. Rajendra Prasad's secretary, Mathura Babu. Rajendra Prasadji had wanted to speak with *him*. "Here I was, a man in my early thirties, recently married and soon to become a father. But climbing the stage to touch the feet of the great Rajendra Prasadji, I felt like an awkward teenager. Rajendra Prasadji looked at me intently when I nervously bent down to touch his feet. He asked in Maithili, 'Are you Rajeshwar Narayan's brother?'

"I could only nod, still half-bent with respect. Rajendra Prasadji smiled and asked my name and then inquired about the well-being of our family. I was tongue-tied but managed to say, 'The benediction of elders keeps us going.' He put his hand on my head in a gesture of blessing: 'Your brother is a great man, did you know that?'"

At this, Shankar chacha slowed his pace so that he could fish for a handkerchief in the pocket of his kurta to wipe his eyes. Then he let out a nervous laugh. Even on the stage, he said, his eyes had brimmed with tears, he felt such pride. Rajendra Prasadji had told him to carry on the good work of fulfilling his duties to the country and the community like his brother. When Mathura Babu leaned in to speak to him, Rajendra Prasadji tore a page from his notebook and wrote,

> *I know the family of Rajeshwar Narayan Sinha and their work for the freedom of the country. Blessings of a bright future to Shankareshwar Narayan Sinha.*
> *Rajendra Prasad*

He handed the paper to Shankar chacha and said, "Take this as my best wishes to you."

Our uncle's composure began to return as he explained how important this brief and unexpected interaction had been for him. Rajendra

Prasadji had spoken of Raja bhaiya in the present tense, so he must have known that he was alive. The rumour of Raja bhaiya's involvement in an underground revolutionary group had always offered the most plausible explanation for his disappearance. It must have been to protect his family. Subhash Chandra Bose had made enemies among the British as well as within the ranks of Congress leaders. If Babu was working for Subhashji, he was not safe anywhere.

This meeting had also encouraged Shankar chacha to become more involved in the political struggle, inspiring him to take part in the Quit India protests that began two years later, in August 1942.

Didi asked Shankar chacha whether he still had the note from Rajendra Prasadji. He had a shelf filled with letters and old pictures, he replied, where he kept the note like a precious treasure. He promised to show it to us when we returned to the house.

Shankar chacha turned around to check on Amma's progress once again and continued much more merrily. "Another gift arrived around that time, when we received a letter from the principal of the Kasturba girls' school in Wardha." She had introduced herself as the betrothed of Raja bhaiya and requested the presence of his family at their wedding.

"Your grandmother was alive but not up to travelling anywhere, much less the eight hundred miles to Wardha." Many in the family were very upset by Raja bhaiya's long silence, and some questioned the decorum of the bride-to-be inviting his family to the ceremony, sidelining the traditional role of her extended family. "Your grandmother listened to all the complaints silently. Then she instructed me to go to Wardha to represent the family, even if it was too late."

Babu and Amma were married in the simplest of temple ceremonies on 14 June 1941, in Wardha. Didi and I had read the letters of blessing from Gandhiji and Rajendra Prasadji.

Shankar chacha reached Wardha a few days after the wedding, with traditional marital blessings in the form of special clothing for the newlyweds. At the time, Babu was working at the Hindi Prachar Samiti and also helping Rajendra Prasadji with the editing of his newsletters. Babu and Amma lived in a simple straw hut in Wardha just like the residents of Sevagram.

"Raja bhaiya's routine was as regimented as I remembered from years ago. He would leave the cottage at three in the morning to practice yoga in the nearby forest. Did you know that your Babu could do a headstand for as long as an hour?"

Didi and I had both seen Babu do this in the sandalwood grove in Ram Niwas Garden in Jaipur, so we nodded enthusiastically. Shankar chacha looked only slightly deflated at not being able to impress us with this piece of information, before picking up the thread again. "Your Amma showed me around Sevagram—a close-knit world of people from all over the country. I stayed there for a few days. It felt like I had made a pilgrimage to the holiest place there could be."

As was customary, Shankar chacha had asked the newlyweds to accompany him to the family home to seek blessings from their elders. Shankar chacha got emotional again as he recalled Babu's refusal. Despite repeated requests, all Babu had offered was, "There is no need for an explanation. I simply cannot return home."

Amma, however, had surprised them both by offering to accompany Shankar chacha to visit the family. She had pragmatically pointed out that her school was closed for the summer break for another month, making it the ideal time to undertake this long journey. Babu had said only, "You are free to do as you wish."

Shankar chacha glanced back again to check on Amma, who was struggling a little to keep up with us in the humid heat. He paused for a moment, fixing an appreciative gaze on Amma. "Do you know that Bhagalpur is known for its tussar silk? But, of course, as followers of Gandhiji, your Amma and Babu would never wear it."

Didi and I nodded. Although we mostly wore khadi cotton, our silk clothes were made only from khadi silk, produced by a method that spares the life of the silkworm, while our sandals, shoes, and handbags were made of khadi leather, tanned from the hide of an animal that died of natural causes.

"But we did not think to consider this," Shankar chacha continued, "when my mother sent the gifts for Bhabhi. All the same, when Bhabhi arrived here, she had draped one of the gifts, a red tussar silk sari, around her shoulders, on top of her khadi clothing." He stopped walking long enough to allow Amma to catch up with us and then added very affectionately, "She and my mother bonded as if they'd known each other in another life."

Amma returned Shankar chacha's look of warmth with a solemn smile. She stated matter-of-factly, "She was the only mother I knew."

We had all stopped walking by then, pausing to catch our breath under the fragrant foliage of a large *bakul* tree. The sun's rays were beginning to lengthen, but they still pricked our flesh in the humid heat. Suresh, who had been bounding a few steps ahead of us all this while, now turned around to join our little cluster, and Amma absentmindedly caressed his head of short, shiny black hair. For a few moments there were no pangs of the past, just the rustling of the leaves in the gentle breeze and the occasional melodious call of the cuckoo celebrating the ripening of sweet mangoes.

"Strange how it all works," Shankar chacha reflected, addressing no one in particular. Then he turned his attention back to his story.

After spending a few days with the family and making new friends in Bhagalpur, Amma had returned to Wardha. Shankar chacha wrote many letters to Babu, trying to reconnect him to the family, but he never received a reply. Amma wrote letters regularly, however. That is how they learned that, in 1945, Babu had decided to leave Wardha and move to Ajmer. He had been contacted by the Rajasthan Sevak Sangh, a group of Gandhiji's followers, who were looking for help in resuscitating the newspaper *Nayjyoti,* which had been banned by the British administration for sedition. A number of the princely states in Rajputana were loyal to Britain and had likewise banned the paper.

Babu found it hard to resist a chance to defy the orders of feudal kingdoms and the British Raj at one and the same time, and he agreed to join the paper's editorial staff. The pay was irregular, unlike the threat of violence and imprisonment, which was constant. It was Babu's dream job. "So Bhabhi left Wardha with toddler Abha and you still in her belly," Shankar chacha said, poking me under the chin with his last remark and making me giggle.

Didi asked a question that appeared to be troubling her. "Why did you never visit us in Jaipur, Shankar chacha?"

"I tried a few times," Shankar chacha replied with a laugh and a twinkle in his eyes. "I would write to your mother about my plans to visit. Always on the eve of the journey, a telegram would arrive from her, announcing her own plans to travel somewhere or other. After a couple of cancellations, I got the message that Bhabhi did not want me to visit Jaipur."

Amma immediately protested, explaining how her life had been uncontrollably busy with the duties of family, the school, the board of education, meetings, and delegations, along with frequent summons to Delhi from Dr. Rajendra Prasadji after he became the country's president in 1950. Amma sounded a bit defensive as she explained how Rajendra Prasadji and his wife, Rajvanshi Devi, were like family and how she felt duty-bound to respond to invitations, even if Babu always refused to accompany her.

The twinkle in Shankar chacha's eyes sparkled a bit more, but instead of making Amma squirm any further, he said with a chuckle, "*Arre,* Bhabhi! Everyone here knows Raja bhaiya. We know that managing him requires more skills than all your social and political causes combined. He drives a hard bargain."

Amma looked down at the grassy ground as though mesmerized by the uneven patterns of the moist earth. After a moment's thought, she said, "I have gained more than I have lost in this bargain. My marital shackles have given me the freedom to live by my convictions."

Shankar chacha disagreed. "*Na,* Bhabhi, you were a political activist long before you met Bhaiya." As though to prove his point, he turned to Didi and me. "Do you know how many times your mother went to jail before she turned sixteen years old?"

"Three times," we answered in unison.

Amma was unimpressed by our coordinated response. "The country may be independent, but an unmarried woman has no freedom in our society. She must remain invisible or constantly defend her life and dignity. It is the protection of marital status that allows me to work for the greater good."

Shankar chacha looked unconvinced but did not argue further when Amma smiled broadly at our little group. "Most important, I have gained a loving family."

"So you have," said Shankar chacha with a sigh, as he motioned for us to continue our walk.

Suddenly, the clusters of vegetation and haphazard buildings in our path gave way to the broad banks of the Ganga. In Jaipur I had come to love the Banganga River, which snaked its way through arid desert until the monsoon season, when it would swell its banks to nourish the fertile basin of the local reservoir, Ramgarh Lake, a favourite picnic spot. During recent travels with Amma, I had discovered the glacier-fed rivers of the mountains—the Alaknanda, the Bhagirathi, the Kosi, the Saryu—which tumbled through passes and valleys to feed the great rivers of the plains, such as the Gomti and Yamuna. These broad rivers provided water for irrigation and supported the countless people who lived along their banks. Never before, though, had I seen a river like the Ganga.

We were standing on the elevated ghat that led down to the water. Like so many other ghats, this one was hemmed in on all sides by temples and teemed with cows, monkeys, dogs, birds, pilgrims, priests, and peddlers. But none of the noisy, chaotic jumble of human and animal life crowding its banks could detract from the awe I felt at the sight of the river itself—its green water stretching to the horizon.

As we stared out across the river, Shankar chacha told us to bow our heads to the holiest river in India—Gangaji, Ganga ma, the Ganges. Rising high in the Himalayas, it flowed some fifteen hundred miles before finally emptying into the Bay of Bengal, and at this point where we stood, it was nearly three miles wide. A boat now drew closer to the ghat, the boatman bowing deeply to Shankar chacha. The boat looked almost as old as the river itself. Shankar chacha helped Didi and me into the boat, one by one, before jumping in himself. Amma looked strangely hesitant for a moment but then took a tight hold on Shankar chacha's outstretched hand and climbed in. Without a word, Shankar chacha raised his arm to point to his right, a signal to the boatman to start rowing.

Once we were riding the current, Shankar chacha allowed Didi, Suresh, and me to take short turns at the oars. It was really hard work, which the smiling boatman made look effortless. Shankar chacha pointed to the farmland that we were passing. A recent shift of the flood plains had yielded another piece of fertile land, he explained, which could grow up to four crops a year. He described a special kind of small-grained rice, *kanakjeera,* so fragrant that its aroma lingered in the courtyard for days after it had been cooked.

Amma was sitting very still, right in the middle of the boat, clutching the edge of her wooden bench. Warming to his topic, Shankar chacha talked on about how much had changed since the days when poor people knew their place and farmers did not dare to pretend to ownership of the land or its produce. Nowadays, though, even a servant could stake a claim to land that had been loaned to him only for tilling, in lieu of a salary. Shankar chacha shook his head despondently. He had lost all hope of saving his family's landholdings, which government policies were bent on redistributing to sharecroppers.

"I cannot fight this battle alone. The soles of my shoes will wear through with all the visits I have to make to government offices, just to get official proof of ancestral property. And who will fight long court battles to evict these sharecroppers—these miserable *bantaidaar?*" The sour note was unmistakable. Although the rest of the family failed to appreciate it, he complained, his presence here was saving the family home. "Otherwise, just like the orchard and the farmland, we would have lost it long ago."

As he spoke, Shankar chacha glanced at Amma now and then, as if in expectation of a rebuke. But her eyes were fixed on the horizon, her face tense and beaded with sweat, and she seemed oblivious to Shankar chacha's monologue—and to our periodic interruptions of it, as we pointed excitedly to unfamiliar-looking birds or fish. Suresh identified different types of carp for us, and he was also good at spotting shorebirds rising from the river's banks. Shankar chacha continued to talk, now describing his travelling duties for the Indian Railways and how much he enjoyed seeing the length and breadth of the country. He was thankful to his father for ensuring that he pursued higher education, he said, since land was no longer a source of revenue. And he spoke of his plans to send Suresh to the engineering college in Patna as soon as he finished high school.

Through all of this, Amma said not a word, sitting so still that I started to wonder whether she might be meditating with her eyes wide open. Finally, discouraged by his inattentive audience, Shankar chacha let the chopping of the oars on the water do the talking. The lull in his monologue gave Didi and me the opportunity to start the singing game of *antakshari* with Suresh, which continued for the remainder of the boat ride. Someone playing the game only needs to sing the first stanza of each song, but when Didi started singing *Tu Ganga ki mauj main Yamuna ki dhara*—"You are the course of the Ganga, I am the current of the Yamuna"—everyone joined in to sing the whole song except Amma, who seemed lost in another world. Suresh and I were on the same team and Didi was on her own, but neither side faltered in carrying forward the chain of songs, and the game ended in a friendly draw.

As soon as we returned to shore, Amma recovered her voice. She embarked on a tirade about the relentless feudalism of Bihar, about men and women still trapped in the dark ages, about distorted human values and exploitative social norms. Her words poured out faster than the river's current, some sort of inner fury visible in the veins throbbing at her temple. Shankar chacha was taken by surprise, but he was not offended. He listened quietly to Amma's rant until she subsided and started walking back toward the path, ever so slightly unsteady on her feet, but in the lead regardless.

Shankar chacha hung back to walk beside me. A slow smile played in the corner of his mouth as he offered me his hand to hold. "Does she echo your Babu often?" At his question, I lowered my head, trying to hide the smile that I did not want my mother to see, in case she turned around to check on me.

We returned home just as the cows were returning from pasture, their copper and brass bells tinkling cheerfully around their long leathery necks. The man by the well was waiting for us, and when we arrived he poured water and handed us soap and towels so that each of us could wash our hands and feet before entering the inner courtyard through the back door.

Shankar chacha then declared that we were about to eat the traditional way. "Not the big-table-small-plate-ways of the big city here, no sir."

The pungent aroma of spices crackling in mustard oil swirled around the courtyard. The hall in the inner courtyard now sported a neat row of low square wooden tables with short carved legs, and there was a colourful reed mat behind each table to sit on. Shankar chacha assured Amma that there was no fish or meat and asked her to join him and the children in eating first. She declined, saying that she would eat with the women, after the men and children. Then she turned to help Chachi and the young woman with the hidden face serve the food.

Buaji's wicker chair had been moved to a spot precisely midway between the row of diners and the bustling action near the cooking fires. Chachi was piling large plates high with fragrant rice, while the faceless one doled out large spoonfuls of steaming vegetable and lentil dishes into individual bowls. The pot-bellied cook was frying crisp little puris, and the thin ladies were filling little bowls with yet more mouth-watering dishes.

Amma asked Chachi not to put so much food onto our plates. Chachi gently said that there was enough food for everyone. Amma objected again that the children certainly could not finish that much rice. When Buaji heard this exchange, she demanded so all could hear, "What are the servants going to eat if the plates are empty?"

At this, Amma turned sharply toward Buaji, her face tight. For a moment everyone was quiet, and Didi and I held our breaths. When she finally spoke, Amma's voice was slow and deliberate: "Abha-Rekha will serve themselves and will take only what they can finish. They have been brought up to respect people and food."

I looked around and noticed that more people in the hall had stopped breathing. I was not sure what to do until Didi confidently stood up, dished out a little rice onto two plates, and, placing one of them in front of me, sat down next to me.

Just as Buaji launched into a strident reply, I heard Shankar chacha's voice rise above her shrill pitch, asking everyone to be quiet. He turned to Buaji and told her not to make something out of nothing. "Peace is as important as food," he declared.

He then gestured to the thin ladies to serve the food. The tension, which had hung in the air like a heavy raincloud, seemed to drift away with that slight turn of his raised wrist. Buaji muttered something, but she took care to keep it low, maintaining a furiously flapping fan between her face and her brother's sharp gaze.

The serving of food only intensified once the plates and bowls were in front of us. One of the walls of the hall was lined with ceramic jars of every possible shape and size. From these, Chachi produced chutneys, preserves, and pickles of a seemingly infinite variety, filling many saucers and asking each one of us to try this or that. Amma warned Chachi about our sensitive throats, but Chachi had already spooned a few of the chutneys and pickles onto my plate, insisting, "Homemade food never makes you sick."

Layers of complex aromas rose from my plate, making me hungrier than I had ever been. The faceless one—whom everyone referred to as *dulhin,* the newlywed—brought in two large serving bowls heaped to the top with different types of puris. I took one small puri and broke it into pieces, planning to scoop up one tantalizing taste at a time. But before that puri was done, Chachi had already put two more on my plate, ignoring my protests. In truth, these were feeble to begin with, what with Amma's instructions never to talk with food in my mouth.

Suddenly, Buaji remembered the taro leaves that she asked the gardener to pick for her. She started giving instructions on grinding, cutting, mixing, rolling, and shallow frying, and before our meal was over this new dish was added to the spread. Everyone got a few scrumptious, crisp rolls on their plates.

This express train of sumptuous delicacies was not supposed to halt until the arrival of dessert. By that time, my stomach was so full that I could not even look at the sweet things that I loved so much. I cast a quick glance sideways to see that Didi had done a much better job than I had of protecting her plate against the serving onslaught.

The rest of the plates were already piled high with delicious leftovers when I realized that everyone was waiting for me. A substantial amount of food still remained on my plate, and I was afraid that my stomach would burst if I tried to finish it. Shankar chacha leaned toward me with a smile and asked me if I was ready to make space for the next course.

My stomach was hurting, in part from the thought of eating any more but mostly from the thought of Amma's disapproval. I was trying to summon some tears, as the quickest way out of this jam, when I heard Amma's voice: "Don't clear her place. I will eat from her plate."

The thin ladies carried all the other plates carefully into the back, where the household servants were waiting in the dark to receive their share of the leftovers. Amma looked away from this sombre procession.

I followed Didi out of the dining area and into the outer courtyard. While we had been busy eating, the man by the well had transformed the space into a fairyland. Several cots had appeared, draped in white sheets, under the ghostly gossamer canopies of white mosquito netting. Light from oil lamps and lanterns cast surreal shadows in this open yet enclosed space. The ground had been sprinkled with water, and the wet earth's musky perfume now competed with sweet scents from the tuberoses, frangipani, and night-blooming cereus that thrived along the walls.

While Amma ate with the ladies, Suresh and I played a game of catch. Didi and Meera didi sat on the steps of the hall, chatting, with Meera didi doing most of the talking. Once supper was over, Amma took us to the room where our bags were stored, to wash and get ready for bed. In the summertime, almost everyone slept in courtyards or on terraces. While Amma sprinkled sandalwood talcum powder on my freshly scrubbed back to keep the prickly heat at bay, I blurted a confession. "Amma, I love that we have real uncles, aunts, and cousins."

She smiled. "You mean all the loving uncles and aunts you have known so far were not real?"

I disagreed with a vigorous shake of my head. "They are real, but not our own, like Shankar chacha is."

Amma looked at me curiously. "Ah, the call of the blood." She paused before adding, "Remember, there is the family of blood and then there is the family of the heart. Your family of the heart is as vast and as real as the family of blood."

Didi interrupted, arms folded across her chest. "Why did you and Babu keep us away from our family?"

Amma's look turned stern. "We can accept privilege and live by its unjust rules. Or we can carve out our own path and fight for what is right. But we cannot do both."

They locked steely stares for a long, sullen moment. Amma gave in first, caressing Didi's head with a sigh. "You will understand one day." I was afraid that Didi would jerk Amma's hand away, but she just stood stiffly and frowned.

By the end of the next day, Didi and I had learned the names of all the people who worked in the house and the garden. Keeping in mind Amma's injunction, just as we had done in Jaipur and Lucknow, we added "bhaiya" to the names of the men and "didi" to the women, or "ji" for either sex. Shankar chacha was a silent witness to this training session, though he hid behind his newspaper. He never failed to smile lovingly whenever I caught his eye.

For the next few days, Didi and I were in heaven. We had the orchards to play in and cousins to play with, and we had doting uncles and aunts—and so many of them. Some relatives travelled from nearby towns to see us. Some who lived in Bhagalpur came to spend the day with us in the enormous house. The kitchen kept churning out delectable delicacies under the watchful supervision of our many aunties.

One lazy evening, Amma asked me to sing a song, and I chose one of Babu's favourites, by Surdas—*Prabhu more avgun chit na dharo*, "O Lord, dwell not upon my shortcomings"—earning high praise for my voice. Didi and I next did a dance skit in the courtyard in which I played the part of the dark, mischievous Krishna, while Didi was his beautiful, gentle consort, Radha. The older aunts made spitting sounds to ward the evil eye away from such magnificent performers. I was elated, and I squeezed my mother in a tight hug to share my happiness with her. She looked down at me, also looking content and happy in the bosom of a family that, despite her discomfort with wealth and privilege, she had missed as much as we had.

Bhagalpur had its drawbacks, too. The heat was much more oppressive than I had ever known. By the time the humidity had started to rise in Lucknow, we were already in cool, mountainous Jeolikot. When temperatures soared in Jaipur, we had simply stayed indoors until the

64

evening, when the breeze always got cooler. During midsummer in Bhagalpur, however, humidity from the great river made the afternoons sweltering. Walking felt like wading through warm tea, even late in the evenings.

And then there was our own enthusiasm for mangoes. At the indulgent insistence of uncles and aunts, we consumed multiple varieties of mangoes every single day, ignoring Amma's calls for moderation. When we paid for our extravagance with rashes and upset tummies, Amma put both of us on a day-long fast of plain yogurt—not the deliciously creamy kind but the regular buttermilk kind—to give our stomachs some relief. She also applied ground neem leaves all over our bodies to heal the rashes, and soon we were enjoying ourselves once again.

Shankar chacha had much to show us in Bhagalpur, as well—the silk factories, the historical monuments, and his favourite, the ruins of Vikramshila, a bus-ride away and over a thousand years old. During the ride, my head and Didi's were crammed with details about the many centres of learning in ancient India and about the rise of Buddhism, Jainism, and the Nyaya, Vaisheshika, and other schools of Hindu philosophy that once flourished in Bihar.

Shankar chacha vividly described the historical significance of the region. He explained that, in the sixth century BC, the city of Vaishali became one of the earliest-known democratic republics, predating the city-states of Greece, and played a key role in the development of both Buddhism and Jainism. A few centuries later, Pataliputra—present-day Patna—became the capital of the Mauryas, who took back the northwestern territories of India from the governors of Alexander and whose empire extended, at its peak, all the way to southeastern Iran. Then there was Ashoka the Great, who built highways and monuments throughout the length and breadth of south Asia in the third century BC.

With an ongoing history lecture, we spent several hours amid the ruins of Vikramshila, one of the foremost universities of the era, as we learned, along with those at nearby Nalanda and at Taxila, near Rawalpindi. Shankar chacha showed us the remains of huge stupas and of the many-storeyed libraries, similar to those at Nalanda. Both Vikramshila and Nalanda had survived as prominent centres of learning until the end of the twelfth century, when they were destroyed by the invading army of Bakhtiyar Khiliji. Thousands of students and teachers were slaughtered, and ancient troves of manuscripts were said to have burned for days after they were set afire.

Shankar chacha's detailed description of the heyday of Vikramshila and its destruction reminded me so much of Babu and his meticulously told histories of the places that we used to visit in Jaipur that my heart started twisting in my ribcage. My tearful eyes made Shankar chacha stop in alarm and pull me closer to look at my face. Everyone thought that I was moved by the tales of horror and carnage, since I offered no explanation for my sobs. But I suspected that Amma understood how much I was missing Babu. I saw it in her sad, comforting smile.

In between memorable excursions and elaborate meals, during the long summer afternoons everyone gathered in one of the pillared halls, where the children romped, the men played cards or chess, and the women read, wrote, or embroidered. An electric fan hung from the high ceiling, but Buaji did not like to use it. She favoured the big, frilly cotton fans that had to be pulled by hand by one of the many servants, while she muttered instructions and admonitions. As I came to understand the language better, I was able to gather that she thought the electric breeze "drying" rather than "cooling" and thus preferred to take her summer afternoon naps under the gentler breeze of a cotton fan pulled by human hands. When she started to doze, though, I would see Amma gesture to Suresh to switch on the ceiling fan and for the servant to stop pulling the cord of the cotton fan.

Buaji was also regularly annoyed at the use of electric lights at night. When she caught anyone reading under the electric lamp, she grumbled that they would go blind in the artificial light: "If God had intended you to see at night, he would have made you an owl." Like most of her other objections, everyone ignored this one, with either a smile or, in the case of one of the boys, a wisecrack.

As our happy visit approached its inevitable end, one last thing remained. We were to receive special visitors on the evening of the day before we had to return to Lucknow. One of Babu's distant cousins, Rai Bahadurji, was visiting Bhagalpur with his daughter, and they had been invited over for dinner. There were more lights than usual, and a big wooden table with the finest chairs of the household occupied the centre of the courtyard. Shankar chacha and Amma had an animated discussion about the arrangements for the evening, and all the children were being given special instructions about appropriate greetings and table manners.

Finally Rai Bahadurji arrived with his daughter, who had just returned from finishing a degree in Singapore. He was dressed in a three-piece suit that struggled to maintain its crispness under the oppressive onslaught of the humidity. He kept dabbing his narrow, bald head with a kerchief, in a valiant battle against streams of perspiration.

In contrast, his daughter, Miss Nisha, a statuesque young woman whose thick black hair brushed her shoulders in shiny, languid curls, seemed totally impervious to the heat. She wore an exquisite silk sari—periwinkle blue, with a faint white floral print—that flowed smoothly along her curves and over a matching sleeveless blouse. In one hand, she carried a dainty black purse and, in the other, a small Japanese folding fan, which she used unobtrusively from time to time. Her flawless skin seemed to glow in the radiance of a magnificent gold necklace, tastefully complemented by a gold bracelet on one slender arm and a gold watch on the other.

The two guests talked to the uncles sitting around the table, while all the servants, dressed in their best clothes, busied themselves with serving the finest that the household had to offer. Didi, Suresh, and I had the honour of sitting at the table in this dazzling company. We had already been given some snacks so that we would not be too hungry to remember our recently repolished table manners. Suresh and I sat very stiffly, not always knowing what to do with our arms and legs. Didi was even more ladylike than usual, looking confidently from speaker to speaker around the table as she dexterously manipulated the rarely used flatware.

As the dessert trays made their way to the table, Miss Nisha asked Shankar chacha about his sister-in-law from Lucknow. Before he could reply, she pointed toward the covered hall with her folded fan and said in her velvety voice, "I hope that she is not hiding in the inner quarters with the women and children."

The bamboo curtains of the pillared hall had indeed been pulled down, and Buaji was presiding over the proceedings from behind them. Despite Shankar chacha's protest, Amma had chosen to stay behind the curtains in solidarity with Chachi, who was too timid to sit at the table with the visitors and was also not feeling very well. I knew that Amma could hear us and wished she couldn't, as Miss Nisha launched into a spirited lecture on the archaic traditions of India and the bravery of the women who had transformed society in Japan, where Miss Nisha was born.

I expected Amma to burst from behind bamboo curtains, but nothing stirred. I wondered whether Miss Nisha was deliberately being provocative, especially when she turned toward the curtains and began to address them directly, extolling the virtues of education and the need for educated women to lead by example. When she paused briefly to take a breath, Amma called out, "Abha-Rekha, please come here."

Amma had an annoying habit of joining our names, Janus-like, sometimes creating confusion about whether she meant one or the other or both. Normally, I ran to her the instant I heard her summons, while Didi liked to wait for confirmation as to whether she was indeed the object of the beckoning. But we had just been given a long lecture warning us to be politely attentive to the guests at all times. Didi and I exchanged glances. Then Didi noiselessly pushed her chair back, excused herself, and walked purposefully toward the curtained hall.

I heard Amma's voice asking Didi to invite Miss Nisha to come and meet the rest of the household. Miss Nisha hesitated momentarily at this invitation but then stood up, assumed her most elegant posture, and walked over to the curtains, one of which was rolled up to admit her. Now too curious to stay seated at the table with my hands folded in my lap, I slipped out of my chair, deliberately not looking toward Shankar chacha, wanting to avoid any signal of disapproval that might thwart my escape.

On the other side of the curtains, my aunts and cousin-sisters were seated on very low and ornate furniture. Everyone was draped in yards of resplendent silk and gleaming gold jewellery, the elaborate *pallu*s of their saris covering their heads and shoulders to varying degrees. As always, the anomaly was my mother, a plump but austere presence, draped in a coarse white cotton sari, sitting with a straight back on a chair in the corner.

With a self-assured smile, Miss Nisha folded her hands in greeting. Amma looked up and returned her greeting with an open smile. Miss Nisha gazed down at the group and then said, in effortlessly polished Hindi that only my mother could match, "I was given to understand that the daughter-in-law from Lucknow was the director of a government department of some sort. But all I see here are women who cannot possibly have much education if they choose to live behind curtains."

There was total silence on both sides of the curtains until Amma asked, "Wouldn't you like to sit down for a moment?" She pointed to the middle of the divan, where space was created as she spoke, by rustling silk saris sliding sideways.

Miss Nisha retorted, "You are asking me to join these women in their lightless and airless world?"

I wanted to give Miss Nisha a good hard shove from behind, but instead I clutched the edge of the bamboo curtain, hard. Didi cast a swift, fiery look at Miss Nisha and then, with that defiant tilt of her chin we all knew so well, went to stand behind Amma.

Amma had sadness in her eyes, rather than the glint of anger I was expecting. "You spoke about the great Japanese women who inspired you. Let me ask you this. How much do you know about the first generation of Indian women who stepped out of their homes for the freedom of their country? Women who could no longer go back to their homes for protection or rest, who continued to spend their lives fighting for social and political justice, not just for themselves, but also for others?"

Miss Nisha opened her shapely mouth to say something, but no smooth words escaped her painted lips. Amma continued, "We don't know each other, but I suspect we have the same objectives. We may have somewhat different paths. Your path starts with personal freedoms that you guard jealously. I admire your desire for independence, but please do not stop at that. Personal freedom is important, but on its own it is selfish and arrogant. Our quest for freedom has to be inclusive, for all women, for all of humanity."

By now Amma was almost imploring. "I am the outsider in this family, but these women you are castigating are your own family members. It is their misfortune that they have not had the same privileges that you have had. To change this, they need someone to champion their rights. Who better to take on this onerous task than someone as bright and fearless as you?" Amma folded her hands at the end of her question.

Miss Nisha looked at once embarrassed, irritated, and bewildered, like someone who had never before been challenged. Leaving her to recover her composure, Amma excused herself, saying that she wanted to check on her sick sister-in-law.

Didi chose to walk behind Amma like a loyal bodyguard, while I stood torn between following them or returning to the dessert that I had left on my plate.

In the end, dessert won.

3

No Easy Path

After that first visit to Bhagalpur, Didi and I yearned to go back. Amma seemed somewhat ambivalent about our reaction, but she did not prevent us from spending very available holiday with Shankar chacha, who, besides welcoming us into the family home and introducing us to our brand-new cousin, another boy named Praveen, would sometimes take us on train rides to other parts of the country. We had found an anchor, a source of stability and dependable love.

Back in Lucknow, we were spending more nights than ever at Lalita mausi's house, where Didi and I had, eventually, made friends with some of the adults and struck an uneasy truce with the younger inhabitants. Dadi ma calmed down perceptibly whenever Didi read aloud from the *Bhagavad Gita* or I sang devotional songs, especially *Jhini jhini bini chadariya,* "Fine, fine, is the weaving of that shawl," Kabir's *bhajan* reminding us that the body is but a delicate shawl that the soul discards at the end of our time on earth. No matter where we were, Didi and I religiously wrote daily letters to our parents, some of which got mailed to Babu once every month. Babu's letters to us arrived only sporadically, and were always

71

devoid of answers. Sometimes they contained a poem he had written or a passage translated from a book he had been reading, and always they ended in blessings of happiness, health, and good karma.

Didi and I had by this point become voracious readers of the Hindi books in our collection, but Babu's library included books in French, German, and Russian, as well as in Bengali and several other Indian languages that neither Didi nor I knew. We wondered why Babu had chosen to study those particular languages, but that was just another of the questions he would never answer, and for the most part we just ignored their presence on his bookshelves. We sometimes tried our hand at books in English or Sanskrit, but they were too much work. In any case, Amma and Babu's ever-growing collection of Hindi titles made up the bulk of the hundreds of books that lined the walls in the living room of the bungalow.

In the meanwhile, Amma was travelling further and further afield, her trips no longer confined to the welfare centres in semi-urban areas. She was now going deeper into rugged wilderness, to rural villages inaccessible by highways or railway links. Reaching these remote locations sometimes involved crossing through territory inhabited by bandits, making Amma's journeys unpredictably lengthy and potentially dangerous. She travelled along unpaved roads in a government Jeep, in the company of Deen Dayalji, who still struggled to not call her "Saheb."

Often, the only rest stops for Amma and Deen Dayalji along the road were the *dak* bungalows for government officers that still stood in some of the more remote parts of the country. Back in the 1840s, the British had begun building these bungalows as staging posts for the imperial mail, the *dak,* and many had evolved into resthouses for travelling British officials. The accommodations ranged from barely functional to utterly ostentatious, some located in spectacular settings and some in godforsaken terrain.

On one occasion, they returned from a trip looking especially haggard. When Deen Dayalji asked Ramu kaka to get him some water, I noticed that he seemed unusually relieved to be home. Only later did he tell us the full story.

The welfare department was planning to open a new multi-purpose welfare centre in southwestern part of the state, in the Bundelkhand area, which borders the ravines of the Chambal badlands. Amma and Deen Dayalji had travelled down to Jhansi and, on the return trip, had set out in their usual government Jeep, heading for Hamirpur, about 125 miles to the northeast. Partway along the route, though, the Jeep had broken down. Since they were not far from a railway station when this happened, Amma chose to ignore the advice of the driver and Deen Dayalji that she spend the day and possibly the night in the nearby town while the Jeep was repaired. Instead, she decided to continue on to Hamirpur alone, by train.

Deen Dayalji tried to explain to her that the Hamirpur train station was not in the town of Hamirpur itself and that, to reach the town, she would have to cut across a dense expanse of forest that was controlled by dangerous dacoits. Amma was undeterred. It was barely midday; the district magistrate and the district welfare coordinator of the area were expecting her. There was much work to be done over the next few days. So she asked Deen Dayalji to join her as soon as the Jeep was fixed and, in the meantime, to phone the office in Hamirpur and inform them that she would be arriving by train that evening.

It took several hours for Deen Dayalji to organize the repair of the Jeep and then find a telephone. Dusk was already falling as he listened to the district coordinator, a young woman, yell at him from the other end of the line. She was hysterical with anxiety at the news that Amma was travelling alone at night in those parts. If the train she had boarded was on time, it would have arrived at the Hamirpur station a couple of hours earlier, but there was no sign of her. The two of them fervently hoped that Amma had decided to wait at the station rather than try to make her way to the dak bungalow through the jungle at night. Sick with worry, Deen Dayalji pleaded with the coordinator to send someone to look for Amma—at least to the edge of town.

Meanwhile, Amma had gotten off at the remote Hamirpur railway station, where the only transport consisted of a few rickety mule carts that rapidly filled with people and their substantial luggage. She took a seat on one of the last ones, which joined the convoy of carts on a narrow road snaking through a patchy network of trees and farmland. They were riding toward the forest that separated the train station from the River Betwa, on the other side of which was Hamirpur. Two policemen walked behind them, armed with rifles.

A few miles from the station, as the foliage began to grow dense and the trees taller, the convoy of mule carts stopped in a clearing, where several people dismounted and unloaded their luggage. Accompanied by the policemen, they started walking down a sliver of a road that led along the edge of the jungle toward the cultivated land of the nearby village of Rampur. The remaining passengers, all men, sat on the ground in a tight group, with piles of jute bags, tin canisters, and other goods in the middle, prepared to wait for morning light before resuming their journey through the thick forest.

Amma, however, refused to get out of the cart and quarrelled angrily with the cart driver, who had promised to take her to Hamirpur. The driver argued that entering the forest at night would be an invitation to death. He would rather take his chances with wild beasts, he said, than die at the hands of dacoits. He told Amma to follow the walkers to Rampur if she did not want to wait with the group of men. Frustrated by their mutual stubbornness, the cart driver and Amma began raising their voices to out-shout each other.

Suddenly, two men appeared from the shadows, the metal glint of their long rifles clearly visible in the flickering light of a small hurricane lantern held by the taller of the two. At this sight, the driver's teeth started to chatter, and beads of perspiration appeared on his forehead despite the chill winter night. The men seated on the ground only a few yards from them froze into silhouettes, like a collection of cowering statues.

The two dacoits were wrapped in coarse black *lohi*s, which allowed them to melt into the darkness of the night. The taller man raised his lantern to peer into Amma's face, meeting her unwavering gaze. The thick silence of the cold, foggy night was broken only by distant howls and hoots from the forest.

Amma looked unblinkingly at the lantern-bearer's hard face, with its stiff moustache curled up at the ends. The man's gruff inquiries slashed the silence. "Who are you? Where are you going?"

74

"Bhaiya," she replied calmly, "I need to go to Hamirpur. The district magistrate is expecting me. Will you help me reach my destination?" Amma explained that she was the deputy director of the Social Welfare Department and told him about the breakdown of the Jeep on her way to the new field site. She said that he might have heard her scolding the cart driver, who had promised to take her to Hamirpur but was now refusing to budge. The cart driver stammered that the bridge gate would be closed by now, and the path through the jungle was dangerous for a woman.

"No danger survives our presence," the tall man rumbled. He took the lantern away from Amma's face and made a sign toward the bushes. At that, two more men appeared, also wrapped in dark *lohis*, the metal barrels of their guns visible above their shoulders. The tall man told the cart driver to stay in the middle of the road and follow them.

So they marched through the forest, Amma and the driver in the mule cart, with two dacoits leading the procession and the other two following behind. Their march was accompanied by loud chants of *Hum hain, hum hain*, "It's us, it's us." After nearly a mile, they emerged from a thicket by the bridge on the river. The flickering lights of the town on the other side were in clear view.

The bridge gate was indeed locked, as the driver had predicted, so the tall man used the butt of his rifle to knock on the door of the little shanty next to the bridge, calling for the watchman to unlock the gate. The watchman appeared with his lantern held high, shivering with cold, or terror, or both. He looked up at Amma in the mule cart and spluttered, "Sister, where are you going with these men?"

Before Amma could respond, the tall man rumbled again, "She is a guest of the district magistrate. Open the gate."

The watchman's trembling quickened, but he bravely held his ground. "I can only unlock the gate at this hour upon written orders."

The tall man's body tensed and his eyes flickered. It looked like he was going to break open the gate himself, probably with the head of the watchman. Miraculously, however, he responded to Amma's firm command to wait, as she fished out her official letter pad from the depths of her cotton shoulder bag and scrawled a note for the watchman—the written orders he required.

Still trembling, the watchman unlocked the chains that held the gate of the bridge shut for the night. As soon as the cart started rolling across the bridge, the four dacoits disappeared noiselessly into the shadows. In stunned silence, the driver steered the mule toward the lights of the town, and the watchman locked the bridge shut again behind them.

At the edge of the town, they met a small group of men with flashlights. When Amma asked one of them if this was the town of Hamirpur, the incredulous man asked her whether she was the deputy director they had been waiting for. He introduced himself as the father of the district coordinator, who was beside herself after learning that Amma was alone in these parts, where not even groups of men dared venture into the forest at night.

The cart driver, who sensed his safety, now burst into loud expressions of gratitude to all the gods and all his ancestors for protecting their lives. With widened eyes, he declared that they had just been escorted through the forest by one of the most notorious dacoits in the region. At this news the townsmen joined in voicing their grateful praise to divine powers for sparing Amma's life. This, she replied irritably, was why the area needed a welfare office.

Deen Dayalji arrived the next day with the Jeep and found the whole town talking about Amma's passage through the jungle, re-telling the story repeatedly to him, attributing Amma's survival to the power of the goddess who must have been with her that night.

Now safely back in Lucknow, Deen Dayalji was pleading with Amma not to bother with any more field trips. They had seen enough to prepare the reports, he said. Amma's brow was furrowed more than usual as she listened from her chair on the veranda, but she let Deen Dayalji finish saying his long piece, which ended with a mention of his little children and their possible future without a father. He stopped abruptly and got up to leave, mumbling something that sounded like either an apology or a resignation. Amma watched him leave and then turned to us to ask about our upcoming exams. I got up from the swing to sit on the floor next to her chair, so that I could hug her legs while she talked and stroked my head.

Even two years after we had left our home in Jaipur, I missed it every day. There, we had been a seamless extension of the various families that surrounded us, never letting us feel alone or unprotected, even when Amma was busy and Babu was away. I could ride my bike wherever I wanted to in the walled city. Everyone knew Amma and knew Didi and me as her daughters. We had learned to expect love, kindness, and respect from friends and strangers alike.

Lucknow was still far from feeling like home, except for the brief periods when Amma was around. Our large isolated bungalow with so little neighbourly contact was a frigid and lonely place. When we stayed with families who had generously made space for Didi and me, it strangely increased our ache for home.

I often had nightmares that made me scream and cry in my sleep. Amma placed a small folding knife under my pillow to keep the vague ghosts of the night at bay, which did seem to help. The cold, sharp steel was strangely reassuring to feel under my pillow every time I woke up at night.

Everywhere we went, our outsider status was loudly announced by our clothes and speech. Except for our school uniforms, Didi and I dressed differently from other girls our age. Amid the colourful dotted designs of *bandhani* silks and cottons in Jaipur, the delicate shadow of *chikankari* embroidery in Lucknow, the golden tussar silk of Bihar, and, for special occasions, the intricately woven splendour of Banarasi *jamawar* brocades, we stuck out in our simple white or beige khadi ensembles, as did Amma. Our fluency in standard Hindi, with its Sanskritic vocabulary, was useful to us in school, but our classmates made fun of the way our tongues stumbled when we switched to Awadhi, the local language. Six years earlier, in 1949, Hindi had been designated one of the country's two official languages, along with English, but, in a profoundly multi-lingual country, the choice, we knew, had been controversial. Speakers of the Dravidian languages of southern India had resented the imposition of one of the Indo-Aryan languages of the north, while, in the north, rivalry existed among various linguistic groups. Awadhi, in particular, had a long literary tradition, and we soon realized that, as Hindi speakers, we were regarded as linguistic interlopers.

We were also no longer the daughters of the principal of the school. My teachers in Lucknow did not expect to talk about our progress with Amma, who was one of the few mothers who ever visited the school for that purpose. The other mothers wore pointy shoes, chiffon or silk saris with fashionable blouses, jewellery, and perfect hairdos. The suited-and-booted fathers did all the talking with the teachers.

Even some of the teachers stared at Amma in her unchanging white saris and flat khadi-leather chappals, which gave way to equally utilitarian khadi-leather shoes in the winter months. The way Amma spoke also got sniggers from the girls in my school. One particularly unkind girl loudly asked me in class if my mother worked for All India Radio, since she sounded just like the evening newscaster. Her remark was followed by muffled titters from many of the other girls. I was embarrassed to the core and wished that Amma would never come to school again.

Unlike in Jaipur, where people's respect for Amma and Babu had protected us, Didi and I were subjects of prying enquiries in Lucknow. Most often, people asked questions about our absent father, but even after we had spent three summers away from Jaipur, away from Babu, we had few answers that satisfied us or them.

On the last day of school before the two-week-long Dussehra holidays, which we would be celebrating in Bhagalpur, I was trying to concentrate on what the teacher was saying, barely able to keep at bay my daydreams about our upcoming escape—the adoring aunties, the affectionate cousins, the delectable delicacies, the generous orchard, the majestic river, and, above all, our very loving Shankar chacha.

The teacher and my daydreams were both interrupted, however, when the school peon handed the teacher a note that summoned me to the principal's office. As I rose to leave, I heard "Gangway for Kali avatar!" followed by snickering behind my back. I kept my eyes on the white marble floor and resisted the urge to drag my shoes deliberately—just to annoy any of the staff who might be watching.

The passage curved toward the principal's office.

I looked up and froze.

In the garden beside the principal's office, on a stone bench under the ancient pipal tree, Didi was huddled next to Shankar chacha. I started running toward them, heart singing and feet dancing. Hearing my stomping footsteps on the cobbled path to the bench, the man's face turned toward me. *It was Babu!!*

I couldn't stop running in time and nearly fell into Babu's lap, where I let out all the tears that had been waiting for over two years. We huddled together and cried until sadness could no longer seep through our eyes.

After what felt like an eternity punctuated by sobs, Babu said in his sonorous whisper, "I have to catch the next train back."

The long silent moment was broken by one word from Didi: "When?"

He replied, "In an hour." The grip of silence tightened around my chest.

We continued to sit on the hard stone bench, with Babu in the middle clutching us close to him. When it was time for him to leave, he lifted our chins, kissed our foreheads, wiped his own tears, and walked away without looking back. The only reminders of his visit were our moist scarves and kerchiefs, which we held close to our sore hearts.

MATHURA, 1956–57

As Amma's travelling increased, our Lucknow bungalow began to seem less and less like our home. The chaotic rhythm of Lalita mausi's house had become part of our daily lives, and the shelves and cupboards in Dadi ma's room were slowly filling up with our school books. Didi and I were still writing letters to our absent parents, but we often devoted more time to entries in our personal diaries. We also kept busy after school with dance, music, painting, embroidery and riding classes. Didi excelled at playing the sitar and graduated to advanced-certificate training. It was hard for me to decide which I loved more—the expressiveness of music and dance, the vivid eloquence of painting, the meditative peace of embroidery, or the exhilarating grace of riding.

All of this changed, however, a few months after Babu's visit to the school, when Amma unceremoniously announced that Didi and I were to move to a residential girls' school in Mathura. Didi, who would be fourteen on her next birthday, was about to start her final year of high school, and Amma wanted to ensure a year of strict and uninterrupted routine. We were packed away within two days of our final exams, despite the high drama to which Didi and I took turns subjecting our mother. We were grateful for not being separated, at least.

In Mathura, then still a small town, Amma had another adoptive family, who lived in a house not unlike our home in Jaipur and embraced us much as our former neighbours had done. Ravikantji was like a brother to Amma, and thus Didi and I addressed him as *mama*. He was a bony man with kind eyes who called our mother Shanti. His three children, wife, and elderly mother lived with him in the three-storey house, on the main floor of which he ran his Ayurvedic clinic. The entire house was permeated with the aroma of the herbs, flowers, and barks that were variously boiled or dried and then mixed, often with the addition of ground minerals, into powders or little round tablets or liquids poured into dark-brown glass bottles. Ravikant mama's practice was strictly not-for-profit. The ground floor clinic and dispensary thus had a constant flow of patients from far and wide.

Ravikant mama was our official local guardian, so we were allowed to visit his house on Sundays and other holidays. The entrance to the building was through a small gate opening into a narrow passage, which widened into a square courtyard. The passage had two doors facing each other—the clinic was on one side, where Ravikant mama sat on the floor behind a traditional *munim* writing desk, and the formal living room was on the other, the only room in the house that was locked up and used only on special occasions. A couple of small rooms around the enclosed courtyard contained the paraphernalia and ingredients needed to prepare Ayurvedic medicines, deftly employed by a husband-wife team of assistants.

The first floor had the busy kitchen and many rooms of various sizes. None of the rooms on the top two floors had any clear demarcation in terms of ownership. Ravikant mama and his wife had only three children, but their hospitable home hosted several visitors at any given time. Even after a number of visits to this teeming household, during which we were affectionately fed and looked after by Ravikant mama's wife, Rani mami, and his old but agile mother, also called Dadi ma, we had difficulty establishing who was living with the family, who was visiting, and how they were related to each other, if at all.

Didi's sitar now lived in Ravikant mama's formal living room on the ground floor, since our room in the school's dormitory had barely enough space for our school books and a few belongings. When Didi was not working on her homework or practicing the sitar, she liked to help the ladies in the kitchen. I looked forward to playing with Ravikant mama's children, little Deepak and Shradha, and the oldest, Gayatri didi, who soon became my good friend. And, of course, we were welcomed each Sunday with an array of puffy puris stuffed with spicy potatoes, peas, or lentils.

Our boarding school was located in a tall and narrow building that enclosed a small atrium, which served as the space for our morning assemblies. The ground floor contained the principal-cum-warden's offices, the kitchen, the dining hall, and a room for the use of faculty. All the classes, from grade 6 to matriculation, were taught in classrooms that filled the second and third floors. The topmost floor under the rooftop terrace was meant for the few girls who were boarders. There were eight small rooms on this floor, accessible through a continuous balcony that looked into the atrium. Didi and I shared one of these rooms with each other, and we shared the two toilets and tiny bathrooms on this floor with fourteen other girls.

The elaborate uniform of our school in Lucknow had changed from navy skirt, sky-blue blouse, maroon scarf, and long white socks in the warm months to navy blazer, sky-blue blouse, maroon tie and white pajama-pants in the winter. Our new school uniform was an unchanging beige sari with a burgundy blouse. In the winter months, a burgundy sweater was added to this ensemble. Unlike the bobs, bouffants, and fashionable braids of Lucknow, there was also a prescribed way to tie our hair in Mathura: a single tight braid folded to a length of no more than eight inches.

On Amma's first visit to our dormitory, I had tried to get her permission to cut my long hair into a "boy cut" to avoid the problem of having to conform to the hair rule by folding my braid twice. When Amma refused,

I had argued with her, calling her refusal ironic, since she told us to not be ruled by external markers of beauty like long hair.

Amma had simply smiled knowingly at my clever attempt to get my way. It turned out that I had only opened the door for a lecture on self-reliance: cutting our hair short would mean that we would become dependent on someone else to style and maintain it, rather than being able to manage it on our own. She stroked the black sheet of straight hair that cascaded over my shoulders and reached my lower back, much longer than Didi's waist-long wavy hair. "You do have beautiful hair, and beauty must be appreciated," she said tenderly. "But beauty is all around us, even in the wispy intricate tentacles of a bug. What I ask of you is not to be defined by specific ideas of physical beauty dictated by others."

I was not too thrilled to be compared to a bug, even in this way, but I did manage to get Amma's permission to shorten my hair enough to conform to the length requirement of the school without having to fold my braid. Unlike Lucknow, Mathura had no salons for women, just some hereditary barbers who went to people's houses to cut the hair of men and children. So Didi reluctantly chopped several inches off my hair.

Also unlike Lucknow, our small school offered no extracurricular activities—no music or dance classes, no sewing lessons, no horseback riding. A big brass gong in the courtyard was struck with a wooden mallet at five in the morning, to signify the start of the day—in other words, the start of the skirmish to use the limited facilities shared among all the girls living on the top floor of the school. The gong was struck again at six, summoning us to the courtyard for an hour of yoga, meditation, and prayers, followed by half an hour for breakfast.

Classes were small, with no more than a dozen girls in each class, and ran from eight in the morning until four. Each class level had an assigned room, and students stayed in the same room in the same seat all day, except during two half-hour breaks. In the evening, the sixty or so day-scholars left the tiresome tower, as we boarders made our way down to the dining hall.

Breakfast and supper rotated between *dalia,* a savoury wheat porridge that was served with lentils, and shallow-fried paratha accompanied by pickles, yogurt, and vegetables. The school also gave the boarders fruit for snacks during the breaks, which the boarders added to the pool of savoury and sweet dishes in the lunch boxes brought by the day-scholars.

From six to eight every evening, we used the dining hall tables to do our homework. At nine we were given a hot glass of milk sweetened with jaggary, just before lights-out. Most girls had supplies of homemade snacks in their rooms, such as sugary *laddu* and flaky *mathri* biscuits, and again we found that the practice here was to share them communally. So Didi and I contributed to this shared pool the contents of our steel jars—almonds, cashews, walnuts, pistachios, pine nuts, sunflower seeds, cantaloupe seeds, and sundry other nuts, roasted in ghee and flavoured with different types of salts and spices.

In the beginning Didi and I were somewhat reluctant to participate in the communal spreads that unfolded on the terrace during lunch breaks, a scene so unlike the vast grounds of our school in Lucknow, claimed by exclusive clutches of girls and their ayahs. Didi and I had just been getting comfortable navigating our way around our complex lives in Lucknow when we were unceremoniously uprooted. By the time we left, we had even made some friends and allies at school, but we always ate by ourselves. Now Didi and I found ourselves trying hard not to be regarded as snooty girls from the big city.

We finally crossed an invisible barrier into a closer circle of camaraderie when someone played a prank on Didi. To be the first to claim one of the two toilets each morning, Didi would shoot out of the room like a bullet the moment she heard the five o'clock gong. The rest of us snuggled down in our cozy beds, even if this meant waiting in line at the toilet. The prank needed only one perpetrator, who crept out in the middle of the night and struck the gong at two in the morning. Didi was awake in an instant, sprinting to the toilet and then leaping into the shower, oblivious to the fact that no one else seemed to be stirring. When she emerged from the shower, she hurried to wake me up. But I was sound asleep and determined to remain that way. As Didi was shaking me and calling my name, her voice rising in exasperation at my refusal to respond, a murmur of laughter encircled the whole floor. Only at that point did Didi finally realize what time it was. Instead of complaining or pouting, she took the prank in stride, even regaling her classmates with the story later that morning. The backslapping and chuckling seemed to dissolve some of the vague tension between us and the other girls in our dormitory.

MATHURA, 1957

It felt like years since I had seen Amma or Babu. I missed them both so much that my whole body hurt. Didi sounded worried as she reminded me that Amma had visited us just the previous week. Didn't I remember the books she had given us? The worry in her voice increased when I showed no interest in reminiscing about the delicious snacks that Amma had brought along with her.

The dormitory warden said that I was delirious with fever and would be going home very soon. I felt the warm streak of a tear roll down the side of my face. "Which home?"

Didi was standing by the bed, applying a cold compress to my burning forehead. I heard the sound of my own tears in her voice: "Can I read you something?" I wasn't sure whether I nodded or shook my head.

Through the haze of my fever, I heard Babu playing a *bhajan* on a cranky harmonium . . . Babu thundering, "It was all a waste. EVERY-THING. Everyone has sacrificed their souls at the altar of personal greed. EVERYONE!" The clop-clop of Babu's wooden khadau . . . the goddess Kali dancing to the rattling of the skulls strung around her neck.

I woke up to the strong smell of holy basil. Ravikant mama was holding a spoon full of basil extract, which was searing its way into my chest through my dry throat. Didi helped me to sit up and then offered me a cup holding something that smelled of camphor. I could barely keep my eyes open and spluttered when I tried to drink from the cup.

When I next awoke, I felt the warmth of a familiar presence—*Babu*? No, it was Amma. Sitting on the bed beside me, Amma had both her hands on my stomach, her eyes closed as if in meditation. I smiled to myself and drifted off again.

Amma at her desk writing in her diary . . . nameless faces in Amma's diaries clamouring to escape . . . a fire searing a hole in my stomach . . . Amma's cool hand on my burning forehead . . . beautiful ochre walls surrounding Jaipur . . . a crowded sea of terraces. . . kite-flying under the mild January sun . . . chasing after the dangling thread of a kite falling from the sky . . . people everywhere, looking at you, looking out for you, all the time.

We had been living at Ravikant mama's house for a week by the time the high fever broke. I had had typhoid, I learned, and it had left me very weak. The principal said that I could stay at Ravikant mama's house for one more week so I could recover my strength. Didi was not allowed to miss classes, especially so close to exam time, but she had permission to stay with us after school. When that week came to an end, it was time for Amma to return to Lucknow.

Didi and I sat on a divan next to Amma to say goodbye, just as we had sat with Babu, holding onto her from either side, like sparrows huddled together on an electric wire in the rain. Didi was wiping away tears, and I was complaining about everything in the dormitory, particularly the oily, insipid, and generally uninspiring food. Clearly, I was back to normal.

Ravikant mama walked into the room, his eyes smiling more than his mouth, as always. "Are we done with tears, or are there more to come?"

I sank deeper into Amma, my pout drooping to the lowest level I could muster. I felt Didi's hand reach for me from behind Amma's back. We linked fingers.

Ravikant mama deposited his tall frame in one of the chairs next to the divan. His kind eyes moved from Didi to me as he leaned back. "Did you know that your mother went to the same school that you do, nearly thirty years ago?" His elbows resting on the armrest, palms apart but fingers touching, he paused to check for our reaction. "It was a different time, a different building, much smaller."

This information prompted me to sift through the many bits of information about Amma's life upon which we kept stumbling unexpectedly. Suddenly I remembered hearing Amma mention her principal, Manoramadevi from Mathura, whom she had called her first ever mentor, and who had taken her to political protests in Lucknow. Mathura!

Ravikant mama didn't wait for us to search our memories further. His smiling eyes shifted to Amma's unhappy face. "I think your Amma should tell you the story of a little girl born in Allahabad many years ago."

I sensed Amma's straight back stiffen even more. "Bhaiya, I am not sure if it's time yet."

His gentle voice urged her on. "Shanti, your little dolls are almost young women. They are wiser than you think. I think the story will help them in these difficult times."

Amma closed her eyes for a long moment. "You may be right."

"Trust me," Ravikant mama reassured her, "just like you did all those years ago." Amma smiled absently at some comforting memory from her unmapped past.

We had been staying in the living room on the ground floor, so that we could to be closer to Ravikant mama's watchful eye and because the upper floors were always such a hive of noisy activity, even this late at night. Amma got up from the divan and shut the door of the living room. It was too late for us to be disturbed by any visitor or patient, but she closed the latch for good measure nonetheless.

Her face a battleground of emotions, Amma walked over to a chair next to Ravikant mama and sat down. She looked from Didi to me as though we were pieces of a jigsaw puzzle that she wasn't sure how to fit in. Her eyes moved slowly from Didi to me until, gradually, we saw resolve set in. Then she began to speak.

In 1918, a baby girl was born not far from Lucknow, in the ancient city of Allahabad, located at the confluence of India's three most sacred rivers: the Ganga, the Yamuna, and the invisible Sarasvati, which, according to legend, has not flowed for four thousand years. Nobody remembers the exact date of her birth, but she was told that she entered the world as a sickly baby at the end of a very hot summer. With a lot of love and care, she even managed to survive a bout of smallpox as a toddler.

In 1926, when she was about eight years old, she went with her three older sisters to bathe in the Ganga at its junction with the Yamuna. Thousands of people came each year to this sacred spot to wash away their past sins, in hopes of attaining spiritual release. For the sisters, the area was familiar terrain, as their great house stood on the elevated banks not far from the place where the two rivers merged in a serpentine embrace. It was an auspicious day for a ritual bath, and the four sisters arrived at the river early in the morning, before the crowds.

The oldest sister had recently been married and was visiting the family for the first time since her wedding. She was also the first one to feel the powerful tug of the eddy in the middle of the river. She tried to warn her sisters not to come near her, but they saw her flailing hands as an invitation to join her. By the time they, too, felt the pull of the swirling eddy and realized the danger they were in, it was already too late. The younger sisters were terrified, but they would not leave their sister to drown. They formed a human chain, trying to use a sari to throw a lifeline to the drowning sister, but they were trapped in the powerful embrace of the two rivers, and dark waters soon swirled above all four of their heads and their long, flowing hair.

The youngest sister had not let go of the sari despite the strong current pulling her into the dark depths of the water. Her little limbs ached with the strain, but just as her nose and lungs started filling up with water, she felt another tug that pulled her toward the surface. She struggled against it. Her body was caught in a net that now dragged her out of the water. The corner of the sari was no longer in her hands.

The fisherman threw the net into the churning waters repeatedly in an effort to save the others, but in vain. As the sun rose on the horizon, he carried one limp little body to the big house on the bank of the most sacred river, a house that was about to drown in a mourning from which it could not be rescued.

None of the riches of the household, the privileges of birth, or the enlightenment of education had prepared the little girl or her family to cope with a tragedy of such proportions. The little survivor was shocked into a stubborn silence—not crying, not eating, not talking. Later that night, as her mother's heart-rending shrieks dulled into aching sobs, the little girl stole out of the house. She ran into the broad orchard that separated her house from the banks of the murderous river that had so cruelly rejected her, seeking to return to its arms.

A pair of strong arms grabbed her little body in flight and knocked the wind out of her lungs. A stout man with a big head of short-cropped *hair glowered down at her. He hissed, "Ai, laundiya, what are you doing out so late in the night? Aren't you from the big house beyond the trees? Why aren't you in your comfy bed?"*

She sat down abruptly on a smooth rock to recover her breath. Above the rock spread a familiar mango tree, in whose wide branches she could hide for hours reading, far from the summoning of concerned parents, siblings, or servants—a tree that had always yielded its sweetest mangoes to her brother's slingshot. In this orchard, she had once run into a donkey with her new bicycle, having not yet mastered the brakes. Now it was filled with sinister shadows and a strange man. Overwhelmed, she bent her head low onto her knees.

She had not shed a single tear since the moment when horror dawned—that indelible moment when she stared at the palm and stubby fingers of her empty hand, the hand that no longer held the sari, that no longer held any connection to her sisters.

Now tears flooded her face. Her little body shook as she wept for her precious sisters, for the cruel spectacle of her mother, fainting at the news, for the memory of her stoic father pounding his heart with his fists to make it stop hurting, for grown men forcibly restraining her brother, who was determined to jump into the river himself to search for his lost sisters.

Her sobbing alarmed the stout man, who tried to calm her. Then, out of the shadows emerged a second man, lean rather than stout, who whispered urgently, "What's wrong, little girl? Have you run away?"

She could only nod her head numbly as she continued to sob, unable to find words to express the impossible vastness of her despair. The two men stood helplessly beside the rock, unsure what to do or how to comfort her.

Eventually the second man addressed the small sobbing figure, his tone clipped. "I don't know if you understand any of this, little girl, but the police are looking for us. We can't risk getting caught. We need to move fast and stay out of jail. We are working for the freedom of our country."

She lifted her tear-soaked face. "Death is the ultimate freedom," she said, not knowing where the words came from.

Her statement startled the men as much as her crying had. They stood watching her for another long moment before the lean man spoke again, much more gently this time. "But you're just a little girl. You have your whole life ahead of you."

Calmer now, the girl asked the men to let her go her way. She said that she would trouble them no further.

So far, the stout man had said little. Now he made a terse offer to the little girl. "I don't know who told you that. But some people think we need to do something good with our life before we die. So why not help us fight for freedom here on earth?"

Pushing his round spectacles further up his nose, the lean man explained that there were many revolutionaries active in the area. They needed to travel far and wide, from one place to another, without raising the suspicion of the police or local people who didn't support their objectives. Their work was dangerous but important; it would mean that the people of India would one day have their own government. All over the country, hundreds of young boys and girls were helping with the struggle for independence.

The two men reminded the girl of the rich and long history of the country in which she was born, and of its enslavement. She had already heard of someone named Mahatma Gandhi, who said that people should spin their own yarn so that they wouldn't have to buy high-priced cloth from British. She also remembered hearing about a massacre in Amritsar, when British soldiers had opened fire on a crowd of unarmed men, women, and children who had gathered for a festival.

She was about to learn much more. The two men told her about a number of revolutionary groups—Anushilan Samiti, Jugantar, the Hindustan Republican Association, and now the Bengal Volunteers—that favoured armed rebellion against British rule. Members of these groups and others targeted the lifelines of the British Empire by destroying railway tracks, telegraph posts, and government buildings. They travelled throughout the country to spread news of the revolution and to connect pockets of rebellion. The men boasted that moral and material support for their activities came from places all over the world: Turkey, Germany, France, Ireland, Russia, Singapore, Japan, and the United States.

The girl listened intently. "But how can I be of any use?" she asked. They explained that the police would never suspect two men travelling with a little girl, especially if they pretended to be a family. Her mere presence would make their movement swifter and easier, since they would not have to wait to move until after dark.

The little girl stood up and declared, "All right. But we have to leave quickly."

Just like that, she embarked on an arduous journey that took her through jungles, remote villages, and ancient towns. She trained in traditional martial arts and was especially good at wielding the small kataar dagger and the curved khukhari blade used by the Gurkhas. She helped to produce nationalist pamphlets and even wrote some of her own, and she learned to hide messages in her clothing. For more than a year, she was on the move, covering the length and breadth of the country by train and by foot.

Radicalism was growing in the cities, but those who lived in the vast countryside of the subcontinent were difficult to reach by either road or radio. Small groups of activists took the message to the countryside by posing as wandering singers, using local devotional songs and religious imagery to spread nationalist ideas. The little girl was not much of a singer, but she never missed a beat, keeping perfect time with a tinkling pair of small brass manjira.

She also enjoyed altering simple folk verses to replace mythical lore with images of the country as the goddess Durga, the British Raj as a demon, and Gandhiji as the ascetic whose penance and suffering would be the means to end the serfdom of the goddess. They had to be constantly on the move, avoiding not only the wrath of the police but also that of the local zamindars—who were unhappy with the effect of the revolutionaries on the tenant farmers who tilled the land.

Then, in 1928, the British government convened a commission to study the impact of constitutional reforms that had been introduced in British India a decade earlier and to make further recommendations. Not a single member of the Simon Commission was Indian. Mass strikes were organized, and wherever the commissioners travelled in the country, they were met by throngs of protesters carrying black flags. British authorities responded with unbridled assaults on unarmed protestors. Crowds of men and women were trampled under the hooves of horses, and tough prison

sentences were meted out at the slightest suspicion of nationalist activity.
Recognizing the increased risk to their lives in this new political climate,
the band of revolutionaries and their network of sympathizers arranged
to take the little girl to Mathura, where she might be safer.

Amma paused, as though she were looking for the right way to continue. Despite her care to maintain a distance from her young self in her storytelling, I could see the little girl in my ever-composed mother. I noticed it in the way her left thumb kept rotating the gold bangle on her right wrist and in the way her toes clenched the cotton rug under her feet, as though the rug were the only thing preventing her from falling deep into the bowels of the earth.

Didi and I sat with our backs straight, slowly letting her words sink in, waiting for Amma to finish sorting through some unknown memory chest and go on. I tried to prompt her: "Why didn't you go back to your parents instead?"

Amma's silence gave way to a resigned sigh. In the end, it was Ravikant mama who broke the silence. "By leaving the family of her birth, she embraced the whole world as her family."

For the next little while, he took up the narration, relieving Amma of the burden of words. He told us how Mathura was a hotbed of nationalist activities, largely owing to the influence of Raja Mahendra Pratap. In 1909, he had started a technical college at his palace near Vrindavan, convinced that education was the key to equality. Prem Mahavidyalaya was free for all students, among whom were many of the earliest social and political activists in the region. During the First World War, Raja Mahendra Pratap travelled to Europe to enlist support for a plan to overthrow the British government of India via Afghanistan and, in December 1915, established a provisional Indian government in Kabul. He subsequently journeyed to Russia, at the invitation of Lenin, and the British finally became so concerned about his activities that they put a price on his head. In 1925, he fled India for Japan, where he lived for more than two decades. His political activism had the effect of transforming Mathura into a centre of nationalist activity, which continued even in his absence. The Congress

Party held many of its meetings there, drawing even devoted householders like Ravikant mama into the political arena.

Ravikant mama looked affectionately at Amma's contemplative face. "When I first met your Amma," he said, "she was a puny little girl, all muscles and brawn. But her eyes had the meditative depth of an ascetic." She joined the household as his supposedly long-lost younger sister. Ravikant mama had acquired two other sisters under similar circumstances. Under his protection, these young women embraced new identities, and the other two settled into domestic lives. But not Amma.

Ravikant mama then told us about the principal of her school, Manoramadevi, a committed Gandhi follower who anointed the little girl "Shanti," or peace—wanting to bless her with tranquillity after the harrowing experiences of a life barely begun.

Manoramadevi was a courageous young widow who used her education to save herself and to help others fighting for dignity. Under her mentorship, little Shanti learned to reconnect with the independence movement, but this time on her own terms. Noticing her advanced reading and writing skills, Manoramadevi encouraged Shanti to study on her own for middle-school certification rather than join regular classes. She taught Shanti that education was the only key that could release the unwieldy chains of custom and religion, especially for women. At the same time, she took her to protest rallies in Mathura and Lucknow.

Drawing upon her love of reading and writing, Shanti wrote her exams. In 1929, under Manoramadevi's tutelage, she earned a middle-school certificate, becoming one of relatively few young women to have acquired such a credential. The same year she agreed to move to Jaipur to become the head teacher at a school for girls run by the Agarwal merchant community. Shanti was not yet twelve years old. But she had been in her new position for only a few months when Mahatma Gandhi embarked on the Salt March.

The heavy taxes levied by the British on the people of India had long been a source of bitter complaint. The most onerous of these taxes was the salt tax, which, in 1930, accounted for 95 percent of the price of salt in India. Especially in a hot climate, salt was an essential commodity, and the burden of the tax fell on the entire population. Rather than focus on exorbitant land taxes or stifling industrial taxes, Gandhiji used this most basic commodity as a symbol of the injustice of British rule and the rallying point for the civil disobedience movement.

On 12 March 1930, Gandhiji left Sabarmati Ashram, near Ahmeda-bad, to walk to the coastal village of Dandi, 240 miles to the west. The march lasted for twenty-four days, passing through four districts and forty-eight villages in western India. Hundreds of thousands of men and women joined the march at various stages, and, before long, the throng of people stretched for more than two miles. Dressed in white, the marchers sang Gandhiji's favourite chant, *Raghupati Raghav Rajaram,* invoking Ram and Allah as two names of the same divine presence, asking for the gift of wisdom for all.

International journalists were watching intently, calling the march a "White Flowing River," relaying images of this extraordinarily peaceful mass movement all across the globe. Upon reaching the coast at Dandi on 5 April 1930, Gandhiji picked up a handful of salt from the ground in defiance of the Indian Salt Act. Then, setting up little fires, the marchers began boiling seawater to make salt.

Ravikant mama seemed momentarily overwhelmed by the power of these memories. The Salt March was, he said, a stroke of genius. It trans-formed the freedom movement into a "poor man's battle," a struggle of the humble against the arrogant. There could be no better illustration of *satyagraha*—a reckoning with the force of truth.

Shanti responded to Gandhiji's call for civil disobedience by resigning from her job and returning to Mathura to attend organizational meetings of Indian National Congress workers. Because of her familiarity with the region, she was asked to go back to Rajputana. At the time, the Rajputana Agency consisted of almost twenty sovereign kingdoms, of varying size, bound by subsidiary alliances with the British Raj. The princely state of Jaipur was one of these semi-sovereign domains. The Maharajas of Jaipur were loyal allies of the British, as, for the most part, were Jaipur's influen-tial and wealthy merchant classes.

Unlike the rest of Rajputana, the city of Ajmer, about eighty miles southwest of Jaipur, was ruled directly by the British, as part of the tiny province of Ajmer-Merwara. The site of military cantonments since the rebellion of 1857, Ajmer was a railway hub as well, and it was here that Congress workers were trying to mobilize mass civil disobedience by organizing protest rallies and the picketing of shops selling British goods or alcohol. As a result of their tireless campaigns, civil disobedience had already spread to many corners of the subcontinent, both British-ruled and semi-independent. Defiance of the unpopular land, forest, and agricultural taxes was widespread.

And so Shanti rejoined the freedom movement, this time in full public view. Mahatma Gandhi had been arrested early in May, and the Indian National Congress and its activities were declared illegal by the British. The onus was now on local Congress workers to keep the nationalist fires burning. Shanti reached Ajmer in August of 1930. We listened in rapt silence as Ravikant mama told us how she immediately took to addressing public meetings organized by Congress workers—speaking without the aid of a microphone, before throngs of men and women gathered in city parks, urging them to fight for their independence. On 13 August, when the police came to arrest Shanti for making seditious speeches, she calmly surrendered, in obedience to the principle of non-violence, and, at the age of twelve, became the first woman Congress Party worker to be jailed in Ajmer.

Ravikant mama went on to explain that the city's Indian residents were outraged by the arrest of a young girl, and the next day a general strike was called. However, Mayo College—the elite boarding school for the sons of Indian aristocracy—refused to show solidarity with the strikers. In response, hundreds of men and women gathered outside the wrought-iron gates of the sprawling campus nestled in the Aravalli Hills. Police armed with lathis attacked the chanting protestors and arrested three hundred men and twenty-five women. Those arrested joined the more than eighty thousand political activists imprisoned nationwide for various acts of civil disobedience that year. Seventeen thousand of those political prisoners were women. An overwhelming majority of these women had stepped out from behind domestic walls for the first time in their lives.

As we were well aware, Amma was deeply concerned about the status of women, the plight of widows in particular, and now we learned that her commitment had a long history. As Shanti continued to fight for the country's political freedom, Ravikant mama told us, she realized that women wore another set of chains. As a tribute to Manoramadevi, she made a vow to champion the cause of the "living corpses" that were Hindu widows at the time. She also vowed to wear only khadi until the country gained its independence, in accordance with Gandhiji's vision of non-violence and self-reliance.

At the mention of khadi, Didi and I looked at each other like conspirators who shared a guilty secret. In Amma's view, despite the Nehru government's industrialization projects, economic self-reliance remained a vital need, especially in rural areas. So, even after the country gained its independence, she had not forsaken her vow to wear only khadi, and, as her children, we had inherited this vow. Yet we were often envious of the clothing that others wore, made from traditional silks or machine-made cottons and chiffons. With their rich colours and often intricate patterns, such fabrics stood in stark contrast our relentlessly plain clothing. Even khadi silk, which does have a certain lustre, is coarser than regular silk, as the process by which it is made produces shorter strands of silk thread.

Now, hearing the story of Amma's vow, I felt ashamed of my attraction to un-khadi fabrics. I also suddenly realized the connection between her vows, made so long ago, with the widowed "sewing ladies" of my childhood in Jaipur. But Ravikant mama interrupted my thoughts.

"Your mother followed the right path, not the easy path," he said. "Are you girls going to be the true daughters of that brave little girl?"

Suddenly, I felt very small and lonely. I wasn't sure that I could ever be my mother's true daughter, no matter how hard I tried.

4

Meeting Babu

The end of our annual exams heralded the end of high school for Didi and the long-awaited summer break for both of us. Didi and I could barely contain our excitement upon finally seeing Amma once again. "Where are we going to spend the summer?" I asked.

Amma had a twinkle in her eyes that I had not seen in a long time. She asked us to guess.

"Bhagalpur?"

She shook her head, and her smile broadened further.

I screamed, "Jeolikot?"

Still no, but she added, "You love this place more than any other."

I slowly exhaled. "Jaipur?"

She nodded and scooped us up in a tight hug, her smile illuminating the room.

We started the day-long journey to Jaipur early in the morning, in a quiet coach all by ourselves. This time, I wasn't the chatty one, for once; Amma was talking to us as though we were her long-lost friends. I loved travelling in the daytime, on trains that cut across farms and cities, snaked

97

along rivers and roads, and thundered through tunnels and bridges. But on this day, as Amma talked, we discovered another landscape, different from the one unfolding outside the gently rocking train.

Ravikant mama had forced open a window into Amma's past that had been boarded up a long time ago. Now Amma allowed us to peek further. She had actually brought along a few of the daily journals that she had kept during her prison terms, and she read passages from these diaries aloud, filling in the context of those turbulent times in her life and in the country.

Amma described the phenomenon of women courting arrest in large numbers in response to Gandhiji's call for mass civil disobedience in 1930. Hundreds of thousands of women stepped out of their homes, defying their families and ancient customs, as well as British law. Women joined picket lines, protest rallies, and *prabhat pheri* marches at daybreak through the streets of cities and towns, singing spiritual songs infused with nationalist fervour. Veiled women made salt on their terraces and in their courtyards, literally shouting from rooftops that they had broken the law.

This dramatic influx of women into the civil disobedience movement posed a logistical problem for the British, whose prisons were not equipped to take in so many women detainees. Hoping to cut to the heart of the problem, the British sent undercover informants into public meetings to identify women who appeared to be ringleaders. Young Shanti's every step was shadowed by the police, and her rousing public speeches were duly noted.

After she was arrested early in the fall of 1930, she was sentenced to six months in prison. With a wry smile, Amma recalled how the magistrate who sentenced her seemed reluctant to do so—she was barely more than a child. She also fondly remembered the affection shown to her, as the youngest inmate, by the other political prisoners, as well as the stream of visitors who came to bless her and be blessed by her.

This flow of visitors had not ebbed when the British authorities decided to transfer Shanti from Ajmer to the Lucknow jail. Here she found a friend in Shivarani Devi, the wife of one of her favourite contemporary Hindi writers, Munshi Premchand, whom Shanti admired for his honesty and realism. She was also touched by the generosity of Kamla Nehru. The prison guards were noticeably lenient toward the handful of women prisoners who had family connections, and Nehruji's wife had been permitted to arrange for the delivery of home-cooked hot meals. These she insisted on sharing with Shanti, moved by the girl's young age and her lack of family.

Most importantly, Shanti witnessed the courage of the many women prisoners who participated in daily meetings and, every morning and evening, joined their voices for an hour in the singing of nationalist songs. The vast majority of these prisoners had no privileged status: they were often from ordinary middle-class families, women with little by way of education who had been arrested for doing what they believed to be right. Many of them—especially those who had small children—were worried about their future after prison. To turn these fears to their advantage, the British authorities offered a pardon to any woman who would apologize for participating in seditious activities and swear an oath to never to do so again. Yet, despite the tempting prospect of official forgiveness and a swift release, Amma could not recall a single woman who accepted this offer.

She sighed briefly. Perhaps because she was still so young, she said, she was one of the more vocal of the women prisoners—she had a fearlessness that adults can ill afford. Irritated by her tendency to speak out, and well aware that she lacked the protection of family, her jailers decided to make an example of her, no doubt hoping to intimidate the other women prisoners into behaving themselves. So, for singing nationalist songs in prison, she was punished with a week in solitary confinement.

Her tiny cell had no light except for a small barred window, no more than a foot wide, halfway up the high wall. She was given a blanket to sleep on, a metal bowl by way of a toilet, a pitcher of water, and two coarse, dry rotis per day. To survive the experience, she meditated as much as possible and ate and drank as infrequently as possible.

Despite my love of snakes, I squirmed and gathered my feet under me as Amma described her visitor one night. No doubt looking for dry ground to escape the monsoon rain, the snake found its way into the cell through a crack near the door. The pale yellow crossbands along its smooth, dark scales shone vividly in the moonlight streaming in through the little window. It was a king cobra. Shanti screamed for help as she struggled to clamber up the rough stone wall toward the window. The guard looked in through the little peephole and told her to shut up, but he stopped short of opening the door, much less trying to remove the snake. Shanti hung from the metal bars of the window for several hours until, at long last, her visitor slithered into some hole in the thick stone walls.

At the end of her solitary confinement, she was not allowed to rejoin the other women prisoners but was instead sent back from Lucknow to Ajmer, where she finished the remainder of her six-month jail term. Immediately after her release, Shanti returned to her family of freedom fighters in Mathura to resume her routine of meetings, picketing, and public speeches.

It was there she learned that Gandhi, arrested the previous May, had also been released from jail and had negotiated a pact with India's viceroy, Lord Irwin, agreeing to suspend the civil disobedience movement in exchange for a series of concessions from the British, including the elimination of the salt tax, the release of political prisoners, and the repeal of ordinances that limited the scope of Congress Party activities. Rumour was that Gandhi would be travelling to London in the fall, to represent Congress at the second of the British government's round-table conferences about India's constitution.

This sounded to her like good news, yet it seemed to make little real difference. Within ten days of her release from prison, she was served a legal notice signed by the governor of the United Provinces commanding her to cease and desist from political activities and ordering her not to travel outside the municipal limits of the city of Mathura. It was not long before undercover police agents began shadowing her again: Shanti laughingly referred to them as her loyal servants. Her well-wishers advised her to go to another province and continue her political activities under a new identity. If she were to be arrested in the United Provinces, it would be regarded as a show of contempt for the governor's injunction and could result in harsh sentencing.

In the meanwhile, India had acquired a new viceroy, Lord Willingdon, and, all around her, the suppression of civil liberties seemed to be intensifying. Congress workers were being beaten up for handing out meeting announcements or nationalist pamphlets. Anyone suspected of harbouring controversial political views was being thrown into jail without benefit of trial. Newspapers deemed seditious were banned, and public meetings and rallies were routinely broken up by armed police.

In Mathura and other cities, the resistance went underground in response to the repression, while villages remained largely cut off from national politics. So, ignoring the advice of her friends, Shanti decided to rejoin the Congress volunteers who travelled into the heart of the rural hinterlands to bring people news of the nationalist tide that was sweeping the urban areas of the subcontinent. Despite the growing danger, she resumed touring villages with groups of wandering singers who sang stories from the great epic poems, the *Ramayana* and the *Mahabharata*, spiked with nationalist messages.

Amma read from her diary a description of their tactics. A drummer would walk through neighbouring villages announcing a day-long program of *bhajan-puja*, devotional song and worship—apparently a harmless religious event. Hundreds of poor and illiterate villagers from nearby areas would attend the event in hopes of spiritual enlightenment and good karma for their next lives. The singers would sing the praise of the gods and sages of ancient times, comparing them to Mahatma Gandhi and Jawaharlal Nehru. They would also denounce the demons and villains of these epics, equating their sinful actions with those of the British—the traders who came to their country and now pretended to be owners of lives and lands that did not belong to them. Into the mythical narratives, the songs often rolled the history of the forcible expansion of the British East India Company's commercial activities, the looting of India's treasures, and the commonplace assumption that killing natives was a ruling power's natural and necessary duty.

Amma recalled several occasions on which she evaded arrest because a sympathetic Indian informant, planted in the crowd as a police spy, secretly warned her group to move on before the police themselves arrived or the local landlord wised up to the singers' political tampering with the holy epics. The seeds of rebellion appeared to be sprouting.

Amma paused her story at every station stop, allowing the crescendo of hawkers, tea-sellers, porters, and travellers to take over the quietness of our coach. As the train lumbered out of each station, leaving the loud voices floating behind, she resumed her story, reading aloud from her diary about the impact of a particularly inspiring meeting. On one of her visits back to her home base in Mathura, she was introduced to Subhas Chandra Bose and Kishan Singh, the father of Bhagat Singh, the young revolutionary who had killed a British police officer, John Saunders, in an attempt to assassinate James Scott, the police superintendent responsible for the brutal beating of Lala Lajpat Rai during what began as a peaceful protest.

Bhagat Singh had detonated a bomb in the Central Legislative Assembly specifically to provoke his own arrest. Members of his organization, the Hindustan Socialist Republican Association, wanted to challenge the apathy of the millions of Indians, particularly merchants, bureaucrats, administrators, police, and army men, whose willing compliance had enabled a handful of Britons to rule over the teeming millions of the subcontinent. While in jail, Bhagat Singh had fasted for 116 days for equal treatment of Indian and British prisoners. His brief but dramatic life, which ended with his death by hanging on 23 March 1931, ignited the imaginations of many young men and women, including that of young Shanti. She was especially struck by his father's courage and determination in the face of such a loss.

Shanti managed to continue her clandestine political activities for the better part of a year without getting caught. But the situation in India was rapidly worsening. Ever since Lord Willingdon had arrived, amidst the swirl of protests that followed Singh's execution, a backlash had been developing among British officials in India, who resented the allegedly conciliatory policies now emanating from London. Taking advantage of Gandhi's departure for England, the British authorities began deliberately violating the terms of the pact signed in March. In the meanwhile, unrest had spread to the countryside, once it became clear that the British government in India would do nothing to alleviate the plight of immiserated peasants. In October, Nehruji had launched a "no-rent" campaign in the United Provinces, where tens of thousands of tenant farmers were now refusing to pay their landlords.

At the end of December, Nehruji left Allahabad for Bombay to greet Gandhiji on his return. But he never arrived in Bombay. Instead, police swooped down and arrested him, along with his travelling companion,

Abdul Ghaffar Khan, leader of the Khudai Khidmatgar and one of Gandhi's most respected friends. Then, as the new year began, Shanti heard that Gandhi himself had been arrested and all Congress Party organizations banned. Everywhere, Congress leaders were being imprisoned, and a brutal crackdown was underway. Shanti knew that it was only a matter of time before she, too, would be back in jail.

On a cold morning toward the end of January 1932, an informant quietly warned her that a warrant had been issued for her arrest. Inspired by Bhagat Singh's policy of indifference to punishment, Shanti decided not to wait for the police to find her and instead devised a plan of her own.

In response to Gandhiji's call for renewed civil disodebience, as well as to protest the wave of arrests, Congress workers in Mathura had planned a nationalist rally to coincide with a festival at a local temple. Protestors would march through the streets to the site of the temple, in hopes of transforming the festival into a mass expression of outrage. Shanti was staying at the house of a physician in Mathura, a well-known Congress sympathizer who was under the watch of the police. A few hours before dawn on the day of the festival, she stole out of the house and made her way to the temple to join the crowds attending the festival.

As the sun rose into the sky, the priest began to recite a religious *katha,* the opening of the tale unfolding as the large inner courtyard of the temple filled with hundreds of women in colourful saris, the long ends draped modestly over their heads and faces, Men sat separately in the outer courtyard, clapping and swaying. Then, as the marchers arrived at the temple, a chorus of nationalist slogans in the street beyond began to mingle with the Sanskrit chants inside the temple. Suddenly, one of the women threw off the *pallu* of her sari, boldly uncovering both her face and the furled flag she was carrying, and started running toward the staircase that led to the terrace of the temple. Once on the terrace, Shanti unfurled the tricolour flag with Gandhiji's beloved symbol of the *charkha* in the middle, the spinning wheel a reminder of the goal of economic self-sufficiency. Immediately, she began to chant nationalist slogans that were soon echoed not only by the protestors outside but also by the hundreds of people gathered in the temple compound.

Reading from her diary, Amma then described the battalion of police in riot helmets and gear that swiftly arrived to quell the disturbance. They seemed momentarily startled when a young woman began a rousing speech from the top of the temple terrace, and then they started raining down lathis on the white-capped heads that had filled the narrow lanes around the temple. The well-armed police had no trouble beating up and arresting the protestors, but it was more difficult to get the girl herself down from the temple terrace. Because the temple was a sacred place, the policemen were not allowed to enter wearing their leather shoes and gear.

An English police officer shouted for the girl to come down from the terrace right that very minute. She continued her stream of seditious speech with renewed vigour, and the masses of people who had been dispersed by the armed police started to gather again. Some of the police went and fetched a ladder, by which it was possible to reach the temple terrace without actually entering the compound. When Shanti kept ignoring orders to climb down the ladder, the policeman started climbing up himself. As he got closer to the girl, the crowd grew restive, and the sloganeering and gesticulating increased. In response, the officer ordered the rest of the police to redouble their attack on the milling crowds. To stop the vicious beating of the protestors, Shanti agreed to climb down from the terrace, but not via the ladder. She descended the staircase into the courtyard, as nationalist slogans reverberated against the ancient walls.

As the police van moved slowly through the narrow streets clogged with people, the lathis danced mercilessly, breaking limbs and battering skulls. Didi and I winced at Amma's description of the violence. We could hardly bear the knowledge that such scenes were sickeningly common during the movement for independence, but she shrugged at our discomfort. The British were struggling to contend with massive waves of non-violent civil resistance. Jails around the country were filled beyond capacity with men and women protestors who were often treated more like criminal inmates than political prisoners, unless they had famous last names.

To discourage women from participating in the movement, she told us, the British authorities were considering the introduction of fines, payable by their husbands, parents, or guardians, although they were worried about the political repercussions of measures that would tend to inflame public opinion. For Shanti, such fines would hardly have been a deterrent, as she had no male protector. For the court record, she gave the name of her father simply as *krantikari*—revolutionary.

As another means of stemming the tide of women prisoners, the British had also resorted to exploiting fears of pollution. Untouchable female staff were employed in jails to make the prospect of imprisonment abhorrent for the mostly upper-caste Hindu women courting arrest. This did not deter Shanti either, as she had been part of Gandhiji's campaign to end the practice of untouchability and refused to use any caste identifiers with her name.

As before, Shanti was duly arrested and sentenced for the crime of sedition under Section 124A of the penal code—but the similarity with her earlier experience ended there. In preparation for her impending jail term, she had stuffed a khadi-cloth bag full of books on or by political thinkers, from Hammurabi, Plato, and Chanakya to Bertrand Russell, Sun Yat-sen, and, of course, Mahtama Gandhi. What she failed to anticipate was that the relatively benign treatment she encountered during her first term in jail was not to be replicated during her second.

Despite her political prisoner status, she was allotted to Class "C," the same category as criminal inmates. When she arrived at the prison, two guards trained guns at her, on the jailer's orders, as a burly woman leapt upon Shanti, tugging at her clothes on the pretext of searching her. In a matter of seconds, Shanti had immobilized her assailant, pinning her offending hand behind her broad back, far from her straining shoulder. Shanti expected the jail guards to split open her skull with their rifle butts at any moment, but the two Indian guards remained immobile, and the jailer ordered the sullen woman to leave Shanti alone.

Shanti tested the patience of the jailer again by refusing to wear the all-black prison clothing given to criminal inmates, demanding the black-and-white striped uniform meant for political prisoners. To her surprise, the English jailer assented to this demand, but he denied her access to the precious duffle bag with all her reading and writing material.

Shanti had been sentenced to eight months of hard labour and was locked up in a dirty cell shared by a number of women who were serving sentences of various lengths for a wide variety of crimes. Amma read to us from her diaries the classification system that she developed to understand the eclectic collection of inmates who shared these filthy, crowded jail cells. She tried to talk with her cellmates to learn about their lives, and ultimately divided them into four categories: a very small number of remorseless women who had deliberately committed violent crimes; women who were framed or who had been foolish enough to be led to commit criminal acts, often by family members; women who had hurt someone in a rage; and women who had no money to pay for a fine or legal defence. Shanti's assessment was that the majority of the women prisoners belonged in the last category.

There was little room for discussion, learning, or camaraderie in the crowded cells, full of fear and filth. The inmates were not allowed to talk while working on the various tasks allocated to them. Shanti was given a large pile of jute fibre to braid into lengths of rope under the watchful eyes and the prickly prods of the women guards. All day long she had to work on the pile of coarse fibre, which cut into the skin of her hands. When the blisters on her hands became weeping sores, the prison doctor ordered that her task be changed to mending prisoners' clothing. She detested this task even more than making rope, for she couldn't help imagining the origins of the stains on these rags, and she gagged at the stench of despair and violence that emanated from them.

At the end of each week, the inmates had to hold a parade out in the yard and stand next to their meagre prison possessions of two metal bowls, a reed mat, and a blanket, to be inspected by the jailer. Shanti refused to take part in this dehumanizing spectacle. The woman guards screamed at her until their voices went hoarse and Shanti's eardrums buzzed. When she did not budge, they went running to complain to the jailer. The jailer appeared on schedule with other prison officials to inspect the parade of inmates. Shanti was called into the yard and her things were piled next to her by the guard. The stern jailer met her unwavering gaze and then surprised everyone by saying nothing more than, "You should have participated in the parade."

Much to the further chagrin of the guards, an order then arrived to change Shanti's assignment to Class B, which promoted her to a cleaner cell of her own and the company of her precious books and diaries. It also meant food that did not look and smell like it belonged in the sewer. In solidarity with the rest of the inmates, however, Shanti insisted on and ate the food served to Class C prisoners. She soon learned that her promotion to Class B had more to do with separating her from the other inmates than with anything related to justice.

Within days of her "promotion," Shanti was bundled early one morning into an empty compartment of an eastbound train, surrounded by prison guards and armed policemen. At every station, large or small, where the train stopped, the policemen would surround the compartment and train their guns on anyone who dared to come close to it. This only fanned the curiosity of onlookers, some climbing onto distant benches and piles of luggage to try to identify the dangerous cargo being guarded by so many guns. It would take just one person to recognize Shanti, and then the nationalistic sloganeering would start, along with jeering commentary about the impotent police who felt threatened by a young girl. Shanti enjoyed the consternation of the policemen, but she strongly disliked not knowing where they were headed, even after several hours into the train journey.

Finally, just as the warm and dusty afternoon was beginning to cool into evening, they stopped at a station where two men approached the head constable and begged to talk to the young prisoner. They claimed to be Shanti's close relatives and appealed to the middle-aged Indian constable's love for his own children, some of whom, they reasoned, must be the same age as the girl in his custody. Their strategy worked well enough that the constable granted them two precious minutes to talk. Amma had understood immediately, of course, that these men who described themselves as family members were in fact part of the widespread network of freedom fighters. They had just enough time to tell Shanti that she was being transferred to the Benares jail, hundreds of miles east of Mathura.

They were there to assure her that the network had not lost sight of her, despite her captors' best efforts.

But Amma had more to tell us, not only about that trip but about her mysterious early years. As she continued to read from her diary we learned how happy she was to hear that her destination was Varanasi, that most sacred of sacred cities, known in ancient texts as Kashi. With a history extending back several millennia, Benares (as the British spelled it) had long been a place of pilgrimage and study, famed for its ghats, where those seeking spiritual release could bathe in the holy Ganga. Several major figures of the early *bhakti* movement—Kabir, Ravidas, and Tulsidas—had spent much of their lives in the city, and even at that young age, Amma explained, she was drawn to their poetry, with its openly emotional evocation of an immediate connection between the worshipper and the divine. She had never been able to bring herself to believe in God as something personal, she admitted, and yet the songs of the *bhakti* poets had never ceased to move her.

Shanti knew, of course, that she could not expect to roam the bazaars of Varanasi, which teemed with merchants trading in jewellery, perfumes, and brocade and with pilgrims from far and wide. She did not expect to witness spectacular sunsets on the Ganga, as the sound of bells, chants, cymbals, and conch shells rose from thousands of temples and mixed with the chirps of countless birds that, every sundown, settled into the orchards and forests along the broad banks of the sacred river. But she was also determined not to let her imprisonment prevent her from reliving her memories of the city.

At this, Didi interrupted. "Memories? Had you been in Varanasi before?"

Amma did not move her eyes from her spot on the page. "Yes, a few times, before I left home."

I was riveted by this and hoped that Amma would tell us more about her childhood. Didi leaned forward in anticipation. But Amma simply continued to describe her jail odyssey.

Much larger than the Mathura jail, the Benares jail was reserved for Class B political prisoners of the United Provinces. Each of the fifty women political prisoners had their own cell and were allowed to organize daily morning events of flag hoisting, singing, and debating. The matron was a gentle Irishwoman who taught English to the children of the inmates in the evening, and she invited young Shanti to join these classes.

This jail also housed nearly four hundred women jailed on criminal charges, most of whom were serving life sentences. Shanti's contact with the criminal prisoners in Benares was limited to interacting with those who worked as servants in the political prisoner section, but she learned what she could of their stories and found that the circumstances that landed women in jail here fit neatly into the same four categories she had observed in Mathura. All of them would be burdened for the rest of their lives by the stigma of having been jailed.

What made matters worse was that the jail term allowed for no education or training for future rehabilitation. Shanti felt particularly sorry for the inmates who, having no other means of livelihood, had turned to prostitution. Although the British strictly regulated prostitution, brothels had remained legal in India until the 1930s. As new bans came into effect, Indian prostitutes were caught between the laws that criminalized them and the forces that lured them into the trade—which, of course, continued to thrive.

In the Benares jail, Shanti also encountered another class of women prisoners, a small number of Anglo-Indian women. They were housed in a separate section, with facilities that were better than the best offered to Indian political prisoners. With individual servants, balanced meals, and books and journals, this section was like a little retreat within the confines of the massive jail. The treatment of the Anglo-Indian women also stood in stark contrast to the way that male political prisoners were treated. Rasping sounds, made by the regular whippings, and clanking sounds, made by the leg shackles attached to rods that prevented the inmates from sitting or lying down, routinely drifted over the bars and walls that separated the men's sections from the women's sections.

We all fell silent at this information, until Amma looked up from her diary. "I learned so much during my jail terms, mostly about the human capacity to inflict and tolerate extreme pain." But in response to what she was learning, she made a promise to herself to work for prisoner education if she came out of her ordeal alive. At this I recalled how Amma had taught evening classes at the Central Jail in Jaipur. I was proud of my vivid recollection, at which Amma smiled and nodded. "It was one of my most fulfilling activities in Jaipur," she commented. "My current position has left little room for that kind of personal fulfilment."

Didi looked a little impatient at this digression. "Yes, yes—and then what happened to you?"

Amma smiled at us both, but, as she often did, she insisted on testing our patience further by embedding her life story within the larger frame of national and world events. She reminded us that when she was back in Mathura in 1932 and 1933, having been released from the Benares jail in August of 1932, Europe was still reeling from the impact of the First World War and the ongoing Great Depression, while the political situation was increasingly unstable. In Britain, Ramsay MacDonald's second Labour government, elected in May 1929, had collapsed in August 1931, leaving MacDonald as the head of a coalition government in which the Conservatives held an overwhelming majority in Parliament.

In the meanwhile, the British stranglehold in India was steadily loosening, and British revenue from India was declining. The report of the Simon Commission, released in May 1930, had met with well-nigh universal condemnation in India, prompting MacDonald's Labour government to convene a series of round-table conferences in London. Congress boycotted the first, which opened in November 1930, by which time the civil disobedience campaign was well underway. Gandhiji was in jail, and so was Nehru, who had been arrested in October. Gandhiji did attend the second round-table conference, which took place in the fall of 1931, but, like the first, it failed to produce significant progress on the question of India's future constitution. In August 1932, MacDonald took unilateral action, announcing the Communal Award, which granted separate electorates in British India to the "forward" castes and to the so-called Depressed Classes, or Scheduled Castes, as well as to Muslims, Buddhists, Sikhs, Indian Christians, Anglo-Indians, Europeans, women, and various other interest groups. Gandhiji was fiercely opposed to any such arrangement. As Amma explained, it was an approach calculated to exploit Indian's ethnic and religious diversity in order to weaken the nationalist movement.

In this attempt to pander to minority interests, however, the British government underestimated Gandhiji's determination to preserve unity among the biggest bloc of the Indian electorate, the Hindu community. Gandhiji had been unable to bridge the growing rift between the Indian National Congress and the Muslim League, which now clamoured for a separate country under the "two-nation theory." This theory, first articulated by the poet-philosopher Muhammed Iqbal, had been translated into a political agenda by the barrister Muhammed Ali Jinnah. Now the Communal Award threated to drive a wedge between "caste" Hindus and those considered to be untouchables.

On 20 September 1932, while imprisoned indefinitely in Yervada jail without trial, Gandhiji began a "fast unto death" to awaken Indian society's conscience to the cruelty of untouchability. The next day, millions of Indians fasted with him for twenty-four hours, as did Shanti and all her associates in Mathura. Gandhiji insisted on referring to untouchables as *Harijans*, or "people of God," a term he borrowed from the fifteenth-century *bhakti* poet Narsinh Mehta, who had used it with reference to *devadasis*. As I learned many years later, the term had appeared at least a century earlier in a poem by the *bhakti* poetess Gangasati, in whose eyes a Harijan was one whose devotion to God remained steady in both joy and sorrow. "The great Mount Meru may be swayed," she wrote, "but never the mind of the Harijan."

Gandhiji was in his early sixties, and the fast swiftly took a toll on his health. So, just a few days later, Dr. B. R. Ambedkar, the leader of the country's untouchable population, met with Gandhiji and other Congress representatives in Yervada to negotiate an end to Gandhiji's fast. Unlike Gandhiji, Ambedkar had supported the idea of a separate electorate for the Dalits—a term he preferred to Harijans. But, under the circumstances, he was prepared to agree to a compromise, which took the form of an agreement signed on 24 September. Under the terms of the Poona Pact, as it came to be called, the Hindu community remained as a single electorate, but a total of 148 seats in provincial legislatures were now reserved for the Dalits, more than twice the number specified in the Communal Award. After an overwhelming vote in favour of the pact at Congress Party meetings, Hindu temples were opened to untouchables all over the country. Gandhiji marked this transformation by replacing his political newsletter *Young India* with the weekly *Harijan,* which continued to set forth his ideas on non-violence and socioeconomic issues.

Despite criticism from some Congress Party leaders that Gandhiji had abandoned the cause of political freedom in favour of social concerns, the civil disobedience movement continued unabated, and so did British opposition to it. In November 1932, Congress boycotted the third of the round-table conferences organized by the British government to negotiate political reform. In January 1933, nationalist activists around the country were rounded up and imprisoned in a sweep that raised the number of people taken political prisoner to 120,000 in fifteen months. The number of women prisoners still held steady at a little under a quarter of the total. Worried about the influence of communism, the British authorities also imprisoned several trade unionists, including three Englishmen, for organizing an Indian Railway strike that the court deemed treasonous.

Shanti was expecting to be arrested yet again, but she still attended a Congress Party meeting in Mathura, where she led the public pledge of independence. The next morning, a band of policemen arrived to arrest her. She was sentenced to six months of hard labour, for which she was much better prepared than before. Our hard-working Amma even commented that this jail term felt like a respite from the punishing schedule of processions, public meetings, and picketing, and from constantly having to witness the regular beatings and abuse of women and children by the police. In prison Shanti joined many women activists who were familiar to her, and they all helped keep each other's spirits up through singing, writing, and reading.

Just before Shanti's six-month term—her third—was to end, Gandhiji suspended civil disobedience in May 1933 for three months. He requested the British government to repeal the draconian ordinances that allowed the police infinite power, and he advocated for the release of political prisoners. He instructed Congress Party workers to continue with individual acts of civil disobedience if they could. He also started a six-week fast to consolidate the gains that had been made on the issue of untouchability. Initially, British authorities ignored Gandhiji's requests, but three weeks into the fast, when his physical condition started to deteriorate, they released him from jail, along with a large number of political prisoners who were close to the end of their terms, including Shanti.

Shanti emerged from prison into a stifling atmosphere of repression and brutality on the subcontinent. Every day the newspapers carried stories of hundreds of young students being thrown out of colleges and universities for their involvement in or sympathy with the nationalist cause. Every day the newspapers carried stories of Indian government officials resigning in protest against a police state that ruled with iron-tipped lathis and bayonets. Meanwhile, Gandhiji had given over his leadership of the national movement to Jawaharlal Nehru in order to spend more of his time on what he identified as the most crucial social issue of the day, untouchability.

There were other, more personal reasons, as well, for Shanti's heightened sense of repression at the time her third jail term ended. Now that she was fifteen years of age, instead of seeing her as a young girl with a divine spark, people around her made her feel like an oddity that needed to be tamed. She was constantly reminded by well-meaning benefactors and near-strangers alike that a woman her age was expected to be married already and bearing children. Still, Shanti tried to continue with her usual routine of activism along with her daily practice of reading and writing. Inspired by Gandhiji's call to end untouchability, she attached herself to volunteer groups to work for its eradication through education. But her unmarried status was now throwing up obstacles for which she was unprepared.

Didi raised an eyebrow. "How could it be harder after all that time? Wasn't it more difficult as a child?"

Amma looked toward the escaping landscape, but her gaze was turned inward. To the train window she explained that the child who ran away from home to join a group of principled revolutionaries was lucky to be protected and supported by a wide network of patriotic men and women who believed her courage to be divine benediction. The young woman emerging from prison journeys was alone in a man's world, considered an empty vessel to be filled by someone else's identity—nothing more than a prize, or a property. She turned some pages of the diary as though looking for something, and then she closed the book to face us squarely.

"Remember, not everyone was fighting for the freedom of the country," she said, her tone rather acid. For every political activist, there were thousands of people who watched from the sidelines. There were also many who supported the British regime, driven by ancient rivalries of religion and region or, sometimes, by plain old self-interest. When Shanti started volunteering as a Congress Party worker, she came across as many crass opportunists as she did genuine nationalists. "The lesson of my life," Amma told us, "was not to trust anyone blindly, not even the demigods of the nationalist movement."

Shanti decided to use the lull in the nationalist movement to earn a high school equivalency certificate offered through Prayag Mahila Vidyapeeth, an educational institution for women, based in Allahabad, that allowed students to study via correspondence. Early in 1934, just a few months after she passed the qualifying exam, a massive earthquake shook Nepal and Eastern India. More than twelve thousand people died in Nepal and Bihar along the foothills of the Himalayas and the northern rim of the Indo-Gangetic plains. Because Agra was on the outside edge of this rim, it was one of the centres collecting donations to be sent on to the worst-hit towns and villages in the region. So Shanti went to Agra to help with the coordination of volunteers and donations. It was during this period that she had to use her Gurkha knife to defend herself from the lecherous soldier.

Following that incident most of her colleagues celebrated Shanti's courage in fighting back, but one sanctimonious local leader of the Congress Party rudely reminded her of the limits of womanhood. He denounced the moral "character" of women who remained outside the folds of family and marriage, an attack that left Shanti more shaken than she had been by the physical assault.

Martial arts training had not prepared her to immobilize wagging tongues, but it had trained her to face her aggressors. She confronted this well-known middle-aged man and asked him to apologize to her and to womankind in general for his malicious and contemptible views on the "nature" of women. Emboldened by the silence of their senior colleagues, he refused to talk to her any further. Shanti was hurt deeply, as much by the silence of other men whom she respected and had trusted with her life as by the words of the obnoxious man who had first insulted her.

Once back in Mathura, she met with influential Congress Party leaders to complain about the incident. Their deafening silence made her realize the limits of their views on freedom, which did not necessarily extend to the freedom of ordinary women. She decided then to contact the highest authority in the organization and wrote a detailed letter to Jawaharlal Nehru. She received a response four days letter, written by Nehruji, expressing his dismay that a fellow Congress Party leader had insulted women workers. He promised to look into the matter as soon as he could, since he believed that such scandals discredited the nationalist movement and the Indian National Congress.

Shanti waited for a week before sending Nehruji a reminder that she was still waiting for a written apology from the offending Congress leader from Agra. Nehruji's next letter stated that he had spoken to the man, who had accepted his fault in the matter and promised not to talk to any worker sister again in such a rude manner. He suggested that Shanti should forgive the man and consider the matter resolved. The callousness with which everyone handled the matter wounded Shanti profoundly.

I felt for young Shanti's wounded pride and shattered trust, but I was not altogether surprised at the meanness of her colleagues. As young as Didi and I were, we were very aware that our lives were filled with quiet, unseen women, dominated by husbands, fathers, and brothers. Some of these men chose to be kind and generous, but none were required *not* to be selfish or cruel. We knew that our Amma was the anomaly: public speaker, working mother, government official, activist for various causes, talking to men as an equal—even standing up to big boisterous Babu. But the discomfort of many men when they met Amma for the first time was not lost on us. Often they did not know how to address her or how to meet her penetrating gaze. They bowed too low and spoke too little, or they looked right over her head and ignored her, which—despite her diminutive stature—was not all that easy to do.

Shanti was worried that the dismissive reaction of Congress leaders to the public quarrel in Agra would encourage other men in the organization to treat her differently. Her concern was confirmed when she was volunteering for the provincial elections held at the end of that year, which marked the first time that Indian women would be able to vote in significant numbers. Shanti was too young to vote, but she was well-known enough to influence people in their voting. Despite her public stature, however, during one campaign meeting another activist in Mathura tried to put her in her place "as a woman."

The only counsel her benefactors could offer in response to such insults was to suggest that she either marry or seek sanctuary in a community of nuns. The thought of our Amma as a compliant disciple in some religious order made me giggle—our Amma, who refused to enter any of the innumerable temples that stood in every city and village we had ever been to, the one who reminded us that god lives within all living beings and not in a building ("Why else do we close our eyes in prayer?"), who told us to revere the sculptors who created the statues and the carvings on temple walls, the one who participated in a hunger strike to end the practice of animal sacrifice at the Amber Devi temple in Jaipur.

At my giggling, Amma smiled through her sourness.

"Is that why you married Babu?" Didi asked.

"No, this was a few years before I met him." Instead, she told us, she had decided to take a break from political activism and focus on her education. She went back to Manoramadevi, who convinced her that education was the first requirement of mental, social, and financial freedom. With the help of her benefactors in Mathura, she retreated temporarily from public life and started preparing for teaching-certificate exams.

Misfortune struck when Manoramadevi passed away quite unexpectedly. Now mentorless and alone, Shanti wanted to honour the memory of Manoramadevi by not giving up the fight for justice and equality. So she decided to follow the example of the nation's moral beacon, Mahatma Gandhi.

In 1930, Gandhiji had abandoned his home of more than twelve years at the Sabarmati Ashram in order to lead the Salt March, vowing not to return there until the country was independent. In 1936, he established new headquarters in a humble shack in a small village near Wardha, in the heart of central India, surrounded by farms and forests: this was Sevagram Ashram, the place to serve. Here Gandhiji maintained a rigorous routine of selfless service, wrote regularly on social issues, and held meetings with national leaders.

Amma's voice softened as her eyes caressed the diary pages that contained the accounts of her Wardha days. "I do not have words to describe the feeling of being in the presence of the Mahatma," she said, almost reverentially.

"The first time I ever saw Gandhiji was in 1934. He was fanning me with a palm-leaf fan as Mirabehn sprinkled water on my face." She smiled at the memory. "I had fainted and then had nearly been trampled by the throngs of people at the Mathura railway station, all trying to get a glimpse of the Mahatma. When I came to, I found myself in a train compartment, and I heard Gandhiji's voice asking, 'How are you feeling now?' I jumped to my feet and declared that I was fine. Gandhiji held me by the arm and took me to the door of the compartment, where he chastised the crowds for not caring for the life of a young girl in their eagerness to see him. Then, instead of addressing them further, he simply returned to his seat."

That brief encounter, she said, cemented her resolve to fight not only against colonial rule but against oppression of any and all kinds. Two years later, she was living at Wardha, not far from the village of Sevagram, where Gandhiji had recently set up new headquarters. Everyone there called him simply Bapu, "Father."

Amma went on to praise the generosity of Jamnalalji Bajaj, to whom she had first written and who had kindly offered her a place at the Mahila Ashram. She also fondly remembered the support she received from the chairman of Wardha's municipal council, Kanhaiyalalji Bhaiya, and his wife, the writer Satyawati Devi. However, it soon became clear that the training courses at the Mahila Ashram were too rudimentary for Shanti. She wanted to work while studying further, but she wasn't sure of her options.

Jamnalalji took her to meet Gandhiji for advice. "You are wrong to think that the exams and courses run by the British government are real education," Bapu told her. She respectfully tried to explain that she could not work in the field of education without the right credentials and that she had worked very hard to gain her high school and other certifications while being in and out of jail. Nevertheless, Gandhiji disagreed that educational credentials were the best markers of a person's suitability for any task, and he dismissed the need for her to write any further exams.

Shanti then sought refuge with another revolutionary brother's family in nearby Nagpur, in order to ponder her disagreement with the Mahatma—and to write the teacher's training certificate exam. Only after having written it a few months later did she return to Wardha.

Jamnalalji, at least, was impressed with the young woman's resolve to educate herself and others. Yet the elders of Sevagram were convinced that Shanti's anchorless past could not be a foundation for an acceptable future. The fiercely independent young girl who pushed all existing boundaries had to make way for a more compliant young woman, one who was prepared to work within the frame of her new community. So Jamnalalji decided to take her on as a project and anointed her "Prakashwati"—one who spreads light. With this new identity, on 26 September 1936, at the age of eighteen, she was appointed headmistress of Kasturba Kanya Paathshala, a primary school for girls not far from the edge of Sevagram.

Finally she was safe under the watchful mentorship of Jamnalalji, loved by her adoptive family of activists, students, and residents of Sevagram and Wardha, fulfilled by the joy of teaching young girls, and humbled by learning from the Mahatma himself.

"At the end of each long day, I hugged the cool mud floor of my straw hut in the Mahila Ashram. I was finally home."

But her sense of happiness and fulfilment was not enough, not even for her well-wishers. Every day she ignored stares, fielded questions, and deflected unsolicited advice related to her marital status.

Soon, the country was ready for its first provincial elections under the new Government of India Act, passed in 1935, which promised autonomy to provincial administrations while firmly keeping the purse strings in British hands. Despite her transition into a new life, Prakashwati received repeated requests to join the Congress campaigns in central and northern India. Eventually, on Jamnalalji's orders, she went back to Mathura to help with the election campaign, but she could not stay away from her idyllic sanctuary in Sevagram for more than a fortnight.

An interim Congress government came to power in eight of the eleven provinces in early 1937. Many people considered this to be the beginning of self-rule on the subcontinent, but many others were suspicious of the powers granted to the British-appointed governors of the provinces. This was history that Didi and I already knew well. But we kept listening when, after checking some dates in her diary, Amma began to read directly from the transcript of a conversation she had recorded all those years ago.

"Nearly a year after my brief trip to Mathura, I was summoned by Haribhau Upadhyay, one of my many benefactors in Wardha. After failing to convince me to get married and start a family, he wanted me to seek counsel from the Mahatma himself. Haribhauji introduced me to Bapu as I bent down to touch his feet. 'This is Prakashwati,' he said. Gandhiji patted my head with a smile. 'Yes, she does indeed spread light.'

"Haribhauji explained my resistance to marriage and asked the great soul to guide me. 'Bapu,' I said, summoning up all my courage, 'I have decided to spend my life serving the country and the community. I believe that it is difficult to manage the burdens of marital life with the demands of my chosen path.'

"Gandhiji smiled. 'So you are scared of following a difficult path then?' When I shook my head vigorously, he continued more seriously: 'With the right partner, married life can be simple and pure. It can become the means to serve the nation and mankind.'

"I was astonished. 'But Bapu, a celibate has no shackles! There are many young women in the freedom movement who have adopted this path so that they can dedicate their lives to working for the good of their country.'

"'You are confusing true celibates with women who avoid marriage to elude responsibilities,' he replied. 'If you do not want responsibilities, you can remain unmarried. But, for a woman, true chastity is not found in celibacy. *Brahmacharya* is a serious vow that should not be used as an excuse to avoid the responsibilities of marriage.'

"I tried to convince him of my intentions. 'Bapu, I need your guidance to serve the greater good in my own small way. My life is not my own. I find no truer purpose than serving others. I am willing to spend the rest of my life at the Mahila Ashram teaching children.'

"But Bapu remained unmoved. 'You may succeed in fooling yourself, and society may be fooled as well. But you do not need my permission to fool yourself. A true celibate is one in many millions. My advice to you is that you find a suitable partner and practice self-restraint, living a simple and chaste life together. Chastity is not mere abstinence. It is the willingness to do one's duty while sacrificing the temptations of pleasure.'

"It went on in this vein for some time. I was distraught. I had failed to convince Gandhiji that I could remain unmarried, dedicating myself to working with and serving others. I had stood proudly by my principles in front of the whole world, but now the greatest man I knew was telling me that a woman could not choose the path of celibacy—that she could be chaste only within the boundaries of marriage. My heart and mind did not agree with him, but I did not have the right words to convince this master of political negotiations.

"I tried arguing with him on one other occasion but faced the same unbending opinion about marriage being the only option for a chaste woman. I did not even protest when he delegated the task of finding a suitable match for me to Dr. Rajendra Prasadji and Jamnalalji. When everyone else had spoken, what did it matter what I wanted?"

The instant Amma stopped reading, Didi jumped in with a question. "So is that when you met Babu?"

Amma closed the diary with a sigh. "No, not right away." She was able to resist the sporadic matchmaking efforts of her mentors for four whole years. Thankfully, marrying off the stubborn young headmistress of a small primary school in Wardha was not the foremost priority for the architects of an independent nation. These men had more important concerns to occupy them—except for one, who took a personal interest in the matter.

With a note of bemusement that perhaps betrayed her fondness for the memory, Amma mentioned the ardent admiration of Pandit Parmanand of Jhansi, a revolutionary who spent a total of nearly three decades in jail and whom she met in Sevagram during one of his rare spells of freedom, not long before the Second World War began. He respected her desire to serve the greater good but insisted that she would need a husband to protect her and could not possibly find anyone better than him. Amma admitted to us that, in response to repeated invitations, she had journeyed all the way to Kanpur to meet with him, but she claimed she had done so only to suggest that, if he wished to protect her, he could adopt her as a daughter, given that he was nearly twenty-five years older than she was. He was back in jail soon after their meeting, but letters from Parmanandji trying to persuade Amma to change her mind about marriage continued to trickle in for some time.

Amma went on to explain that she met Babu during the Second World War. When the war broke out, Lord Linlithgow, the viceroy of India, unilaterally declared that the country was at war with Germany. Recognizing that Britain needed the support of Indian troops, many nationalists, Hindu and Muslim, saw the war as an opportunity to press for independence, although others felt that India should join the fight against Hitler. As the war escalated, Gandhiji resisted calls to relaunch mass civil disobedience, declaring that he would not seek India's independence out of the ashes of Britain.

One of the fiercest opponents of support for Britain, Amma told us, was Subhash Chandra Bose, known to many as Netaji, "Respected Leader." In 1939, Bose had been elected president of the Congress Party, but he openly advocated the use of force against Britain, a position that put him at odds with Gandhiji. As a result, he was effectively ousted from Congress and formed his own radical faction, the All India Forward Bloc. When the war began, the British placed him under house arrest, but, in January 1941, Netaji escaped and travelled to Germany, where he solicited Nazi support for the cause of Indian independence. Amid swirling rumours of Netaji's secret meetings with Hitler and other Axis powers to launch guerilla warfare, a mysterious man arrived at Gandhiji's ashram.

Amma described how everything about this man was enormous—his muscular body, his booming voice, and, above all, the stories circulating about him. She heard that he was from Bhagalpur and used to edit Dr. Rajendra Prasadji's newsletters in Patna before joining the revolutionary wing of the freedom movement. One story said that he worked in a secret outfit that provided intelligence to Netaji. Another story said that he had deserted Netaji after his overtures to Nazi Germany. Yet another story maintained that he had returned to Dr. Prasadji because a bomb he had planted to damage government property killed a person, causing him to question his chosen path to freedom.

Amma paused. Clearly, she was talking about Babu, and she seemed momentarily flustered, as if suddenly presented with emotions that she had long ago mislaid. I did not want her to stop peeling away these layers of her past, but I waited with her, hoping she would continue.

And, almost blushing, she did. At Wardha, she said, Babu had worked at the Rashtrabhasha Prachar Samiti, the institute for the promotion of Hindi as the national language. When he was not writing at his desk at the institute or reading in his small room in the Harijan hostel, he would walk through patches of emerald-green rice fields into the dense forest of teak trees that stretched toward the Dham River, to practice yoga and meditation for hours on end.

"How did you know his routine?" I asked, ever curious.

Amma's sideways glance was accompanied by an obliging smile. "Our paths crossed a few times." He was a recluse who did his best to avoid social contact. But it was not easy to ignore his silent, formidable presence in prayer meetings, the only daily ritual he deigned to participate in at the ashram. The ashram was abuzz with rumours about this disenchanted revolutionary, about his evening swims in the Wardha River, his hour-long headstands in the teak forest, and his prowess in stick fighting, which he periodically taught to the boys at the hostel. But since he was clearly not interested in joining the close-knit community at the ashram, Amma—as she claimed—ignored him.

A few weeks after his arrival, as the carnage of the Second World War filled the news, Amma was summoned by Dr. Rajendra Prasadji to his cottage. His wife, Rajvanshi Devi, sat her down with her usual affection. Prakashwati had immersed herself in the ashram and school routines, away from the political milieu that seemed to have no place for her, but she was not aloof from the simmering anger and the dread all around. She wondered if Rajendra babu wanted her to get more involved in the public arena again.

"I was surprised, and honestly a bit disappointed, when he started a lecture on social norms instead." He ended his speech with a suggestion that "to anchor your restless life and his" Prakashwati should join the new ashram inmate in holy matrimony.

Then I heard that rare, rollicking laughter. "All I could manage to say was, 'Why would such a handsome man want to marry someone like me?'" Didi and I joined in the laughter, tickled by Amma's rocking mirth, even if we were not quite sure what was amusing her so much.

The train was slowing down as it approached the next stop, on its unhurried way to Jaipur. I was grateful for the pause, which gave us time to savour the sweetness of our collective smiles. Typically, we would be counting the railway stations and talking about the historical significance of every settlement we crossed. But this train ride was all about an altogether different journey, through Amma's life via her diaries.

As the train inched onward to pick up speed again, I wanted to take us back to that joyous flash of a moment ago. "So what did Rajendra Prasadji say in answer to your question, Amma?"

But the train had mysteriously left the station of joy. "Rajendra babu said, 'Rajeshwar will do as I tell him to, because I have his best interest at heart. I hope you trust me enough to accept my suggestion too.' I could not argue with that."

Amma turned again to read from her diary, but her pace was halting. "Sinha saheb was waiting for me after the evening prayer meeting. We talked as we walked the short distance to my hut in the Mahila Ashram. He pointed to his short-cropped salt-and-pepper hair. 'I am not a young man. Most of my life, I worshipped a god I no longer believe in. The only solace of my wasted life is the written word. I like to immerse my tortured mind and soul in others' writing to stop trying to make sense of this world. I know nothing about marriage, but we have both received the same instruction. I need you to know that I am labeled a fugitive and a deserter by my long-time associates. My family thinks that I am an irresponsible wanderer, and I generally regard myself as a useless burden on this earth. I will do as I am told, but I need you to know that I cannot be the protective husband you might have in mind.'

"I was livid at his presumption of my expectations. I stopped in my tracks, looked up at his startled face, and told him, 'I have survived raging rivers, fought off man-eating beasts, and defended myself from men as big as you. I do *not need* protection, much less marriage. It's what everyone else thinks I need. Nobody cares what I want.'

"We locked stares until he closed his eyes and asked, 'What do you want?'

"I was still angry. 'All I want is to walk the path that gives me peace and purpose. All they care about is the stamp of respectability and chastity. If only marriage can provide that stamp, so be it.'

"Sinha saheb did not open his eyes, but through a half-smile he said, 'Well, then, Prakash. That can be arranged.'"

Didi's face bore a mix of emotions. "You two should have just lived your idealistic lives. Why bring children into this world?"

Amma tried to gulp away her wretchedness. "You may be right. I wish I had known then what I know now. But my life had not prepared me for a lot of things. I was naïve enough to believe that all I needed to prevail were well-grounded convictions and perseverance. After we got married, despite your father's ever-present flight risk, I discovered that my desire to have a family to call my own had been rekindled, and I could not conquer it."

Amma looked from Didi to me, imploring us to understand. "You two are like my two eyes. I could not have carried on without either of you." I sprang from my perch on the berth to hug Amma, tears stinging my eyes. Didi's eyes were moist too, but she remained glued to her spot. She pulled her sullen silence around her like a muggy blanket.

It was time to break the silence, and nearly time to end our journey. So I looked at Amma's watch to see the time and pointed out that we had barely touched the snacks that Rani mami and Dadi ma had packed for us so lovingly in Mathura. Gingerly I opened one of the paper wrappings, stained slightly despite the many layers, to discover a most exquisite delight—a small pile of flaky-soft puris, kneaded with milk and spices, deep fried in ghee. We each helped ourselves, and then I leaned across Amma's lap to look out the window. The fields that rushed toward the train were parched from the summer heat. The tall *arjun, ashok,* deodar, and *saal* trees of the United Provinces had given way to scraggy stunted acacias, *khejari,* palm trees, and thorny bushes. I inhaled the dry breeze, savouring its hint of fine sand. My excitement at going to Jaipur, the city of my birth, had been restored.

"Amma, why did you leave Wardha?" I wrapped a puri around a spoonful of the tantalizing shallow-fried potatoes, anticipating the flavours of cumin, coriander, chillies, and dried mango powder.

Amma's sad eyes were riveted to her diary, but she was reading from an invisible book. Slowly, even reluctantly, she told us of her bereavement at Jamnalalji's sudden passing, in February 1942, at Wardha. Six months later, following the declaration of the Quit India movement, Gandhiji was arrested, along with most other senior Congress leaders, and he remained in jail for nearly two years. Even after his release, he mostly lived in Delhi, and his absence made the ashram seem soulless. As Amma got busier with school and the infant Didi, Babu grew more restless. "When the news of Netaji's death in an air crash arrived in August 1945," she told us, "your Babu was more distraught than I had ever seen. It even brought us close, momentarily."

Even though Amma was pregnant with me, Babu decided to move to Ajmer to take up the cause of a nationalist newspaper there, the *Nayjyoti*. Amma's mentors found a job for her in nearby Jaipur, as principal of the Shri Veer Balika Vidyalaya, a private school for girls that, much like the one where she had taught when she was barely twelve, was operated by a wealthy merchant community, in this case the Jains. So she followed Babu to the western frontier of the country, with a toddler in her arms and a baby in her belly. Her new position came with a good salary, as well as accommodations in a large house, to which Babu made periodic visits.

After the end of the Second World War, the struggle for independence entered its final phase. A note of bitterness crept into Amma's voice as she recalled Gandhiji's ultimately futile efforts to prevent the country's partition—a hope shattered forever in July 1947, when the British government passed the Indian Independence Act. Pakistan was created on 14 August 1947, and the following day India celebrated its own birth as an independent nation. But Gandhiji saw no cause for joy. He spent the day fasting, praying for an end to the frenzy of violence that was already gripping the newly born.

Four and a half months later, he was dead. Her voice sinking almost to a whisper, Amma remembered listening in horror as Nehruji's voice floated out of the radio: "The light has gone out of our lives," he began, "and there is darkness everywhere." Amma read from the last few pages of one of her journals, sharing her personal anguish at the loss of her cherished ideal, her Bapu—killed by a madman, Nehruji had called him, who had robbed an infant nation of its father and source of inspiration. And yet, even in her grief, Amma knew that the bullets of the fanatical Hindu nationalist Nathuram Godse could not snuff out the light of Mahatma Gandhi, whose ideals would continue to guide her life and that of her many mourning comrades.

After independence, when it was no longer treason to read it, Babu lost interest in the *Navjyoti* newspaper. He did come to live in Jaipur for a while, where he found work with another newspaper, *Rashtradoot*. But his resignation letter was in his pocket, always.

"No draws of family or job were ever strong enough to tie Sinha saheb down." Amma's eyes searched our faces. No doubt she could see how much that reminder of our inability to make Babu stay with us had stung. "Of course, we also had the most wonderful neighbours, and the trusty Mangi bai." Ah, yes.

"Amma, will we see Mangi bai and Bai ki ma? And my friends— Poorna, Anita, Pramila?" I was chirping again, and Amma's eyes sparkled.

"Yes, indeed. You will see them and more." She then asked cheerfully, "So who remembers the year Jaipur was founded?"

I raised my hand and spoke at the same time. "I know! The oldest fortification of Jaipur is more than a thousand years old, but the new city was built by Maharaja Jai Singh II in 1727."

Amma looked to the unresponsive Didi, who was focused on her puri and potato combo, and tried another strategy. "Who can tell me about your earliest memory of Jaipur?"

At this, my mind was transported to a memory that I had not thought about for a long time. I was perhaps two and a half years old, and Didi just over six. In those days we used to accompany Amma to the refugee camps on the outskirts of the walled city. There were hundreds of women and children there, people with missing limbs and missing family members, women staring with vacant eyes who screamed hysterically at the movement of a shadow. Amma led a band of women, organizing those who were not too hurt or sick to cook, clean, and teach the many children in the camp. Everything was covered in a thick layer of firewood smoke and despair that pricked at the insides of our throats and eyes.

I had learned later that nearly fourteen million people had been uprooted for practicing the wrong religion on the wrong side of the border. Nearly one million had died in the bloodletting that accompanied the partition of the subcontinent after two hundred years of colonial rule. The violence of partition was vividly captured by a stark image on the cover of a magazine among Babu's books that showed an angry goddess Kali stabbing herself, beneath which was the caption "India: Liberty and Death."

I pushed this memory aside and found another one: Mangi bai sitting on the floor outside my room beside the stubs of her smoked-down *beedis*, eyes now closed in sleep. I had tried to steal past the snoring sentinel but somehow made a noise that startled her awake. Her knobbly knees knocking against each other, Mangi bai's arms had flung out as if to hug the trunk of a giant tree, and then she spat out a stream of curse words. Then, terrified of Babu or Amma ever catching her smoking or swearing, she admonished me never to use the words that had come hurtling out of her mouth not a moment ago. I saved the details of the cursing and related to Amma and Didi how much the episode had made Mangi bai and me laugh.

Finally, Didi obliged us with her memory: the rectangular tins, decorated with colourful pictures of telephones, automobiles, or animals, that lined the highest shelf in Amma's office and stored Amma's favourite roasted and salted nuts. Amma used to take a handful of the hidden bounty and stuff it into our pockets before we would leave her office for class every morning.

By this time the uneven string of fields was starting to be replaced by signs of urban development. The expanse of arid, sandy terrain outside our window gave way to flat-roofed brick and stone houses, as Jaipur rushed toward us. As the train pulled into the station, Amma began anxiously to scan the crowd of people waiting on the railway platform. At last she spotted a tall figure. Without letting her eyes leave the towering form in the crowd, she spoke loudly so we would hear over the noise. "Sinha saheb has resigned from the college in Shillong. He promised to meet us in Jaipur."

Babu! I was overjoyed. Didi and I immediately joined our faces with Amma's to peer through the metal bars of the one window that separated us from the man who was now walking effortlessly alongside the train. When the train jerked to a halt, Babu placed one hand on the cold metal of the bars of the window and slipped his other hand through the bars into the compartment. Didi and I held onto it with all our might, fighting back our tears.

5

City of Conquests

JAIPUR, 1957–58

After a long exile, we were finally home. Babu had had enough of a stuffy government college, and Amma had resigned from her job with the UP Social Welfare Department, with its relentless hours and multiple frustrations. She had been offered a position as the "founder-principal" of her former school—which was now the Shri Veer Balika Uccha Madhyamik Vidyalaya. The Shri Veer Balika Vidyalaya had existed since 1925, but it had only recently received accreditation as a full-fledged high school. Amma had originally been hired to guide it through its transition, and she was pleased to be back to celebrate its success. This was where I would continue my education.

We were reunited with the ageless Mangi bai, whose face had not lost its toothy grin ever since our arrival. My teary reunion with Poorna and the rest of Bai ki ma's clan soon gave way to storytelling and laughter—accompanied, of course, by a welcome assortment of Rajasthani snacks. Everything seemed a little smaller, everyone was a little older, but the feeling of peaceful protection that I experienced in their midst was unchanged.

Didi, who was approaching her sixteenth birthday, enrolled in Maharani College for her undergraduate degree, studying Hindi literature—an obvious choice for Didi, who had always been fond of reading—and instrumental music, so that she could continue to study the sitar, which had been her passion for as long as I could remember. Now she was one of only two students in a class taught by Pandit Shashi Mohan Bhatt, a disciple of the renowned Pandit Ravi Shankar. To these she added economics, only because she needed a third subject, and there were very few to choose from at the college.

Not surprisingly, most of Didi's childhood friends were already married. Even my friend Poorna was engaged to be married at the end of the year. Didi's only remaining single friend was Jatan didi, the middle daughter of a wealthy jeweller. Her father much admired Amma, to the extent that he had defied the intense social pressure to marry his daughter off, sending her instead to college at Amma's insistence. With her father's protective support, Jatan didi had even continued her private lessons in Kathak dance, although she rarely performed in public, and only after Amma encouraged her to do so.

We initially moved back into our old rented accommodations around a shared courtyard, but Amma wanted some permanence this time around, as well as more privacy. Then trust managers told her about a house on their books that had been long empty, since it was believed to be haunted. Naturally, Amma wanted to see this house.

It was a two-and-a-half storey house wedged between two four-storey houses in a narrow bystreet, further dwarfed by the high rear walls of a sprawling Devi temple. The house was conveniently located only three streets away from the school where Amma worked and I studied, one street away from the bustling broad avenue of Johari Bazaar, and a short rickshaw ride away from Didi's college.

Like other homes in Jaipur, the house was hidden from the street by a thick outer wall of stone, punctuated by small windows, wide enough for a head but not a torso. A narrow stone platform ran along the length of the front wall, about five feet above street level, in the middle of which was a *chhatri,* a decorative dome supported by slender pillars, that provided an elevated front entrance accessible from either side by short flights of steps. From this entranceway, a heavy wooden door opened onto a large courtyard surrounded by spacious halls with chunky sandstone flooring. The uniformly high ceilings were supported by stone pillars with lotus bases. Each corner of the ground floor had a small, enclosed room, no bigger than ten feet square.

An enclosed staircase on the right side of the building took you to the first floor, which had the characteristic overhanging balcony encircling the courtyard and another set of open halls with pillars. The only rooms with doors on this level were, again, the small ones in the corners. Despite the absence of real windows, the open courtyard and the lack of walls made the living areas very airy and bright. From this floor, another staircase led to a broad rooftop terrace. On the left side of the terrace were the crumbling remains of a large room, which ran the breadth of the house. On all three floors, the walls had once been covered with a smooth, lustrous lime plaster, which, now several centuries old, was falling away, revealing the underlying stone, a good two feet thick in many places. On the first floor, some of the lime-plaster flooring still shone like marble through the rubble, while in other places the base layer of lime mortar—mixed in the traditional way with slaked lime, a powder made from under-burnt bricks, sand, jaggery, fenugreek, and other organic additives—was now visible, cracked and crumbling from years of neglect.

Amma did some research at both the royal and municipal libraries to establish the history of the house, and several long-time residents of the neighbourhood confirmed her findings. As the ornamental *chhatri* at the entranceway suggested, the house had originally been a *haveli,* a stately home or mansion, meant for an official of the royal court. Rights to its occupancy had been granted to one of the many hereditary *kotwals,* rulers of local forts who evolved into senior police officials appointed by the Maharajahs of Jaipur. When the last *kotwal* died without an heir, a religious order had requested permission to use the house as a monastery for its small clutch of female ascetics. For several decades, the former mansion provided shelter to these *sadhvis*—young women seeking refuge from poverty in religion, older women hoping for salvation or relief from cruel social practices, and sundry other abandoned women who might have found some measure there of solace or camaraderie. The *sadhvis* had very limited contact with the outside world. A small well on one side of the courtyard meant that they had no need to venture forth even to draw water.

At the turn of the century, however, a scandal broke out when it was discovered that one of the nuns had not only become pregnant but was secretly raising her illegitimate child within the walls of the building. Soon after her sins were exposed, the dishonoured *sadhvi* jumped into the well with her infant. The remaining *sadhvi*s were moved to a new location, and the trustees of the religious order that had been granted use of the house permanently sealed the well. Despite this effort to keep spirits from escaping, neighbours on all three sides of the house reported hearing sobs and sighs emanating from the depths of the empty courtyard, and, on moonless nights, the shape of a woman dressed in white could be seen on the rooftop terrace, rocking a baby in her arms.

Amma had no belief in ghosts, and she negotiated a deal with the religious trust to buy this house. The trustees were relieved to have the house off their books and hastily drew up the paperwork, which required Amma to pay in installments spread over several years. The contract even granted her permission to organize a public event to raise money for repairs and modifications.

I was not sure how to interpret the quietness of our father in the midst of the clamour of moving. Babu did not want to go back to teaching or college administration; that much was clear. There were many public and private educational institutions in the city, but Babu's missionary zeal for education as a life-long quest for knowledge found little space in the regimented structure of classes, programs, degrees, affiliations, and administration.

Yet he was also not prepared to go back to his old job at the newspaper in Ajmer or Jaipur. He argued with Amma when she suggested it, insisting angrily that a newspaper was a sacrosanct part of the media that should be devoted to critical enquiry and public education. He was not prepared to reconcile his ideals with the demands of a publishing environment that predicated the survival of a newspaper on political patronage and commercial support.

They were at an impasse. In our temporary accommodations, Didi and I had been witnesses to many conversations in which Amma and Babu discussed the future, made and remade plans, and savoured being together after so long. Now the four of us sat quietly, Amma in the middle of her bed, Didi and I perched on opposite ends of it, the three of us facing Babu, who sat in Amma's wooden chair. The four of us made a little rhombus of humans, joined together by a fragile hope.

Babu surveyed the gathering and then closed his eyes. His normally booming voice almost quiet, he spoke to Amma as if the two of them were alone. "Is this what we fought for, Prakash? Replacing the shackles of British rule with the chains of profit at any cost? This is not the *swaraj* that Gandhiji dreamt of. This is the colonization of greed."

Didi and I looked at him in alarm. Could we be losing him again? I looked at Amma's bowed head, silently beseeching her with my eyes. *Please say something that will make him stay.*

Amma raised her head, slowly looking from Didi to me. "We have to carry on for the sake of the girls. We could find a way to combine your passion and experience right here in Jaipur."

Babu's eyes were closed, but he appeared to be listening intently rather than preparing a rebuttal. Amma's suggestion came out with a studied effortlessness. "What about starting your own newspaper? That way you would not have to work for anyone else. You could finally use your own vision and voice."

Babu's silence tested Didi's and my ability to hold our breaths. I stole a glance toward Amma, whose eyes were fixed on the weave of the milky-white coverlet on the bed.

At long last Babu sighed. "Perhaps we could use the main floor of the new house for a printing press."

Amma continued to gaze at the coverlet as Babu mentioned the bank account where the college had deposited his salary. He had had little use for this money, which would be well spent on starting a newspaper venture. At this, Amma opened a folder to show him a long list of tasks and materials required to fix the house. These repairs would need to be made not only before we could live in it but also before it could house a printing press. Babu told her to go ahead and do whatever was necessary.

I was still getting used to the deep timbre of Babu's voice, which rang on in contained spaces long after he had left. My gaze followed him as he left the room, but I lingered with Amma and Didi. When Amma looked up from her reverie, the relief I felt was clearly reflected in her own tired but relaxed face.

Except for the bungalow in Lucknow, we had always lived in big houses with shared spaces. Whether we stayed in those houses for a few months or many years, however, Amma always insisted on putting matching curtains on all doors and windows. Like us, our houses were only allowed to wear khadi.

Amma was now spending all her spare time trying to find the right people to do the repairs and remodelling—craftsmen trained in traditional methods who would nonetheless be willing to work for a reasonable price. She had already rejected many of those recommended to her when she met wiry old Surajji and his crew, which consisted solely of his young nephew, Radhe bhaiya. Surajji had been raised as a proud *sainik mali,* born into an hereditary clan of gardeners and cultivators who trace their roots to Rajput warriors. Unfortunately, the crumbling feudal system and the inadequate land shared among his large family had forced him to look for more reliable sources of income, so he had moved to the city to learn a new trade and provide better opportunities for his three sons. His wife had cleaned houses for other people while Surajji became an apprentice stone mason.

They had sent all three sons to school where their brilliance shone. Their hard work earned them scholarships and, later, well-paying jobs. Now married and settled in their own homes, the sons were ashamed of their sunburnt father, his rural dialect, the smell of unrefined tobacco that followed him loyally, and his perpetually coarse hands. Surajji was grateful that his wife had died before the ungrateful sons severed their ties with him. He was training his young nephew in the craft that he had come to love, hoping to be able to pass on his knowledge and his skills, which were now considered slow and outmoded in this era when brick and cement buildings were sprouting up everywhere with reckless speed.

Amma was thrilled to have found a craftsman with traditional masonry and plastering skills. Babu loved his stories and spent hours talking to him in Marwari, sharing meals and tea with Surajji and Radhe bhaiya. Didi and I were exhilarated by Amma's enthusiasm. We planned and discussed things with her as soon as she returned from work each day, only occasionally reduced to squabbling.

During this time of preparation and planning, one of the old sewing ladies came to Amma to present her son. He has just won a scholarship to study for a professional degree; her sewing, we learned, had supported her son's education, despite the objections of her affluent family, who would rather have had her hidden in a dark corner and her son living on the unreliable charity of relatives. She thought her sewing days would be behind her soon, and she wanted to pay her debt of gratitude to Amma by stitching the curtains and bed linens for the new house. Amma declined this generous offer, pointing to Didi and me. We were old enough to test our own sewing skills and creativity. Besides, nobody would have the time to travel this summer because of the renovations. However, Amma did promise to contact her if we found ourselves running behind schedule.

And then there was the movie problem to solve. Amma did not want to sink all of her and Babu's savings into the repair of a house that did not yet belong to us. Fortunately, one of the board members of the religious trust owned the most magnificent movie theatre in Jaipur, and he had offered to let Amma do a charity screening of a Hindi movie to raise money for the repairs. This, he insisted, was his way of expressing his appreciation to Amma for returning to teach a new generation of girls in his community, and he wanted to help Amma make Jaipur her permanent home. Amma respected Golchaji, but she disliked mainstream Hindi films, so the prospect of using one for her own financial benefit presented her with a moral dilemma. She had requested some time to think about his offer.

Since India achieved independence, the country's rapidly growing movie industry had been churning out hundreds of commercial productions each year, including musicals. Even though some of these popular films were quite moralistic, with plots that focused attention on social issues, both Amma and Babu were deeply uncomfortable with most of these movies, which they regarded as frivolous, melodramatic, and too often preoccupied with romantic entanglements. I could count on the fingers of my two hands the number of films that Didi and I had seen— and these only after they had been carefully vetted not only by advisory panels responsible to the Board of Film Certification but then again by Amma. As Amma and Babu saw it, cinema should be a medium for public education, just like the newspapers, not a form of entertainment.

Besides their moral objections to cinematic storylines, our parents also had aesthetic objections to film music. Babu still followed the evening routine of singing *bhajans* to the accompaniment of his harmonium, but he could not stand the sound of a show tune, walking away from the offending noise as soon as he could. At home, if Didi or I let the sound of the radio travel outside our room, he would demand that we turn it off, his voice thundering to be heard above the music.

Amma was gentler in conveying her disapproval, but she was equally vehement. Our parents' love of music had ensured that we were given music and dance lessons wherever we lived. The trouble was that they considered music to be a high art form that needed to be cultivated through disciplined practice and with due respect for traditions. Amma had often told us that her love for classical music stemmed from memories of her family hosting noted singers on special family occasions, and she had often rued the quality of what passed for music in the modern day.

As she debated whether to accept Golchaji's offer, Amma complained to us about the very high pitch at which female recording artists were expected to sing, a style she blamed on the influence of European operas. Women's voices should be low and melodious, she declared, not piercing and shrill.

"But you can't just say that we should go back to the past," Didi countered. "At least now everyone can enjoy music, not just a handful of rich patrons." As she pointed out, until quite recently, professional musicians were mostly male, and they had few opportunities for reputable employment. And the situation was even worse for women. The only female performers were Nautch girls, who danced before the watching eyes of men, in the lavish homes of kings, nawabs, and zamindars, or the lowly *devadasis* who served in temples, singing and dancing to please the god.

Amma had to agree that the secularization of music and dance had brought performers out of temples, palaces, and mansions into a wider world. She was also willing to admit that the popularity of commercial film songs had contributed to the growth of music as a profession, making it possible for performers, especially women, to earn a living without sacrificing their respectability.

"So then what's wrong with film music?" I asked.

"The pitch and the poetry are what's wrong with film music," said Babu, who had just walked into the room. "Music is the melodious expression of universal human emotions, not the shrill pitches of wailing banshees, devoid of either the refinement of classical music or the simplicity of folk music."

"But I have read that film music is a bridge between folk and classical music," I protested. "Even Gopi Krishna and Sitara Devi have performed in films." I had never been permitted to see any of their movies, but I had once watched these two icons of classical Kathak dance give an electrifying performance that had lasted until the wee hours of the morning, and the experience was still fresh in my memory.

"Yes, but a bridge made up of what?" Babu roared his question. "The emphasis on pitch rather than tone, the clatter of instruments that drown out the melody, the substitution of rhymes for poetry?" He particularly objected to the unending refrains of personal love. To him they were not only crass but also a troubling sign of increasing individualism in Indian society.

Eventually, Amma did agree to screen a movie to raise money for the house repairs, but on two conditions: she would pick the movie to be screened, and the movie theatre would have to arrange to cut any scenes that she told them to cut. Golchaji was relieved by Amma's decision and happily agreed to both conditions. Amma settled on the preachiest tearjerker released that year, minus a song sequence in which the dashing hero and the pining heroine looked like they might be about to kiss.

The ground floor of the house was the easiest to repair, as the solid sandstone floor needed nothing more than a good cleaning. Only the closed-up well site in the northern corner received a new cement floor and was walled off with a metal grill to create a space for storing the smaller machinery. Surajji and Radhe bhaiya did a good job of repairing the lime plaster on the wide walls, largely leaving the open floor plan unaltered.

The unobstructed space turned out to be ideal for the paraphernalia of printing that was invading the house—two gigantic German platen printing presses, a paper-ream cutting machine that weighed tons and lived like a monstrosity by itself in one of the rooms, machines for binding and perforating paper, and dozens of wooden stands with trays containing hundreds of pounds of various fonts in both Hindi and English. The ground floor also had an unpaved area right in the middle of the courtyard, twelve feet square, filled with fertile soil for growing hibiscus, roses, aromatic herbs, and other small bushes that thrived in the mix of sun and shade.

The first floor of the house was eminently livable after the open halls had been converted into rooms of various sizes. Except for Amma's and Babu's, all rooms on this floor opened onto the continuous balcony that overhung the courtyard below.

The southern side of this floor was an enclosed veranda open to the sky, lined with many potted plants, a large cement water tank for storing the water supplied by the municipality, and a small wooden screen that separated the laundry area in front of the tank from the rest of the patio. The west hall, which directly faced the staircase, was converted into a drawing room, complete with large wicker chairs and a divan. It was a spacious room, though awkwardly divided by an original pillar about one-third of the way in. Across from the ouside wall of this room, with its row of small windows, stood a series of three wide metal screens, covered in colourful curtains and strings of bead, which connected a row of pillars to create a new wall that now enclosed the room.

Amma chose as her bedroom a small room accessible from the drawing room, in the northwestern corner of the house. Only ten feet square, the room had just enough space for her mattress and a low *munim* desk. I inherited Amma's large writing desk, since she was, increasingly, doing her reading and writing while reclining on bolsters, due to chronic pain in her legs and back.

The long hall in the north was divided into a spacious dining room, accessible from Amma's room as well as from a wide door that opened onto the balcony, and a kitchen, with an L-shaped sandstone counter and deep cupboards. This still left room for a small storage area in the northeastern corner, separated by a wooden screen, for our trunks, steel almirahs, holdalls, and other such items. This neat little box-room was also very useful for keeping our clothes and linens organized, since there were few cupboards in the rest of the house.

Mangi bai had rebelled against the counter and the gas stove; she stuck with sitting on a low stool to cook, using either the portable coal-fired *sigri* burner or the wood-fired *chulha* out on the open first-floor veranda. She also grumbled about the kitchen cupboards, complaining that their extra depth and height made them hazards for children who might want to hide in them.

The large eastern hall yielded a big square room that Didi and I shared. It had enough space for our two divan beds along opposite walls, two desks, Didi's sitar, my five-stringed *tanpura,* and an aisle. A large rug in the middle of the room separated our beds and belongings, but it was not the most effective barrier between our very different routines and temperaments: The door of our room was flanked by two large, elaborately carved *jali* inserts on the walls. Our room connected to Babu's through two side-by-side doors, which could be latched closed from our side of the wall.

Babu's long, cavernous, windowless room was in the southeastern corner of the floor. At the far end was a bench for his harmonium and a metal trunk containing no more than two sets of clothing, which he washed himself. Amma had to keep an eye on the contents of the trunk as well as the one pair of shoes that he owned, since he often gave these away to beggars and homeless people on the street, returning home without shoes or sometimes even without his kurta. His mattress-less wooden bed with its stone pillow was placed right in the middle of the room, flanked on one side by a desk that held neat stacks of paper and books and on the other side by a low wooden *chowki*. He liked to sit down there for his meals, rather than at the table in the dining room with us.

Surajji and Radhe bhaiya efficiently restored most of the walls and flooring, but they were unsure what to do about the large room, now in ruins, that had at some point been added on the rooftop terrace. Rather than waste time and money on efforts to rebuild it, Amma instructed them to replace it with a brick and cement structure, covered with a corrugated asbestos-cement roof, which was supposed to be much more temperature resistant than a metal roof. Much to Amma's dismay, however, they left a series of small, narrow gaps all along the southern wall of the new room, designed to allow fresh air in. She protested that the gaps would give easy passage to the sandy dust of the desert, but Surajji pleaded the case for proper ventilation, even in a room that was intended to be a library. This was the first time there had been any friction between Amma and Surajji, and time and money were both at a premium, so Amma decided to ignore the library's inadequacies for the time being—a decision with consequences none of us could imagine at the time.

Near the southwest corner of the library was a set of narrow double doors, each consisting of an acacia-wood frame with a solid panel of asbestos at the bottom and metal mesh at the top, which was covered by dark khadi curtains to keep the heat and dust out. A small desk and chair occupied one corner near the entrance, and a broad wooden bench was parked outside the room for basking in the cool winter sun or snoozing on summer nights. Aside from the desk and chair, the library held nothing but books, stacked on haphazard shelves along all the walls.

Amma had hired a carpenter to make some oversized bookshelves for this room, but Babu shooed the poor, protesting man away, while thundering at Amma for forgetting simple living and giving in to frivolities and pretence. Amma tried to argue that they had too many books in cloth bags and boxes, and far too few shelves that had survived their many moves. So Babu set about adding layers of bookshelves, improvised from discarded planks and lengths of slate propped up by brick or stone all along the walls of the library on the terrace.

Onto these makeshift shelves went Hindi books on history, philosophy, and music, as well as classic and modern literary texts from many parts of the world translated into Hindi or English, organized thematically all along the long northern wall. The top-most shelf on the short eastern wall was home to scores of Amma's notebooks and diaries. Her collection of biographies, histories, and political treatises occupied all the middle shelves. Paper remains of her involvement in the freedom movement—files and folders containing old letters, telegrams, newspaper cuttings, and photographs—were stacked in the lowest reaches of this wall.

Babu hung a waterproof plastic sheet over the gaps in the long south wall, defeating Surajji's object of providing ventilation. This wall then was lined with books from Babu's inaccessible past: hundreds of volumes in Bengali, Marathi, Marwari, Gujarati, Sanskrit, French, German, and Russian, islands of foreign scripts in a sea of Devanagari.

Babu named his new printing business Vaishali Press, after the earliest-known republic in eastern India, founded in the sixth century BC. He then spread word among his former publishing colleagues that he was looking to hire a foreman for his press. The only qualification was that the candidate had to be Dalit or Muslim, since they had the hardest time finding jobs in Jaipur. Babu was prepared to train and employ someone without any experience. Thus the eighteen-year-old Shafi Muhammad, or Shafiji, entered our lives.

The oldest of eight siblings, Shafiji had dropped out of school after grade 5 to help his father, who owned a little shack where he kept fire going under two vats, dyeing cotton, silks, and wools in vibrant colours, following his ancestral profession. Already married and the father of a little boy, Shafiji wanted his children and younger siblings to go to school.

Despite his rudimentary reading and writing skills, he was an eager learner. Babu hired Shafiji as the only employee of the press with a monthly salary, teaching him the basics of composing and printing as well as book-keeping. Together they hired compositors on daily wages, depending on the volume of the work. Babu paid compositors the highest per-line wage in the city; thus every morning there was a group of men waiting for Shafiji to open the doors of the press.

Thanks to Amma's and Babu's long-standing associations and many acquaintances, the press got printing orders from local literary societies and regional educational institutions. Vaishali Press was one of only a few printing presses in Jaipur, although people in this wealthy city had a variety of publishing needs, from personal invitation cards to political pamphlets. Babu initially objected to printing anything but a newspaper, but relented when Amma pointed to the family needs of the many whom the press could potentially employ.

Shafiji always arrived on the dot of seven, just as Babu returned from his hours of yoga in Ram Niwas Park, hollering, "Rekhu, what's for breakfast?" It did not matter to him that dear little "Rekhu" might be on her way to school on weekdays or that she might still be in bed on holidays— or that she never, ever made breakfast.

Amma settled into a gruelling schedule that took her from school to meetings to delegations to rallies, and still found time for her to teach prison inmates at the Central Jail twice a week and write in her diary every night. Every now and then, Amma got up at dawn to practice yoga and pranayama on the terrace, but her schedule of frequent late nights and early morning commitments got in the way of her routine. I could always tell when Amma had had a chance to practice yoga and pranayama by the brightness of her eyes and the fluidity of her movements that day. But her daughters' pleas to slow down were dismissed. "These aches and pains are just the dharma of the human body. The body has to do its karma, I have to do mine."

The rest of us developed our routines as well, as we settled into the new house. Mangi bai resumed her role as the trusty caretaker of the home and hearth. Didi and I enrolled once again in music and dance classes, rehearsing hard for the upcoming Independence Day celebrations at Jaipur's stately Albert Hall Museum, with its domes and ornate arches. For many decades, the musuem had hosted private events for the Maharajas of Jaipur, and Didi, Jatan didi, and I, who had been asked to dance, were thrilled to be among the first to perform there as part of a public event.

A number of different political factions had been approaching Amma, asking her to run in local elections, but Amma firmly declined any invitation to compete for office in municipal or provincial elections. Her argument was that elected officials had little choice but to engage in political bartering, a necessity that would only be an obstacle in her work on social issues. Despite this skepticism, however, she continued to support the Congress Party.

Amma's loyalty to Congress was an enormous bone of contention between my parents, especially after she agreed to serve as president of the Jaipur chapter of the party's Women's Wing. Babu often helped Amma to write petitions and speeches, but he erupted like Krakatoa any time a Congress official came to the house to meet with her. Refusing to emerge from his room, Babu would launch into a loud monologue in which he denounced all Congress associates as Gandhi's murderers, foot soldiers of the Nehru empire, worshippers of power, sole cause of the misery of two whole nations, greed personified, looters, and so on. If Amma tried to calm him down, he would call her a traitor like the rest of them and storm out of the house. Awkward witnesses to Babu's fiercest side, the visiting official would wait with Amma, who sat with her head lowered, until Babu's private but nonetheless deafening explosions finally ran out of steam—although never before he had given his audience a guided tour of his rich vocabulary.

About a year after we returned, just before Independence Day in 1958, large-scale public protests erupted over the dissolution of the Jaipur bench of the Rajasthan High Court. In 1949, the state of Rajasthan had been formed from a patchwork of nineteen former princely states and one British province, but regional feudal powers still wielded substantial clout, and the evolving legislative and judicial institutions of the new state had to navigate deeply entrenched power structures. Originally, high courts existed in Bikaner, Jodhpur, Kota, and Udaipur, as well as in Jaipur, the largest city in the state, which, in 1949, became its capital. In order to consolidate the state's judicial structure, but also to appease regional rivalries, Jodhpur was chosen as the principal seat of the Rajasthan High Court.

The judicial benches in Bikaner, Kota, and Udaipur had been abolished in 1950, but the Jaipur bench—the busiest court in the state—had continued to operate. Now it, too, was being dissolved, a decision that provoked lawyers' strikes and public demonstrations. When the police opened fire on a rally of striking lawyers, the whole city responded with a general strike, protest marches, and some violent conflicts with police.

All forty members of the municipal council resigned in protest, prompting the state government to dissolve other local boards, including one on which Amma served as an appointed member. Unruly public protests and police retaliation ensued, to which the state administration responded by declaring a curfew in parts of the city and closing all educational and public institutions. Babu's view was that such disturbances were to be expected in the early days of a new nation, one in which some 560 princely states had formerly existed alongside British-controlled territories. Amma's position was that the heavy-handed police action during these protests reminded her of colonial times, and she was determined to travel to Delhi with a delegation to petition the prime minister.

Amma returned exhausted and anxious from her meeting with Nehruji and his chief of staff, his daughter Indira Gandhi. He had rejected the petitioners' request to have the dissolution of the High Court bench in Jaipur reconsidered. Amma was hopeful that she might have been able to appeal to Nehruji's love of children by describing the police attacks with lathis and rubber bullets on groups of unarmed student protestors, but in the meantime, while she waited for him to take action, every relaxation of the curfew only led to further rioting and escalating tension between civilians and the police.

Just outside the narrow bylane in which our house stood, Amma was getting into a government car with the national flag on the hood. Seeing this, Didi and I ran to the Devi temple through the back entrance opposite our house and climbed to the terrace above its imposing entrance in Johri Bazaar. From there we could see a cavalcade of official cars with red beacons on them and one vintage Rolls-Royce that clearly bore the crest of the Maharaja (which depicted his heritage as a descendent of the sun god). We were less than half a mile from the Badi Choupad square, where Sukhadiaji, the chief minister, Nawab Luharuji and other members of the legislative assemble, and assorted other dignitaries were due to address the largest public rally either of us had ever seen.

The row of stone poles that ranged all along the length of the street, each crowned with an image of the sun god, was strung with loudspeakers. The curfew had been lifted that morning, for just a few hours, and the broad street and the narrow bylanes had been filling with people ever since. I was grateful to be able to watch what was going on from the safety of the temple terrace rather than from within the crush of people in the street. We could not quite see the faraway stage but hoped to be able to hear the speeches via the loudspeakers. People were pushing toward the stage in the square, chanting angry slogans, drowning out the sounds that came periodically from the loudspeakers. Clusters of curious children and veiled women had formed at windows and on terraces that overlooked Johri Bazaar.

Then I heard a strange roar above the din, audible in the spaces created by the chanting's rise and fall. It was my Amma's voice, passionately reminding the massive gathering of their civic duties, chiding them like errant children. I was filled with pride and a strange dread, as the restless mass of humanity began to take note of this intrusion. Amma's voice grew clearer, because the slogans were no longer rising as one voice. She sternly commanded people to sit down wherever they were and listen to the remaining speech of the governor, Gurmukh Nihal Singhji. People listened to her and obeyed, as grown men do an overbearing mother.

For the next few minutes, nothing more than a low murmur from the crowd accompanied the sedate address of the governor. However, as soon as the next speaker took the mike, someone threw a shoe toward the stage, breaking the brief spell that Amma had cast. Pandemonium broke out. I could see that the part of the crowd closest to the stage was no longer sitting. They were on their feet now, held back from the stage by a battalion of the same paramilitary police that had been enforcing the curfew in Jaipur.

Amma's voice rose again, the voice of the only woman in what looked like a planet of men. A number of well-respected residents of the Johari bazaar had bravely entered the melee by this time, and we could see them calming people down at our end of the street. The speeches could no longer go on, but Amma and the community elders between them did manage to disperse the agitated crowds and disentangle them from armed law enforcement, so close to the brink of another violent conflict.

JAIPUR, 1959

Jaipur was built on the edge of the Thar Desert, surrounded on three sides by the Aravalli Hills, the eroded stubs of an ancient range of fold mountains that extends southwest from Delhi across Rajasthan and into Gujarat. Seven imposing gates provided the only passage in and out of the walled city, which, for well over two centuries, had been home to centres of trade, the arts, and learning. Within the city walls, hundreds of thousands of people—royalty and commoners included—lived and worked together in the terracotta-pink, multi-storeyed residences that lined the broad avenues, linked by their terraces and courtyards. The overlapping living and working spaces served the needs of social life, of work, and of the numerous festivals that the city celebrated as one organism.

Amma remembered the royal splendour and the sense of open space of Jaipur in the 1930s, when it was home to less than half of the nearly four hundred thousand people who now lived here. She remembered the city gates being closed every night to keep wildlife at bay. A wilderness, arid but teeming with wildlife all the way up into the hills, had then surrounded the city. One of the few exceptions to this inhospitable landscape was the emerald greenery of Ram Niwas Garden, which jutted out of the walled city like a single arrow projecting into the future. The Albert Hall Museum sat in the middle of this luxuriant oasis, the most exquisite jewel of Rajputana architecture and, for us, the site of many memorable walks with Babu.

Since the end of British rule, however, the walls of the city had become unable to contain the surge of people headed to Jaipur. Desperate tides of humanity ravaged by colonization, refugees uprooted by the botched division of the subcontinent and impoverished farmers chasing the promise of a better life in the urban centres of the country came in waves, eventually forcing the city to expand into the harsh territory beyond its ornate high walls. The systematic containment of the city began rapidly to give way to mushrooming residential areas, called "colonies," though named after one leader of the freedom movement or another. These observed neither the patterns of city planning nor the aesthetics of architecture that the city proudly preserved within its ancient walls.

Long before this chaotic development, a number of *haveli*s and palaces, belonging to feudal lords, courtiers, and other beneficiaries of royal land grants, had been built outside the city walls; in fact, some of them predated the city by centuries. Land reforms enacted over the past decade had enabled the state to acquire some of this land in order to build housing for a rapidly growing population, so that islands of feudal splendour were now surrounded by a sea of haphazard colonies.

For Amma, there was much work to be done in this city, where, despite modern reforms, few middle-class women were seen in public spaces without purdah. Her incessant meetings, petitions, speeches, and committee work were all united by the single goal of women's empowerment. Didi and I worried about Amma's groans as she climbed the stairs, the swelling around her ankles, and her frequent headaches. But Amma refused to make any changes to her diet and relied on herbal self-medication, attributing her aches and pains to her irregular practice of yoga and pranayama.

Even at home, Amma worked toward women's empowerment, as she often had to challenge the many lessons in womanly behaviour with which our numerous temporary guardians dutifully filled our heads. Amma was particularly upset whenever Didi and I were reminded about the impurity of the female body—its untouchability during menstruation and pregnancy. She always told us to ask questions rather than comply with injunctions on what to do and how to be. There was fire in her eyes whenever she talked about women's issues; her speech grew slow and measured, laden with layers of meaning that sometimes became apparent only over time.

On occasion, the intensity of her gaze could warm my skin. "Do you remember that woman in the valley, who was worshipped for her power to summon Devi Mata?" I distinctly remembered the terrifying spectacle of a woman who rotated her head in impossible circles, thrashed her long, kohl-black hair in front of a crackling fire, emitted animal sounds from the depths of her lungs, and hoarsely chanted the name of the local goddess.

When a terrible nightmare woke me up that night, Amma gave us both a long lecture on hysteria and the suppression of women in society. I did not remember much of the content, but I did remember being thankful for Amma's lecture, which had kept me from going back to sleep, back to the terrifying nightmare.

"Remember what happened after her trance was over?" We nodded, recalling the image of that same woman, her trance over, surrounded by gifts of food, clothing, and flowers and by prostrate villagers. People had come to seek her blessings and advice. The divine connection had catapulted her from being silent, invisible, and unequal to one who was feared and respected. The villagers would feed her and worship her, maybe even build a temple in her honour, as long as she showed evidence of being more than a mere woman. "For me," concluded Amma, "this is an example of a woman trying to be her own person, rising above the social norms that force her into a sub-human existence." Amma wanted us to understand and challenge these unjust norms, not with the unreliable crutch of divinity, but with the understanding and confidence we could gain through learning and education.

Since we had returned to Jaipur, Didi had received a number of marriage proposals, all of which Amma had refused to consider. She wanted Didi to earn at least a master's degree and then pursue a career that would provide her with an income of her own. Didi had given many sitar recitals in the city on special occasions: at the Governor's House, at some of her college functions, and at provincial youth festivals. She and I were also regularly invited to take part in classical dance recitals at receptions for visiting dignitaries. Didi and her friend Jatan didi would perform rhythmic Kathak compositions based on the legends of Krishna and Radha, while I gave solo performances of graceful Bharatnatyam, a dance form once confined to the temples of southern India. I was drawn to the emotional purity of Bharatnatyam, in which the emphasis falls on mood more than on storytelling.

Didi had grown to be very beautiful, with large, almond-shaped eyes, long, lustrous hair that was naturally wavy, and a petite but curvaceous frame. She carried herself like a princess at all times, her appearance was never less than immaculate, and she never forgot her manners for a moment. Didi was always soft-spoken, though sometimes a bit stiff.

I made a striking contrast to my elegant sister. At fourteen I was already taller than Didi but too skinny, and I liked to laugh too loudly, chatter too often, run up and down the stairs too much, and ride my bike everywhere. Without much encouragement, my straight hair had grown down to my hips, and I was content to have it knotted, braided, or tucked back, just as long as it didn't get in my way. I was in my final year of high school, waiting impatiently for the tyranny of my drab school uniform and the all-day routine to be over.

I often asked to borrow items from Didi's wardrobe, and she never hesitated to share them, albeit with repeated warnings to look after them carefully. Somehow, though, they always looked out of place on my darker-skinned, lanky body, which had a habit of colliding with lurking nails and unexpected corners. Whenever I sheepishly returned a scarf or shawl with a rip or a snag, Didi would exclaim that I must have thorns instead of bones in my body. Yet if I asked to borrow something again the very next day, she wouldn't refuse, and the cycle would inevitably repeat itself.

Shafiji had planted a sickly looking jasmine plant right in the middle of the courtyard on the ground floor. At the time, the compositors laughed at the idea that this plant might survive the competition from the lush little shrubs around it to grow into a respectable bush. Still, Shafiji ignored all skepticism and dangled a rope from a nail on the outer wall of the library on the terrace, two floors above.

This arrangement looked ridiculously ambitious until the jasmine took the hint and started climbing the rope. Its top was beyond the first floor by the end of its first year. In its second year, Shafiji fashioned a network of metal wires between the east and west terraces that then supported the horizontal growth of this bush-turned-tree. We were all incredulous at the birds, butterflies, and other visitors that this green canopy brought into our courtyard, even in the middle of Jaipur's sandstone jungle. Surrounded by walls and balconies, the jasmine made a beautiful contribution to the green tapestry that filled our home, enhancing the shrubs in the courtyard and the innumerable potted plants of *champa, chameli,* clematis, marigolds, roses, basil, coriander, curry leaves, lemongrass, and mint that filled every space in the house ever touched by sunlight.

Shafiji was also a rescuer of note, bringing sundry little creatures to us for care and nursing—an injured baby squirrel that had fallen from a tree, birds that had been entangled in razor-sharp threads during the kite-flying season, baby rabbits whose parents had been claimed by an animal or someone's dinner pot. Babu and Amma never refused to accept any of these creatures, deputizing Didi and me to help with the nursing. The aim was always to release them into the vast green spaces of Ram Niwas Garden once they were strong enough, but the ones who took too long to heal often ended up living with us on a permanent basis. By this point we had a large cage in the veranda for a parrot that refused to fly away, a couple of rabbits with no survival skills, and a few visiting cats, from whom we had to protect the smaller creatures.

Babu's experiment with a subscription-only newspaper, *Praja Sandesh,* "message of the people," had taken off reasonably well. It generated continuous work, at any rate, though revenue was unreliable. Fortunately, because many of Amma and Babu's former colleagues were involved with Hindi literary and educational institutions in Rajasthan, a steady flow of book-printing orders subsidized the newspaper and sustained the press's staff.

Babu insisted on serving tea and snacks to anyone who dropped by the press, a practice that ensured frequent tea breaks for the staff. It also meant numerous trays of food and drinks travelling up and down every day, in addition to the steady stream of unannounced visitors to the family. So Mangi bai now had a helper—proud, loud, but efficient Kesar bai. She came every morning to sweep the main floor and wash clothes. Every evening, her demure daughter, Prem didi, arrived to do the dishes.

Mangi bai was very possessive of our brass-and-steel cooking pots, cleaning them to a shine with white coal-ash herself. She did not care much for non-metal utensils such as glass and ceramic; in her view these were impure—much like Kesar bai, who was from a caste of launderers. Amma had to have a long talk with Mangi bai about her loud objections to Kesar bai's polluting presence, just as she had had to do when Mangi bai objected to Shafiji's entering "her" kitchen. Mangi bai could not over-rule Amma, but she never lost an opportunity to assert her higher status. The affable Shafiji cheerfully ignored all attempts at intimidation by the diminutive cook, but Kesar bai would sometimes rise to the bait, and the two would get into a sharp verbal duel.

What Mangi bai found most hard to adjust to, however, was Amma's decision to employ an untouchable sweeper to dust and sweep the halls of the press and the two terraces. The sand of the Thar Desert invaded every public and private space in Jaipur, effortlessly defeating the high walls of the city. It had to be banished from the house as often as twice a day. Badami bai was a good-natured addition to our household whose normally smiling face beamed even more whenever Babu called out for someone to serve the sweeper a cup of tea. At such moments Mangi bai would grumble under her breath and comply only through an intermediary, even if it happened to be Shafiji. She refused to have any direct contact with Badami bai.

What with our classes, studies, and rehearsals, Didi and I had very little time to help at home, but we were not expected to, as Amma and Babu insisted that we use all our available time for reading, writing, and self-improvement. Even when he was sitting in his office downstairs, Babu seemed to know when we lingered too long in the kitchen after mealtimes. His loud remarks about burning our books in the *chulha* fire always sent us scurrying back to our desks.

At his own desk downstairs, Babu found much to write about in current events. At the time, the newspapers and radio were full of reports about the Tibetan uprising. Earlier in the year, Tenzin Gyatso, the four-teenth Dalai Lama, had fled Tibet and was granted asylum in India. Up until now Babu had been a staunch critic of Nehruji, condemning every one of his policies, but he agreed with his support of the Dalai Lama. However, he also worried about its consequences, and in his editorials for *Praja Sandesh* he speculated about the Chinese response, noting President

Mao's impatience to return China to its historic glory through the Great Leap Forward. Babu believed that Nehruji's plans for catching India up to the modern world were no match for Chinese policies, which were driven by deep convictions about China's rightful place in human history.

The editorials in Babu's paper that commented on local and national politics were supplemented by commentaries on international events— the new Castro government in Cuba, the referendum in Switzerland that denied female suffrage in the same month that women voted in Nepal for the first time, the independence of Cyprus and Singapore, martial law in Laos, the senseless assassination of Ceylonese Prime Minister Bandaranaike, and the reforms of Nikita Khrushchev in the USSR after the Stalin era.

Babu had opinions on everything, and they were strongest when it came to Amma's involvement in local politics. When several municipal councillors arrived at the house, hoping, once again, to persuade Amma to run for public election, Babu's wrath was unbridled. He did not even wait for the delegation to leave before denouncing Amma for prostituting her social conscience for political glory, for selling her soul to devils who sacrificed ideals to expediency. Amma politely declined their request.

Kamala mausi was back in our lives, although the defiant sparkle in her eyes had dimmed. Even her mischievous laughter now rang hollow. Toward the end of our time in Lucknow, Kamala mausi's daughter, Kanti didi, had finished college and then married a man whose family home was in Wardha. The marriage gave Amma the opportunity to take Didi and me on the long journey to her former home—the place where Didi was born. Wardha was the site of so many cherished memories, and Amma had revelled in the effusive welcomes we constantly received.

Amma had known the family of Kanti didi's new husband during her Wardha days. Pratap bhaiya had been very young when his father, a well-respected political figure in Wardha, died unexpectedly. After being swindled out of their family's share of the ancestral property, his mother had supported Pratap bhaiya's education by publishing books of short stories, poetry, social commentary, and histories of women whose strength and influence had helped to shape the country's history. Nevertheless, in an ironic testimony to the lingering power of caste, she had balked when her only son sought to marry a woman whose social rank differed from their own, and it had taken considerable effort on Pratap bhaiya's part to persuade his mother to accept Kanti didi as her daughter-in-law. In honour of our long association with Pratap bhaiya's family, we were invited to attend the wedding as guests of the groom, so in that role we welcomed Kanti didi into her new home as Kanti bhabhi.

With her daughter settled, Kamala mausi could no longer ignore the pleas of her brothers to move back to Lucknow, so she had spent her limited savings on a two-room addition to the terrace of the ancestral house and moved in—an arrangement that had worked reasonably well for everyone until her father's death, just a few months ago. After that, things changed. Her sisters-in-law started objecting to her presence in ways both subtle and overt, while her brothers bore witness to her humiliation in silence. There were no open conflicts that she could confront in her customary direct way, just a nagging series of gestures and comments clearly intended to wound her. Angry and unhappy, Kamala mausi had tried to retreat into her high perch at the top the house, into her books.

Finally, realizing that she could not remain where she was if she hoped to preserve her self-respect, she had decided to move out, and she began to look for a teaching position in one of Lucknow's many newly founded schools. However, her brothers got wind of her plans and insisted that she not move out of the house, since such a brazen action would disgrace the family. To Kamala mausi, this argument, while true enough, had been the last straw. Evidently, to safeguard family honour, she was expected to accept whatever abuse came her way, as if she were a servant rather than a member of that family.

She was too proud to ask her brothers to reimburse her for the money she had spent on the addition to the house—a request that, in any case, would doubtless have been refused. Until she could find a job, she was destitute. Kanti bhabhi and her husband had offered to take her in, but custom forbade a daughter's parents from accepting even so much as a drink of water from their in-laws. In Kamala mausi's eyes, such customs—designed to sever a married daughter's relationship to the family of her birth—were long overdue to be discarded. But, while she was prepared to bring dishonour upon herself, she was not willing to expose her daughter's new family to social scandal, nor did she wish to place her own independence at risk. She was here with us now because Amma was her last resort, and she hoped that her anonymity in Jaipur would allow her a new freedom. Her timing was perfect, Amma assured her: the school needed to hire a new Hindi teacher for senior classes. She asked Kamala mausi to apply.

When the school trustees received her job application, however, they were not as impressed as Amma had expected them to be, and her brow was more furrowed than usual when she returned from her meeting with them. The hiring committee was not in favour of hiring Kamala mausi because she was not from their region or their community. Neither was Amma, but when she pointed this out, one of the trustees magnanimously assured Amma that she had proved her worth and loyalty over the years. Kamala mausi's qualifications and experience were much stronger than those of the other two applicants, but that did not sway the committee. It was only after Amma appealed to their sense of duty toward those who had fought for the independence of the country that the board finally agreed to offer Kamala mausi a one-year probationary appointment.

What bothered Amma most, though, was the infuriating remark she overheard on her way out of the meeting. The trustee who had been most antagonistic had mocked Kamala mausi's contribution to the fight for freedom with the dismissive comment, "As though Gandhiji needed the help of these dim-witted creatures."

Amma did not regret that she had confronted that sorry individual and given him a fiery lecture on the role that ordinary women had played, beginning long before Gandhiji became the leader of the movement. She had rattled off the long list of names of women who had, with her, participated in protest rallies and courted arrest during the civil disobedience movement. She questioned his notion that any political activist could function without the active support of mothers, wives, sisters, and other women in their families. Some men, she pointed out, had only served the nationalist cause after they were shamed into it by the women of their families.

Finding no support from other members of the board, the offending individual had made a hasty retreat, but Amma worried about the implications of this confrontation for Kamala mausi's job prospects at the school.

Hearing this, Kamala mausi guffawed. "Haven't you learned? Only men's actions are worthy of being celebrated as achievements. A woman must be quiet about her own contributions. Otherwise she is arrogant and conceited." Through another round of mirthless laughter she reminded Amma: "How many people really know what it meant for an ordinary woman to be thrown in those jails?"

This led to a passionate discussion of the harsh personal consequences faced by women who left the bounds of the sacred domestic threshold. We listened to the two of them recall how much harsher their lives had been, both inside and outside of jail, compared to the lives of women from prominent political families. Together they recalled the names of women they knew personally whose acts of resistance had never made it into local newspapers, even when a newspaper set out to publish painstakingly compiled lists of the acts of civil disobedience in their area. Amma attributed this neglect to the editors' paternalistic wish to protect the identities of women political activists, but Kamala mausi drily asserted that women activists were considered unworthy of being named unless in association with a famous man. With a tired smile, she reminded Amma of the words of the revolutionary Urdu poet, Faiz Ahmed Faiz: *Aur bhi gum hain zamane mein mohabbat ke siva* ("There are many kinds of pains in the world, not just the ones inflicted by our loved ones").

Our storage room had ample space for Kamala mausi's small trunk and her large cloth bag filled with books, and the divan in the drawing room became her temporary bed, but she refused to move in with us permanently. Instead, she decided to withdraw her application for the teaching position at Amma's school and found both work and accommodations elsewhere. By the end of the year, this fiercely independent woman had joined the staff of a primary school just outside one of the city gates, run by a different business community. On her meagre salary she could only afford to rent a small room in a crowded neighbourhood just outside of Jaipur's walls, a former refugee camp that had turned into a haphazard mix of shacks, shops, and houses of all shapes and sizes. She spent much of her time at our house during school holidays, in order to avoid the stifling heat of her rented room, which turned into an oven during the hot months, as well as to avoid the landlord's family, who shunned her. But that was all the help she would accept.

JAIPUR, 1960

I was rather relieved to be finished with high school. No longer would I be obliged to live under a microscope as the daughter of the principal—or so I thought. But then came college. The Maharaja College for boys had been established in 1844, by Maharaja Sawai Ram Singh II, but the Maharani Intermediate College for girls was established only a century later, by the glamourous world-travelling Maharaja and Maharani of Jaipur. The two colleges now occupied imposing Indo-Sarcenic buildings that stood directly opposite each other. The lecturers at Maharani College were part of a close-knit group of women who had known each other since the days when Maharani Gayatri Devi had first held meetings to plan for the expansion of women's education in the city. Moreover, the principal of Maharani College—the redoubtable Mrs. Savitri Bhartiya, for whom education was nothing short of a mission—was close friends with Amma. So I still felt that I was under scrutiny.

I chose history, painting, and vocal music as my majors at Maharani College, the subjects that appealed to me most in the very limited selection of arts and science courses that girls were offered. Despite the familiar sense of surveillance, I enjoyed the delicious freedom of not having to wear a uniform and having fewer classes to attend in a day. It was also oddly liberating to step outside the world of the wealthy business communities that largely made up our social circle in Jaipur. The majority of the girls in my college came from families whose ancestry lay in other parts of the country—Bengal, Bihar, Himachal, Kashmir, Maharashtra, Punjab, Uttar Pradesh—and whose lives more closely reflected my own middle-class background.

Karuna was my new best friend and my opposite in more ways than one. A quiet mathematics and science student, Karuna came from a large, multi-generational family of cousins, uncles, and aunts who shared one large compound located at the other end of the walled city from ours. Their ancestors had come to Jaipur from Uttar Pradesh many generations ago as public record-keepers, administrators, royal scribes, and writers. Soon I was spending a lot of time at her house, sometimes long past my curfew-hour, until an irate Didi would phone to summon me home. But the easy conversations I could have with Karuna's many family members, their enjoyment of popular music, and their adoration of my singing prowess all kept pulling me back.

By this point I had lost most of my school friends to early-onset matrimony, which changed their lives, and mine, irrevocably. Much to Amma's satisfaction, Jatan didi got to finish her college degree before getting married and moving to Bombay. Poorna had been the first of my friends to get married, to a newly minted accountant, who had then moved with her to distant Bombay. She was quickly followed into marriage by Anita, who was from one illustrious family of jewellers and her new husband from another.

Their weddings were the most fun I had ever had. I loved getting to dress up and participate in the rituals and ceremonies that went on for days. Afterwards, since all my married friends had extended families in Jaipur, they often came to visit, especially during the numerous festivals that dot the Hindu and Jain calendars. Although I got to see them, however, we no longer got to spend much time talking. Even when they were in Jaipur to visit, they spent most of their time confined to their large households, the kitchens in particular, where the cooking fires were never out for long.

One of my school friends, Pramila, lasted nearly a full year of college before being married to the scion of one of the wealthiest families of the rich city of Jaipur. Soon after her lavish wedding, she caused an uproar by refusing to observe purdah. Her father-in-law was one of the trustees of Amma's school, yet he was mystified to hear his new daughter-in-law pontificate against the segregation of women. Pramila was pressured to conform by both her parents and her in-laws, but she stood her ground, quoting Gandhiji's challenge to all: "If you love peace, make injustice visible." I was amazed at my friend's outspoken revolt in a household where even my unmarried head felt the need to be bowed, if not covered.

At four o'clock on one misty morning, Pramila's mother-in-law made the journey across three streets to our house. She walked shrouded from head to toe, protected from prying eyes by four women who held curtains up around her. Didi and I listened from the dining room to her bitter complaints about her daughter-in-law, whose head has been filled with such strange ideas by our mother that she shamelessly revealed her face in front of elders of the family.

Amma had many weapons in her arsenal, but she used the gentlest ones on this tortured woman. She repeated the history Didi and I had heard so often of the purdah system in the region and explained why it had become so prevalent in the business communities. Amma reminded her of sages, queens, and women warriors of India, such as Gargi, Laxmi Bai, Razia Sultan, and Keladi Chennamma, and then she spoke of modern women leaders such as Sarojini Naidu, Aruna Asaf Ali, and Indira Gandhi. In a voice that was calm but firm, Amma delivered all this information in Marwari, her visitor's own language.

The shrouded lady left, dismayed and silent. Amma knew that this was not the end of the battle but the beginning of one, so she asked me to let Pramila know how proud she was of her courage. Amma always hoped that the sparks she nurtured in her school would catch and spread through the conservative business community of the city that her school mainly served. She found it so rewarding to open the eyes of the girls she taught to a world that was vast, exciting, and interconnected, so unlike the enclosed little spaces that now amounted to the whole world for most of my childhood friends.

Amma's passion for education showed in everything she did those days, it seemed. Elections under the new procedure of the 1959 Municipal Act were going to be held soon, and once again, despite Babu's continual insults and her own repeated refusal to get involved in local politics, Amma was facing pressure to run for office. Instead of giving in, she devoted her energy to working with Rajasthan's Board of Education to revamp secondary education in the state.

Shankar chacha was coming to Jaipur with Suresh and Meera didi! I was ecstatic, and even Didi's smiles were broader than usual. Our only disappointment was that Chachi had to stay behind in Bhagalpur to look after their daughter "Baby," born just over a year ago, and our other younger cousins. Since moving back to Jaipur, we'd stayed connected to their lives only through Shankar chacha's regular letters to Amma. We'd been excited when, in a recent letter, he'd mentioned his desire to visit Jaipur with Suresh and Meera didi, before they finished growing up and left home. And now we received a telegram, sent just before they were to set out on their three-day journey by train. The short notice gave us very little time to prepare for their arrival, but it also prevented Amma from finding an excuse to head off their visit.

Figuring out how to make room for three guests in our rather cramped household wasn't easy. We decided that Shankar chacha could sleep on the divan in the drawing room, usually occupied by Kamala mausi. Didi and I gladly agreed to give up our divans to Kamala mausi and Suresh and to add a large mattress in the empty space in the middle of our room that the two of us could share with Meera didi. Didi was put in charge of planning meals, while I was the designated tour guide. We were in our room, happily chatting about the impending visit, when we heard Amma's voice in Babu's room next door, breaking the news to him. The smothering silence that followed was broken only by the sound of Babu's heavy steps as he made his way out of the room and down the stairs and then by the sound of the main gate closing behind him.

Didi and I stared blankly at each other. Then Didi barged into Babu's room through one of the connecting doors. "What's his problem now? Aren't they his family too?" she demanded.

"Yes." Bitterness made Amma's voice cold. "But they fulfil *our* emotional need for family, not his. What's the point of getting angry? Besides, we have work to do." With that, she turned and left, evidently heading for the kitchen, where Mangi bai was cleaning up for the night. We could hear their subdued conversation as Amma admonished her not to pick a fight with Kesar bai in front of the guests.

We had little choice but to try to recover our own excitement about the imminent arrival of our uncle and cousins. Didi drew up a menu for every meal of the week they would spend with us, featuring our favourite Rajasthani dishes, complemented by the simpler but spicier fare of eastern India. The easiest part was desserts, since Johri Bazaar was rightfully famous for its shops full of sweets.

Meanwhile, I planned our sightseeing tours. For the sake of historical sequence, I decided that we should start with an excursion to the fort and palace complex at Amer. The capital of the Kachwaha dynasty for nearly seven centuries, prior to the founding of Jaipur, Amer lies in the nearby Aravalli Hills, at the mouth of a rocky gorge. A steep climb up a serpentine cobblestone stairway leads to the palace, built of sandstone and marble, and its resplendent pavillions and courtyards, embellished with frescoes, sculptures, and precious stones and metals. The nearby forts of Nahargarh and Jaigarh, also perched high above Jaipur in the Aravalli Hills, offer panoramic views of the valley. Together these forts and palaces would make for a whole day of sightseeing.

But I was also determined to show off our beloved Jaipur itself—the "Pink City," so called because, in honour of a visit from Prince Albert in 1876, most of the buildings were coated with a red-ochre paint. Some two and a half centuries ago, when increasing water scarcity had begun to affect the higher reaches of the Aravalli Hills, Maharaja Jai Singh II had decided to abandon his magnificent palace complex at Amer and move his capital into the valley below. Designed by the Maharaja's chief architect, Vidyadhar Bhattacharya, Jaipur was a masterpiece of city planning, laid out in a grid pattern of nine large squares, in three rows of three, that together form a *mandala*—a diagram of the cosmos. I enjoyed imagining how I would introduce our guests to its bazaars, squares, hospitals, parks, palaces, and *haveli*s and its neat rows of multi-storey houses lining broad, well-lit avenues and streets. We would certainly visit the centremost square, the site of the royal palace, around which cluster other opulent buildings lavishly decorated with latticed screens, ornamental domes, and graceful arches.

One place I really wasn't sure I wanted to visit, despite its iconic status, was the Hawa Mahal, an ornate five-storey structure with an intricate façade consisting of rows of semi-hexagonal bays, each constructed of sandstone latticework and topped with a dome and finial. The latticework is punctuated by miniature windows, more than nine hundred in all, behind which the women of the royal household, suitably hidden from view, could peep out onto the world from their drab, sparsely furnished quarters.

However, the Hawa Mahal was part of the City Palace, where the Maharaja and Maharani still resided with their family and retainers, and I did want to take our guests there. I never tired of its glorious maze of gateways, gardens, courtyards, and audience halls or the way its many buildings, added over many generations, blended Rajput, Mughal, and European influences. I was especially keen on the City Palace Museum, which housed the most wonderful collection of ancient paintings and texts, textiles, carriages, and weaponry. We could spend a whole day there but for the magnetic pull of the observatory next door, Jantar Mantar—a collection of stone or marble structures that functioned as astronomical instruments. This was the only monument in the city where I would need the help of a tour guide to explain how these instruments were used to predict eclipses, to track the shifting position of stars, or to mark the passage of time. Our last stop in this complex would be the temple of Govind Devji, the protector deity of Jaipur, who sits, adorned with gold ornaments, on a silver throne in a temple made of sandstone and marble. At the back of the temple is Talkatora Lake, with its floating water lilies.

I could easily think of other temples, monuments, and palaces that we could visit, but I would just have to wait and see how well our guests could handle outings in the desert heat.

Shankar chacha had told us not to try to meet them at the railway station, since he couldn't be sure whether the train would be on time. So we waited anxiously for the sound of a rickshaw or a tonga stopping at the edge of the street. Finally, after what seemed like forever, they arrived.

Suresh had grown to be taller than me, and Meera didi was shyer and quieter than when we last met, but, despite these changes, we quickly picked up from where we had left off three years before. Suresh had recently started college, and Meera didi was already several years in, so we chatted about our assorted studies. Shankar chacha engaged in his customary friendly banter with Amma, who had taken time off from her hectic schedule, and it was so nice to see her smile. And, to my delight, they all quickly fell in love with Jaipur.

Amma apologized repeatedly to our guests for Babu's absence, and I fervently hoped that he would come home before their all too brief visit came to an end. But I knew that hoping was useless. True to form, Babu reappeared only after his brother, niece, and nephew had returned to Bhagalpur.

Amma, photographed in Wardha in 1941, around
the time of her marriage to Babu. As so often, the
faraway expression on her face is hard to read—a
sober commitment to building a future, with a
hint of past sorrows in her eyes.

Rajeshwar Narayan Sinha (Babu) as a young
man. Born into a landowning family in Bihar,
Babu abruptly left his ancestral home when he
was barely in his mid-twenties, moving first to
Patna and then vanishing into the revolutionary
underground.

Shankareshwer Narayan Sinha, one of Babu's
two younger brothers, then in his early
twenties. The fifth of six sons, Shankar chacha
assumed responsibility for the family estate
in Bhagalpur, which gradually dwindled in
size during the land reforms following India's
independence. Although Babu was estranged
from his family, his daughters loved their
visits to their uncle in Bhagalpur, where they
were embraced by the warmth of their kin.

Rekha, aged eight, in the hill station of Nainital, not far from the government training centre at Jeolikot for which Amma—then the deputy director of UP's Social Welfare Department—was responsible. Many years later, Rekha acquired a puppy of her own, whom she named Neelu ("Blue"), for the sparkling colour of his eyes.

Rekha's older sister, Abha ("Didi"), at the age of sixteen. Rekha often envied Didi's beauty and poise, although she did not share her sister's quiet determination to be a "normal" girl—Didi's own way of rebelling against two decidedly atypical parents.

Didi, with her early object of passion—the sitar. Both daughters were given lessons in music and dance, but it was Didi who dedicated herself to the study of a single instrument, Her long hours of practice perhaps allowed her to escape into a private world, away from the emotional cacophony of her family.

Rekha (*top left*) and Didi (*top right*), in a family portrait taken in 1964 around the time of Didi's marriage to Hamir Chand Choudhary. Following the wedding, Didi moved with "Jijaji" ("sister's husband," as Rekha called him) to his family's opulent home near Dhar, in western Madhya Pradesh—some 600 kilometres distant from her friends and family in Jaipur.

Rekha in 1966, at the time of her graduation from the master's program in music at the University of Rajasthan. Initially attracted to the study of painting, Rekha discovered herself increasingly drawn to classical Hindustani music, the field in which she ultimately earned her doctorate.

Bir Bahadur Prasad Sinha, at the age of twenty-nine—the man destined to become Rekha's husband. At first, Amma refused to consider the match: "I would rather push my daughter into a well," she declared, "than consider a marriage proposal from a zamindar family in Bihar." She came around, however, once she realized that the proposed groom had firmly rejected the feudal attitudes that still prevailed in much of eastern India.

Rekha and her husband, whom she addressed as Sinha saheb, in their home in Dhanbad, not long after their marriage, in 1970. Located in the coal-mining districts of eastern Bihar, Dhanbad came as something of a shock to Surekha—the place where she faced the blunt force of traditional social hierarchies.

Amma with Rekha and her infant daughter (and author of this book). Although Amma lived to celebrate the birth of her first grandchild, she died of a heart attack the following year, at the age of only fifty-four.

6

——

Battlegrounds

L ife in Jaipur continued on its course for another year, before the next
time we were suddenly reminded of our parents' scattered families.
One day, a letter arrived unexpectedly from an ashram not far from
Poona. As soon as Amma opened it, she and Babu retreated to her room,
while Didi and I sat in the drawing room, hoping to overhear what was
going on. From fragments of conversation, we gathered that Amma had
been informed of someone's death—a young man, by the sounds of it. He
had been staying at the ashram, and, after he died, Amma's address had
been found among his belongings. Now the head of the ashram wanted
to know whether she could send someone to collect his belongings.

Amma was weeping, and Babu was evidently trying to help her decide
what to do. At one point, he said something about a family friend in
Poona who might be willing to help. Amma struggled to speak between
sobs. "What good are the material possessions of a dead person?"

A little while later, we heard him try again. "It might mend your heart
to see the last place your brother lived."

Occasionally, Amma's voice would rise in volume. "They abandoned me," she said. And then, "This is not on me."

Only later were we able to find out the whole story. The letter concerned Amma's nephew, who had died at the ashram not too long after his father, who had lived there for some time. Her nephew had come upon her address as he was sorting through his late father's things and had written her a long letter expressing his regret that they had never met and explaining that his father had always claimed not to know her whereabouts. He said that he would like to visit her but mentioned that his health was poor and he wasn't currently able to make such a long trip. Amma had not answered his letter, which had arrived just a few weeks before this latest letter from the ashram, bringing news of his death.

Babu tried hard to persuade Amma to go to Poona herself. But she steadfastly refused. Instead, she announced that she would take Didi and me to Bhagalpur for our summer break, and this time the trip was to include a stopover in Allahabad on the way back.

Now it was Babu's turn to refuse. When we left for Bhagalpur, he remained behind. Despite his concerns about Amma's rift with her family, nothing could stir his interest in a visit to his own. I remember wishing that they would both stop being so stubborn.

After two weeks of loving indulgence from aunts, uncles, and cousins in Bhagalpur, we found ourselves on a train bound for Allahabad. Amma had been vague about the purpose of the trip, merely reminding us that the city of her birth was very ancient, dating back to the Vedic period. Now she fidgeted constantly, straightening the pleats of her sari or rotating the gold bangle on her wrist. I wasn't sure just why she seemed so anxious, but I knew it would be pointless to ask.

It was not long before the reason became apparent. Upon our arrival, a tonga took us to the home of the family with whom we'd be staying. The family lived in Daraganj, an old neighbourhood on the banks of the Ganga not far from its confluence with the Yamuna.

At the house, Amma was given a warm greeting by Bhuvan mausi, whom she introduced to us as a dear friend. But we had barely arrived when we left again, to walk the short distance to a small house in a shabby compound. Its crumbling walls were overgrown with the lush vegetation that blesses the banks of the Ganga. Amma turned to us before opening the rusted metal gate of the compound. She adjusted the length of my scarf, tucked in an errant curl for Didi, and reminded us of our manners, explaining that we were about to meet a great poet, a pioneer of the Chhayavaad movement in Hindi literature—Suryakant Tripathi Nirala. Didi, who adored Niralaji's poetry, was too amazed to respond.

Niralaji had been very ill, we were told, and Amma wanted to see him before it was too late. The short metal gate creaked painfully on its worn hinges. When Amma knocked on the door of the house, we heard a feeble voice say, "The door is open."

Inside, we found a man with a bushy beard and long silver hair, propped up by several pillows on a humble *charpai* cot, the angles of his wiry body poking through ill-fitting clothes. We folded our hands and bowed our heads in greeting. His piercing gaze fixed on Amma. "It's you!" His gaunt face was all smiles as he pointed to the jute stools scattered around the room, the only pieces of furniture aside from the bed.

Niralaji chided Amma affectionately. "You are visiting after so long. Have you stopped coming to Allahabad?"

Amma seemed embarrassed. "No, I still visit the city, but rarely."

He chuckled. "So visiting me must be even less than rare."

They spent the next several minutes talking about people they had known, whose names Didi and I recognized—the poets and patriots Ramdhari Singh Dinkar, Sumitranandan Pant, Mahadevi Verma, and Subhadra Kumari Chauhan. Didi was soaking up every word. After several minutes of reminiscing, Niralaji turned to Didi and me to ask whether we had any interest in literature. Amma said we did and proudly told him about Didi's plans to do a master's degree in Hindi. Niralaji looked pleased to hear this but politely declined when Didi asked his permission to take his picture with us. "First, do something good with your lives," he said.

I was stunned by the difference between the man on the bed and the photographs I had seen: a round-faced young man, with mesmerizing eyes and soft, curving lips, now reduced to these bony remains. He was obviously very sick, but the bright, burning light in his eyes and his straight spine, now supported by lumpy cushions, made me lower my gaze.

Soon his attendant arrived with a physician, signalling the end of our visit. As we left the house, Amma turned around to cast one more look through the open door at the dying man. "End of another chapter," she said quietly, as if to herself.

From there we walked along the streets of Daraganj, with Amma commenting on the bewildering density of new buildings in the area. After stopping to orient herself in a lane full of houses still under construction, she looked around in dismay. "This jungle of bricks and cement was an orchard as far as the eye could see," she told us. We walked by a few more hastily built houses and down more jagged, narrow streets, eventually arriving at the ancient temple of Nag Vasuki, the serpent god, on the banks of the Ganga.

Amma walked the length and breadth of the temple's sprawling compound, with Didi and me hanging behind, investigating the carved arches and pillars of this ancient mossy edifice, from which a long flight of stone steps led right into the wide river. Amma climbed down a few steps of the ghat to sit above the green waters. Didi and I climbed down as well, to sit on either side of her. Even in the scorching heat of June, there was a deliciously cool wind blowing from the north, caressing the vast river flowing peacefully below us. This was the last ghat before the Ganga met its sister river. We sat there in silence, not talking, not thinking, just feeling the despair of an eight-year-old girl long ago.

The river stretched before us in the quiet of the midafternoon heat. Only a few brave birds flew overhead; curious fish gathered around our shadow in the water, and a few deer rested in a cool grove at some distance. After a few minutes, Amma walked down the remaining steps of the ghat. She stopped before her feet could touch the murky water, but she dipped her hands into it and then touched the water to her eyes and forehead as a mark of respect. Then, folding her hands, she recited the Mahamrtyunjaya Mantra. We listened in silence to the ancient prayer:

Oṃ tryambakaṃ yajāmahe
sugandhiṃ puṣṭivardhanam |
urvārukamiva bandhanān
mṛtyormukṣīya māmṛtāt ||

We worship the three-eyed Lord
Who is fragrant and who nourishes all beings.
As the ripened cucumber is freed from its bondage,
May he liberate us from death to immortality.

When she had finished, Didi and I followed her to the edge of the water, where we paid our respects to the mighty river by touching the water and bowing.

Only a couple of hundred yards away from the river's banks was our next stop: the ruins of a mansion, where a tall arch stood like a gap-toothed ancient sentinel, protecting crumbling walls. Only one of the panels of the bulky door, laden with brass latticework and wooden studs, remained. Through this gateway we entered an enormous courtyard, where we walked along beside the high wall that had blocked our view of the courtyard from the outside. The inside of the mansion was in even worse condition than the exterior: chunks of stone, wood, and bricks from its ancient walls had been removed, and violently, not by the ponderously slow hands of the elements.

Amma walked without speaking through the nooks and crannies of what survived of the interior. With her, we toured the remains of alcoves and stared as imposing door frames without doors, windows no longer protected by ornate bars and curtains, rooms without roofs, and crumbling walls that glimmered in the glow of the lustrous moss that grew on every surface. We watched as Amma caressed the mutilated walls, the wounded vestiges of what was—we now realized—her lost childhood home.

The screeching of a flock of parakeets filled the sky above the courtyard, reminding us of the approaching dusk and snapping Amma out of her trance. "The cowshed used to be in the back," she said.

We followed her out of the house through another passageway, which opened into a backyard, now overgrown with unruly bushes and wise old trees. There was indeed a neat row of three walled stone-and-mud enclosures that looked like unused animal sheds. Where this row ended, a narrow hut stood forlornly, its door closed, a faint light escaping through its uneven wooden slits. Amma knocked on the wooden door just once and stepped away quickly, as though the door knocker were a live snake. A thin old woman with a bent back, a hurricane lantern in one hand, opened the door. "Who are you?" came her rasping voice. "What do you want?"

Amma could barely say the words. "I used to live in this house, many years ago . . ." She pointed helplessly toward the ruins as her voice trailed off.

The old woman came closer, raising her lantern to Amma's face, screwing her eyes up for a long moment. "Parvati?"

Amma nodded. Her sobs and tears flowed freely as the old woman hugged her, trembling, exclaiming, crying. Amma wailed, her mouth turned to the darkening sky. "*Ha, re!*" Didi and I rushed to her side when we saw Amma's legs buckle under her.

Helplessly, we watched our mother wailing and sobbing, seated on the bare earth, mourning with her whole being, without restraint. Amma's tears mixed with the water in the steel mug that the old lady produced and was forcing her to sip from, while holding her hand and rubbing her back.

Through her own sobs, the old woman kept repeating, "It's all gone! Everyone! Everything!" Bit by bit, the story emerged in her feeble, scratchy voice: Amma's parents died. Her brother left and never returned. The servants were all gone. This elderly woman was cursed to live out her days looking on helplessly as looters took away furniture, fixtures, bricks, stones, and even trees from the orchard.

As the strong current of aching emotions subsided, Amma noticed Didi and me, as though for the first time, leaning close to each other against the rough stone wall of the hut. Amma wiped her tears and summoned us closer. "Abha, Rekha—many generations of this woman's family served this household."

Didi and I folded our hands and bowed our heads to accept the blessings of this feeble link of a broken chain, who showered us with guttural blessings for long lives, marriages, and many sons.

We left this lost world swathed in the dark night, to return to Bhuvan mausi and her family at the other end of Daraganj. As we made our way back, Amma explained the connection. When her eldest sister drowned, the man to whom she had recently been wed was left a widower. He had later married Bhuvan mausi and had been a political activist himself, although he'd passed away not long ago. Strange though it might seem, Amma told us, this family had been her refuge in more ways than she could count.

Bhuvan mausi treated Amma like a little sister, scolding her for not looking after her health. Amma should get more exercise, she insisted. She asked pointed questions about Babu that no one we knew had ever dared to ask. She also lectured Didi and me about Amma's past and our future, until we escaped to the kitchen to help her two daughters-in-law, who were always busy taking care of the large household.

I was wide awake just before dawn. I went looking for Amma and found her on the quiet terrace. The rest of the household was still asleep in their snug beds downstairs. I was not sure how long Amma had been there, writing in her diary, which now sat open in her lap, though her pen was still. I picked up the flashlight near her. Its batteries were spent.

I sat on the wicker chair next to her and rested my chin on my knees, listening to the early-morning bird calls, feeling the reverberations of brass bells from faraway temples, savouring the cool breeze and the whiff of the sacred river the breeze brought with it. "Amma, why didn't you go back to your home?"

She exhaled. "I did."

Startled, I tried to see Amma's eyes in the misty light of dawn. "How could they not accept their little girl back? How could they not welcome her with tears of joy?"

Amma looked away from the page she had been writing. "Tears were shed, but not for the lost little girl. They were shed for the scandal that would follow her return. Not for the sullying of childhood innocence, but for the tarnishing of the family name." She paused. "I could have stayed, reincarnated as a distant relative, given away in marriage with a big dowry, hidden from eyes and minds forever. But it doesn't matter now, does it? The present, this moment, this very breath, is all that matters."

With this, the little girl was officially banished once again. But the anguish was not so easily dismissed, silently announcing itself in her averted gaze, her tightly pressed lips, and the slump of her normally squared shoulders.

In February, Prime Minister Nehru won the third general election in another landslide victory, a win that earned him much annoyed commentary from Babu. *Praja Sandesh* expressed disappointment in the system of electoral democracy, in which less than 55 percent of the population had voted. Yet Babu and other contributors to *Praja Sandesh* also commented hopefully on the ongoing movements for democracy in restive colonies of the Caribbean, Africa, Asia, and Oceania. In other opinion pieces they expressed concerns over East-West polarization since the Bay of Pigs invasion in Cuba and the push and pull of distant forces on Afghanistan and East Pakistan, both now witnessing incursion of the military into civilian politics.

Despite his commitments to the paper and the printing press, however, Babu's sporadic disappearances continued unabated. Sometimes he reappeared after two days, sometimes after more than a week, never following a recognizable rhythm. We had by then perfected the art of pretending to ourselves and others that this was normal. We had mastered the art of hiding the anxiety it caused us to keep up appearances and the worry we felt over whether he would return this time. When home, Babu retreated more and more into his books. Shafiji took on a wider variety of printing orders to sustain the publication of the newspaper, whose subscription base was declining.

Kamala mausi's frequent visits provided respite for a grateful Amma. On her visits, Kamala mausi effortlessly took charge of the household, skillfully managing the menagerie of small animals, the streams of visitors, and the eclectic collection of domestic helpers. She was the only one who ever harassed Babu for sticking so stubbornly to his clockwork schedule of yoga, meditation, reading, writing, and singing, punctuated by breakfast, lunch, and evening snack, which did not match with the routine of anyone else in the household.

She also liked to loudly debate national and international politics with Viyogiji, one of the regular editorial contributors to *Praja Sandesh*. Viyogiji was a freelance journalist and writer in his mid-forties who went by only his pen name, which meant "bereaved." He wore an eternally bereft look on his oblong face, and his thinning hair and saggy skin were always shiny from overly lavish applications of oil. His disappointment with the world was as genuine as Babu's, but the world had not turned its back on Viyogiji. His ancestors had been minor officials in the royal court, and on this basis he had been given a small land grant in what was now a highly sought-after area outside the walled city. He lived with his wife and four children in a large old house in the centre of a very posh colony.

Kamala mausi considered both Babu and Viyogiji to be delusional. She often read her new poems to us, and she encouraged Didi and me to keep writing. Recently she had also begun compiling the stories of women freedom fighters in the province. This project led to a heated argument between her and Babu, who questioned the cult of personality that, in his opinion, these individual stories would promote. A bristling Kamala mausi planted herself squarely in front of Babu's desk, stiffer than her starched white sari, now wilting somewhat in the summer heat. "Aren't we a culture of 'cult of personality'? Isn't this why millions of gods thrive in our pantheon? Or are you objecting to these stories of mine because they do not include goddesses and princesses?"

I enjoyed watching Babu try to sidestep these duels. Since he couldn't avoid this one, he tried to appease her by listing the number of books that had already been published on the Indian freedom movement. Her stare only grew steelier. "You mean the volumes on the heroism of prominent men that mention no women other than the few who had famous fathers and husbands?"

From there she launched into a lecture on the futility of celebrating the fifteenth anniversary of independence when the real heroes and heroines of the struggle for independence had already been forgotten—the ordinary people who paid high personal prices for their defiance and whose lives had changed little since independence. These are the people who need to be remembered, she argued, not the handful of leaders whose goal had been to gain political power and who were now busy creating their own legacies.

I knew that Babu agreed with much of what Kamala mausi was saying, yet he looked annoyed. He tried a different tack. "Independence is not just a moment in history. There are no clean little beginnings and neat little endings. It is an ongoing struggle toward justice for all. Hero worship in any form is individualistic and undemocratic."

Undeterred, her left eyebrow and right hand rose in a dance mudra to emphasize her point. "*Accha?* Is that why you sing the *bhajan*s of social rebels every evening?"

"The *bhakti* poets were more than just social rebels," Babu protested. "Their lives and writings are compelling stories that reveal new meanings every time we return to them."

Kamala mausi looked at him triumphantly. "Aha! But what is more democratic than believing that everyone's story is compelling?"

Babu closed his eyes, but his slight smile acknowledged that her point had struck home. Yet he pushed her further: "If a story is compelling, it will find a way to be known. It doesn't need your help or mine."

"In a perfect world that may be true. But in a man's world, women have no opportunity to tell their stories." She argued at length about the need to collect and preserve these stories, to show that history is more a complex patchwork tapestry than a neat series of actions. Ordinary men and women needed constant reminders of their stake in political change to prevent the privileged from gaining absolute control. Entrusting power entirely to the ruling elite made it easy to go the way of neighbouring Pakistan, where the tug-of-war among powerful elites had allowed a fragile democracy to fall into the grip of military rule.

Kamala mausi had taken me along on some of her expeditions to pore over accounts of the freedom movement in the region, to compile names of women activists, and to try to locate them within the closed confines of busy households. She had faced genuine surprise, hostile questions, and sometimes outright refusal to help her document the experiences of women activists. Now I was holding a bulky file containing notes from her library research and from interviews with the few women who had agreed to talk to her—reluctant testimony given under the watchful gaze of a stern patriarch, a bitter rant from a dark forgotten corner of a decrepit house, a self-effacing account interrupted by an all-knowing spouse, all these memories now bound together with loosely spun jute twine. I was certain I knew how the debate with Babu would end. I shuffled my feet to keep them from going numb and waited patiently.

Kamala mausi had compiled her research into the notebook she was holding, which she now pushed toward Babu. She continued speaking passionately as she handed it to him, reminding him of the limited social and public space that existed in India for women from less-privileged backgrounds. Despite Gandhiji's campaign, she lamented, the keepers of these stories were mostly men who needed convincing to preserve and share these women's experiences. She pressed Babu to help her edit and publish her manuscript, which she had titled *Azadi ki mahila sipahi— Women Who Fought for Freedom*.

To my amazement, Babu agreed.

Throughout the summer, we had been hearing sporadic reports of skirmishes in the distant Himalayas, along the northeastern section of the border between China and India. Nehruji seemed confident that the situation was under control, as did the army's chief of staff, but Babu was skeptical. In his opinion, not only were the country's leaders underestimating the impact of India's decision to grant political asylum to the Dalai Lama three years earlier, during the rebellion in Tibet, but they also failed to understand that the Chinese viewed Nehru's Forward Policy as an expansionist threat.

On 20 October, the Chinese proved him right, launching attacks in two widely separated areas—along the northeastern frontier as well as far further west, in Aksai Chin, a remote area in Ladakh where the location of the border was also a matter of dispute. India was caught off guard. As the fighting escalated in the frozen Himalayan heights, reports of heavy losses filled the news. Amma and Babu worked virtually night and day, trying to raise funds to help the families of the dead or wounded, addressing local meetings, printing pamphlets to quell rumours of imminent state collapse, and organizing rallies in an effort to dispel the fear hanging over the city. In a fundraising effort, Amma had stayed up nights writing two inspirational plays—*Ma ki pukar* (*A Mother's Cry for Help*) and *Aavahan* (*Summons*). Babu and Viyogiji printed up copies of both and also churned out regular editorials in *Praja Sandesh* on India's foreign policy.

Only a month after its initial attacks, China unilaterally declared a ceasefire and retreated from most of the Indian territory it had occupied. India had suffered a humiliating defeat, losing thousands of soldiers— some killed, some dead from exposure. As the nation struggled to come to terms with this tragedy, Amma embarked on a third writing project: her autobiography. Again, her intention was that proceeds from the sale of the book would go to benefit the families of those killed or severely wounded in the war. She titled her story *Smriti ki shrinkhalayen* (*A Chain of Memories*).

The book, which consisted of a loosely linked selection of episodes and events drawn from Amma's diaries, was something of a whirlwind effort, in which everyone participated. Amma wrote, and, when she had finished a section, the typesetters composed the pages, and Shafiji printed a set of proofs. Didi, Kamala mausi, and I divided the first round of proof-reading among ourselves, and then Babu proofread a second time. Amma also read the proofs, making various amendments, before the corrected proofs were sent back to the compositors. In the meanwhile, Amma would be working on another section, and the cycle would be repeated. It was supposed to work like a tightly organized relay race, but, what with power cuts and other interruptions, the various stages of the cycle kept running into each other, causing much confusion and sometimes more work. Finally, though, the book was in print.

I could hear Amma's voice speaking on every page, but I was hoping that she would divulge more about her early life. She opened the book with a vivid description of her visit the previous year to her ancestral home in Allahabad, but she said almost nothing about the family of her birth—she didn't even mention the family name. She made a few tantalizing references to a man she called simply "*bhai,*" who had lived first in Jaipur and later in Ajmer, and she also referred briefly to a *bhai,* also unnamed, who worked for the forest department in Nagpur. But Amma had only one biological brother, and I wasn't sure whether he was either of the two mentioned. Our own family was also conspicuously absent. Babu barely appeared in the book at all: he was mentioned by name only twice. Didi and I appeared in only three places in the book, mostly as children accompanying Amma to visit famous authors and leaders. That didn't bother me all that much, but I was really disappointed that she had chosen to say nothing about her time with the revolutionaries after leaving her childhood home. Yet when I questioned her about these omissions from her story, Amma answered only, "The time has not yet come." When I persisted in my efforts to pry answers loose from her, she put an end to my questions with a smiling challenge: "Perhaps the time will be right once you're writing your own books."

In her book, Amma mentioned that she had been writing daily diary entries since she was about eight years old, and I knew this was true: dozens of notebooks of various sizes now lined the topmost shelves of the library on the terrace. Amma had never expressly forbidden me from reading them, but I couldn't bring myself to do more than take a quick peek at one of them before, feeling like a guilty trespasser, I closed it and returned it to its place on the shelf. I knew, though, that many of the answers to my questions were waiting to be discovered inside those cloth-and-cardboard-bound diaries. One day, I promised myself, I would take them down from their high perch on the bookshelf and organize them, so that Amma could write the full story of her life, a life I knew was in many ways remarkable.

JAIPUR, 1963

Didi and I were both very busy with school. I was in the final year of my undergraduate degree at Maharani College, and my social life was suffering under the demands of music practice, painting projects, and library work for my history courses. Didi, meanwhile, was finishing a master's degree in Hindi literature at the rapidly growing University of Rajasthan. Maharaja Man Singh II had made a generous land grant to the university—more than three hundred acres, about two miles from the city centre. At the time, though, the campus was still under construction, and much of the site was little more than a vast sandy expanse dominated by thorny trees, bordered on the east by the scraggy Jhalana Hills, with the hilltop fort of Moti Dungri lying to the north.

For her final-year thesis, Didi had chosen as her topic the early-twentieth-century nationalist poet Maithili Sharan Gupt. Still alive at the time, and currently one of the nominated members of Parliament's upper house, the Rajya Sabha, Maithili Sharanji was a well-known freedom fighter from western Uttar Pradesh who, beginning in the early decades of the century, used poetry as a vehicle for social and political commentary. Although Braj Bhasa had long been the preferred language of literature in northwestern areas of India, with Awadhi holding sway further east, Sharanji chose to write in Khari Boli, a vernacular dialect of Hindustani spoken around Delhi and in the region between the Yamuna and Ganga rivers—the dialect on which the standardized form of Hindi was later based. Sharanji also preferred the fluidity of non-rhyming couplets, and, at a time when writers typically drew on male mythical and historical figures for inspiration, he had dared to compose poems that centred instead on female figures.

Didi was especially fascinated by one of Sharanji's most famous poems, *Saket,* which focuses on Urmila, the wife of Lakshman, Rama's younger brother. Rather than celebrating the fraternal loyalty of Lakshman, who chose to follow his older brother into exile, Sharanji describes the sorrows of the devoted Urmila, who awaited her husband's return for fourteen years. Similarly, in *Yashodhara,* Sharanji declines simply to retell the familiar story of Prince Siddhartha, the Buddha, who rejected material bonds in search of spiritual enlightenment, and instead explores the anguish of Yashodhara, Siddhartha's wife, whom he left one night as she slept, their young son at her side. Sharanji's examination of the female perspective became the focus of Didi's research and analysis.

In whatever time we could spare from our studies, Didi and I continued to hunt for reading materials in the room Amma had had built on the terrace, but we did not spend much time in it. The asbestos roof had proven no match for the desert heat in the summer or the bone-chilling cold in the wintertime, which made it impossible to convert the space into a functional library. Amma had long since given up on her grand design of wall-to-wall shelves; instead, Babu's plank/stone/metal contraptions, of uneven although sturdy construction, lined every inch of the library's walls. Babu had also recently started creating an island shelf for the middle of the room, to house his regular new acquisitions on philosophy and music. Didi and I would pause periodically during our forays into the library to clean off some of the layers of dust and cobwebs that were always gathering, but that was the extent of our attempts to impose order.

Other matters seemed so much more important. The swelling in Amma's ankles was no longer responding to hot oil massages. Kamala mausi took it upon herself to badger Amma to see Dr. Vohra, pointing to her shortness of breath and to the recurring pain in her neck, arms, and back; in response, Amma invoked her usual philosophical arguments about the nature of the human body—*sharir* dharma, she would say. She adhered to Gandhian objections to modern medicine: she believed it good for superficial ailments, infections and injuries, but not for systemic imbalances. Finally, however, and only after many heated debates, Kamala mausi used one of Amma's own arguments against her stubborn refusal: "Yes, your body is doing its own dharma. But *you* are responsible for its well-being. That is *your* dharma. It is not self-indulgent to expect your feet to carry you and your spine to support you."

At this, Amma agreed to go with her to see the holistic *vaidya* near Sanganeri gate, who practiced Muslim Unani medicine combined with Ayurvedic treatments. They returned from the visit with a bag full of elixirs and powders, and Kamala mausi gave detailed instructions to Mangi bai about Amma's new salt-free and oil-free food regimen. She banned the nuts, fried in ghee and seasoned with salt, that Amma had relied on for so long to get through a busy day without a meal break. At first, Mangi bai grumbled at the unfairness of putting the hard-working Amma on such a tasteless diet, but she was silenced when Kamala mausi threatened to hold her personally responsible if anything were to happen to Amma's health. Amma was supposed to get more rest, too, but she refused to make such a promise.

In the meanwhile, another marriage proposal arrived for Didi, this time delivered via Babu. Babu had always liked the pleasant young clerk at the local khadi distribution shop. When the young man's uncle recommended him as a suitable match for Didi, Babu was pleased, and he brought the offer home to discuss. He reasoned that this was a healthy young man from a decent family who made a meagre but steady income.

Since Didi was about to finish her degree, he thought, she could eventually get a job as a teacher to help support them both.

However, Amma reminded Babu that they had been rejecting far more appropriate matrimonial matches for Didi since she was in high school. She then revealed that she had been approached by their old acquaintance Ramkrishnaji, who had been contacted by a wealthy zamindar family in Dhar about a possible match with Didi. Ramkrishnaji was from one of Rajputana's many erstwhile royal families. Although he was an active volunteer in the grassroots wing of the Congress, the Seva Dal, his other life kept him connected to exclusive clubs in different parts of the country, and this was how he had come to know the zamindar family. He vouched for the gentlemanly dispositions of Thakur Nihal Chand and his only son, Hamir Chand Choudhary, who had a degree in agricultural engineering, and said that caste would not pose a problem. Neither Amma nor Babu was remotely concerned about caste, but those who arrived with proposals of marriage generally did not share their indifference. And so, like this one, most of the offers came from families whose caste matched our own.

Ramkrishnaji had said that he would be very happy to act as go-between in this alliance, and he had assured Amma that Thakur saheb knew all about Amma and her family and was very keen to have someone just like Didi as his daughter-in-law. Babu was unimpressed and scolded Amma for conveniently forgetting the role of the feudal system in the enslavement of the masses by foreign invaders and local oppressors alike.

Rather than argue the point, Amma tried to steer the conversation back to the issue at hand, namely, the young clerk. Didi and I pretended to be deep in our books while our ears strained to hear every word of the conversation in Babu's room next door. Amma was worried that Didi had shown no interest in teaching or any other career. She had few friends, and, aside from her classes, her books, her sitar, and her meals, she showed little interest in anything. Amma wondered whether this introversion was some sort of quiet rebellion against the assertive, outgoing personalities of the rest of the family. But Babu seemed barely to be listening to what she said. Instead, he launched into another lecture on the regression of hard-fought social values and the preponderance of elitism in our lives.

Amma let him finish his rant. "You and I came from the same kind of families, but we managed to break free from the feudal mindset. What makes you think that others cannot do the same?" She declared that she intended to find out more about this zamindar family before writing off the marriage proposal; she would meet the family of the khadi store clerk, she promised, but only after making a trip to Dhar. True to form, Babu refused to take any part in this fact-finding mission, so Amma announced that she would enlist me as her second-in-command.

Amma then headed toward our room, armed with a picture of the young man. It became very hard for us to keep up our pretence of disinterest at this point. Didi had cast only a brief glance at the picture before I snatched it out of her hands. The handsome face wore a stern expression. "That boy looks a bit old," I teased. "He's probably grumpy, too." Amma's eyes searched Didi's face, while Didi simply ignored my taunts and remained silent. She kept her eyes downcast too, but we could see that she was trying to hide a small smile. This was enough for Amma, who promised to investigate the marriage proposal further.

After Amma had informed Thakur saheb of our visit, she and I made our way to the heart of the country, travelling some three hundred miles south to Ratlam by train, where Thakur saheb's son was to pick us up in his car so that we could cover the remaining sixty miles to their home in Dhar. We freshened up after the long train ride in the waiting room of Ratlam station, while, with characteristic small-town simplicity, the station agent asked us questions about where we were coming from and where we were going. When Amma mentioned Thakur saheb of Dhar, he was very impressed and began telling us stories about the family's wealth, but the more his enthusiastic monologue gathered steam the more restless Amma grew. Finally she interrupted him to inquire about the next train back to Jaipur. I was relieved to learn that it wasn't due until the next day, and our return reservation was for the day after that. I was tired and extremely curious, so I pleaded with Amma to continue on, now that we were there.

Reluctantly she agreed to emerge from the station and head toward the only car, a Volkswagen, parked directly outside. A dashing young man, nearly six feet tall, wearing a Gatsby hat, a tweed waistcoat over a white

T-shirt, and pleated slacks, was leaning against it. A narrow, immaculately trimmed mustache completed the effect. He looked like a model from the cover of a film magazine. Amma stood stiffly at first, but she allowed herslf to smile when he rushed forward to take our suitcase, making polite inquiries about our train ride.

As we drove past picturesque countryside, Amma asked Hamir Chandji about his childhood. An only son born after four daughters, he had barely lived at home. At the age of eight, he had been sent off to Daly College, an elite boarding school in Indore, which, for close to a century, had been educating the sons of India's aristocracy. After finishing there, he had gone to Poona to study agricultural engineering. His return home had coincided with the death of his loving mother after a brief illness. His sisters were much older than he was, and all four of them were already married with children.

Since his return home a few years ago, he had spent his time helping his father manage the estate, taking long drives across the country, visiting his numerous friends from school, and playing tennis. He described his father as a well-travelled man and a voracious collector of books, but someone who was most comfortable in the old world that he inhabited. In his late twenties now, Hamir Chandji was currently making plans to start an industrial plant in Dhar that would manufacture heavy agricultural equipment such as tractors.

From the back seat, I could not make out from Amma's profile whether she liked what she was hearing. After a while the biographical details ceased, and they carried on an uncomplicated conversation about the farmland and the clusters of forests we were passing through. I chimed in with questions every now and then, flaterred at being called "Rekhaji" by our gracious guide.

The string of forests and farms, some of these home to hunter tribes known for their archery skills (and sometimes employed to rob highway travellers), eventually gave way to the picturesque town of Dhar. As we entered, Hamir Chandji pointed to the remains of an ancient earthen rampart that once had marked the boundary of a circular city surrounded by a series of water tanks and moats. The city had existed since the sixth century BC, surviving many invasions, lootings, burnings, and annexations to remain a wealthy centre of culture and learning. It had emerged as the capital of the region of Malwa during the rule of the Delhi Sultanate, but then the many wars during the period of Mughal-Maratha rivalry in the region had diminished the city's fortunes. By the time it came under the British rule in 1818, Dhar had become a nominally sovereign princely state under the Pawar dynasty. Hamir Chandji was born into one of the twenty-two noble zamindar families in the region, all of them holders of large estates.

The haphazard network of ancient streets lined with dignified old houses led to a huge compound in the middle of the city. A tall archway led to a narrow, curving driveway that must have been a quarter mile long. The driveway ended at a metal gate through which we entered a rectangular clearing nearly as big as a cricket pitch, bordered by a lush green orchard to the east and a three-storey mansion on the west. At last the car stopped under a high porch supported by Greek-style pillars.

"Welcome to Bada Rawla!" We were greeted as soon as we stepped out of the car by an an older man who had just come down the wide staircase that led to the first floor. Thakur saheb was nearly as tall as his son. His bald ivory head blended seamlessly with his ivory silk kurta and its glinting gold buttons. The tight *churidar* slacks revealed slightly bandy legs. "From my excessive love of riding," he offered with a chuckle, noticing my stare.

I was deeply embarrassed and tried not to gawk at anything else as the elders exchanged greetings and introductions. My resolve was put to a sudden test, however, when I saw a young woman descending the staircase. She looked as though she were made of spotless marble, a lovely combination of fine features, statuesque figure, and poise in a sari. Thakur saheb introduced her to us as his eldest daughter, Jayanti ben. "My horse-riding, boar-hunting daughter has recently had her third child. She is now recuperating in her father's house," he said with paternal pride. Jayanti ben greeted us sweetly, but despite her warm welcome I glanced nervously at Amma, knowing that the hunting reference could not have been well received by this lover of all creatures big and small. To me she appeared to be struggling to reserve judgment.

Nevertheless, the pleasantries continued, and we followed Thakur saheb and his two children upstairs while two servants scurried to unload our small suitcase from the car. I noticed that Amma was climbing the stairs a bit stiffly, so I moved closer to offer her the support of my arm. This also gave me the opportunity to whisper excitedly, "Amma, his daughter is so beautiful!" But her sharp pinch on my arm said, "Not now."

The staircase led us to an opulent drawing room, furnished with a magnificent sofa with a silver frame, side tables whose marble tops were inlaid with semi-precious stones, and an intricately carved mahogany two-seater in the shape of two peacocks, their interlocked plumage unfurled in all its majesty. A row of photographs and paintings of the past few generations of Thakur saheb's family looked down at us from the upper reaches of the wall, and an enormous oil painting of Thakur saheb in a three-piece suit sat importantly atop a mantel fitted with numerous shelves. These shelves were filled with delicate porcelain figurines and gold and silver knickknacks of all kinds. The collection, as we were later told, had been gathered from all over the world, including Europe and the Far East.

From the high wood-panelled ceiling hung a number of chandeliers that swung gently in the breeze that entered through four open doors, one in each corner of the enormous room. There were eight more doors, all closed. A vast Persian carpet lay across much of the polished sandstone floor, and along one of the walls ran a broad divan covered in gold brocade and a neat arrangement of oversized bolsters. The divan would have seemed very inviting were it not for the large tiger skin draped over its centre.

Thakur saheb politely asked us to sit and make ourselves comfortable after the long journey. Amma chose the sofa closest to an entrance, as though preparing to leave any minute. Thakur saheb took my hand and led me toward the lap of the peacocks across the room, where he sat down beside me, while his son and daughter sat next to Amma.

Soon silver trays laden with freshly made sweets, savoury snacks, and cool sherbet arrived, which Jayanti ben stood up to serve. As we savoured these treats, Thakur saheb asked one of the servants who had carried in the trays to check whether the guest room was ready and our bags unpacked, but Amma protested that we were used to doing such work ourselves. Thakur saheb smiled courteously in response to her abrupt interjection and asked Jayanti ben if she would escort Amma to the guest room so that she could freshen up after we had finished our refreshments.

He then turned to ask with a mischievous smile, "Are you also tired, young lady? Or do you have the energy to see the house? Let's leave your mother here for a chance to snack and talk to the family." Of course I wanted to see this amazing place that looked like a living museum. Amma nodded her permission, but her countenance remained clouded.

Under a wide overhang, a long balcony ran the outside length of the drawing room, connecting to a large enclosed hall with decorative metal grilles encased in a fine wire mesh. "So that the women can see what is happening in the yard below without being seen from outside," Thakur saheb explained. I raised an eyebrow at this, but said nothing. The airy hall held a stocky dining table for ten, with ornate high-backed chairs. Glass-fronted wooden display cases lined one wall; they housed a haughty-looking collection of fine bone china, which came from Britain and Belgium. A mesh-encased door opened onto a square open terrace, directly above the carport.

The western wall of the dining room was lined with heavy wooden doors, but I saw no sign of a kitchen. Three of these doors opened onto the billiards room. Above the custom-made billiards table hung the largest chandelier that I had ever seen outside of a museum. The three doors on the other end of the billiards room opened onto another square terrace and a balcony, this time overlooking the inner courtyard of the mansion.

Next we went to Thakur saheb's library, wedged between the drawing room and the billiards room. Babu and Amma's could have competed with it in the number of titles it contained, but nothing else. Neat rows of wooden bookshelves with glass doors lined the walls. An antique writing desk and chair sat invitingly in a corner near one of the six doors. All the books were hard-backed, many in leather covers, and nowhere did I see any of them stacked in multiple rows or packed horizontally on top of book standing vertically in rows.

Next we tracked back to the dining hall and into a short passage connected to another staircase, which led us to a new area of the house that Thakur saheb said has just been added on, intended for his son and his future bride. The new section had large connected halls, each one with numerous doors and windows fitted with stained glass from Italy, the walls accented by porcelain tiles from Britain. Only one of the rooms in this section was furnished, and this had been chosen as the guest room for Amma and me. And all this was just in the east wing of the first floor.

The south wing of the building held the working areas of the house, something like what I remembered from the house in Bhagalpur, but on a totally different scale. Different activities involved in cooking and food preparation were divided into different rooms—grain storage halls, potato and root storage halls, rooms where the grain was stone-ground, rooms with only large cooking pots, one room for cleaning the variety of vessels, a room for storing water in variously sized earthen and metal containers, and finally a large kitchen that held everything necessary for cooking, whether with wood, dung patties, or gas fire, and where, as I was told, the fire never died.

A large, bare room with lots of folded mats and small square stools in a corner was described by Thakur saheb as the dining area for the women and children. We skipped the tour of the west and north wings, since they were, apparently, much like the south wing. Periodically, one of his four married daughters would come for an extended stay to deliver a child and recuperate in the paternal house, and the south wing was where they generally stayed.

All four wings of the house were connected through covered passages and staircases descending into the inner courtyard. A high arch in the east side connected the inner courtyard with the outer one. An impressive black-stone entryway, shaded by a pink cassia tree, led to the office of Thakur saheb, who was a lawyer by training. It held a mahogany table with a swivel chair, and the table was surrounded by bookcases that held long rows of law books in leather bindings.

Through the metal-grille front of this office, I could see the building's third storey with its slanted roof, sitting like a crown on top of the east wing. Thakur saheb saw me looking up at it and promised to show me the army of cupboards on that floor, which, he claimed, contained the most fashionable clothes and fabrics that could be purchased in Europe or

America. He then pointed to the humble ground-floor rooms all around the courtyard, explaining that they were either empty or used as storage.

"To store what?" I ask.

"Oh, this and that," he grinned. "Let me show you something."

I followed him into another large hall behind his office, this time with a black granite floor and a raised stone platform at one end. This room, he explained, was for the religious festivals that his family observed in elaborate detail. We crossed that hall into yet another room and finally arrived in a small, windowless room. In front of us stood a metal chest as big as a full-sized bed, only higher. When Thakur saheb opened the heavy lid, I saw that the chest was filled to the brim with silver plates and bowls in all sizes and shapes. He suggested I lift out a few plates while he held open the lid.

In obedience I wedged my fingers under the curved corners of a pile of about ten plates, but when I tried to lift them out I groaned at their unexpected weight. Thakur saheb laughed and told me to put them back, then raised his voice in a "*Koi hai?*"—the nameless way to summon those who serve us. A lean man in a turban materialized noiselessly at the summons and stood with his head bowed while Thakur saheb instructed him to take the plates upstairs and to see if Amma was ready to meet him in his office. The servant picked up four or five of the plates with great effort, then retreated backwards a few steps so as not to show his back to us, in a mark of extreme respect.

Still puzzled, I followed Thakur saheb back into his office, where he asked me if I wanted to sit in the swivel chair. That was when I noticed that there were no chairs facing the desk, and I imagined the ghosts of supplicants past standing there with bowed heads. I had never ever sat in a swivel chair, though, so I guiltily accepted this tempting offer and tried to sit in my most ladylike manner, while he sat on a wooden bench in the far corner near the entrance.

To make some polite conversation, I thanked him for the tour and complimented him on his beautiful house. He looked bemused but thanked me for the compliment. How many people lived in this house, I then asked, and was astonished when he said that he and his son were the only permanent residents. The rest were either visiting members of the extended family or staff.

"Such a big house for just two people!" I exclaimed.

He smiled again as he informed me that there were two hundred rooms in total. Not only that, but there was yet another block of rooms at the back of the mansion, unattached to the main building, where some of the servants lived, and then of course there were also the stables and the grain storage. As I tried to digest all this information, I began to swivel back and forth in the chair without meaning to. Only when I heard him laugh indulgently and ask me to try a full twirl did I realize what I was doing. After one hesitant twirl I twirled again and again, only to stop cold when Amma's form loomed in the doorway.

I expected at least a look of disapproval, but she was totally focused on Thakur saheb. She accepted his invitation to sit on the bench, but maintained maximum distance between them. She thanked him for his hospitality and told him that her intention had been to meet everyone in person, but she had seen enough and would like to take her leave soon.

Thakur saheb was quiet for a moment and regarded the wall behind me with great interest. He spoke softly, almost apologetically.

"I have an inkling of what you must be thinking. We have not hidden anything from you about our lives. We have heard a lot about you from Ramkrishnaji. I admire the values that you and your family personify, and would be honoured to have your elder daughter as my daughter-in-law."

Amma focused her frown on the granite floor. "There are just too many differences."

"Not all differences can be bad," he protested. "There must be something you liked about us."

Amma looked up quickly. "I have no doubt that you and your son are extremely nice people." Then her tone grew stern. "But we live in different realms. In your world, it is like the fight for freedom never happened. It is like the country was not at war just a short while ago." Her voice rose in volume. "When we were burning imported fabric from Britain to protest the death of textile manufacturing in our country, you were ordering fur coats from Europe. When our soldiers were sacrificing their lives to protect the frigid borders of the country, you were busy protecting your own wealth accumulated through the toil of other people."

I sank into the swivel chair as low as I could, but Thakur saheb squared his shoulders for battle. While Amma inventoried her accusations, he never flinched. When she was finally done, Thakur saheb spoke respectfully but without apology. He assured Amma that his ancestors had carried out many public projects in the city, and that he and his son intended to continue the tradition. He admitted that their actions and choices may not have been driven by idealistic values like Amma's. But that was exactly why they needed people like Amma in their lives. He thought Didi as his daughter-in-law would bring new depth to their lives if she has absorbed even some of the lessons of Amma's life and upbringing.

Thakur saheb's words totally deflated Amma's rage. She looked at him in amazement but made no immediate reply. At her hesitation, Thakur saheb repeated his request: "We hope that you will reconsider your plans to return to Jaipur. Please spend at least one full day with my family."

At that, Amma recovered her voice enough to say firmly, "If you know anything about my life and values, you must also know that I do not believe in the degrading practice of dowry. Neither am I capable of conducting a wedding that will match your opulent standards." He merely said that it would be an insult to him and to her to have such expectations.

Amma's arsenal was empty for now. She agreed to spend another twenty-four hours in Dhar. She also warned Thakur saheb that this could not be an alliance decided upon by the family elders. The final decision would rest with the two people who'd be expected to promise their lives to each other.

I noticed that Thakur saheb's grin had returned by the time he asked Amma's permission to show us around town.

An hour later, father and son drove us to the ponds and public buildings that bore the names of their ancestors. We visited the picturesque Kalika temple, on top of a hill foregrounded by a lotus pond, and several other ancient temples and mosques, the historic remains of the various ruling dynasties of Dhar.

Finally, we got to the site where Hamir Chandji was planning to build an industrial plant for agricultural machinery. He explained the project in detail. The initial plan was to import the technology and then to manufacture the parts in keeping with local conditions and requirements. Some of his childhood friends were investing in the factory, for which he has recently hired a project manager. Of all things so far, this project was the one thing that hit all the right notes for Amma. She remarked at the signs of decay in this once proud and prosperous historic town, and commended the family for planning to create employment and economic self-sufficiency.

Thakur saheb joked about the legendarily mild-mannered Malwi culture, which had complacently borne invasions and annexations by Turks, Mughals, Marathas, and then the British. The raging fires of the freedom movement had cooled down considerably, he claimed, by the time they reached the higher altitudes of the Malwa plateau. But this was not something Amma felt inclined to joke about. Instead, she disagreed that being mild-mannered should be equated with complacency, citing the examples of the philosopher king Bhoj, from a thousand years before, and the Maratha queen Ahilyabai, from two hundred years before, who had both ruled the Malwa region with great vision and acumen.

Our last stop was a small circular reservoir and a deep well, which marked the eastern end of a large tract of farmland and grazing ground owned by Thakur saheb. The family owned vast stretches of land given to them through royal grants, he told us, but he was worried about the recent land reform laws and new tenancy policies, which would take away land that had been in his family for generations. Amma's response was a mini-lecture on the country's feudal agrarian structure.

She was not even looking at Thakur saheb as she instructed me on the plight of the vast majority of cultivators, who did not have any rights as tenants, mostly leasing land for subsistence, paying more than half of their produce to the zamindar as rent. Amma believed that the ongoing land and tenancy reforms would finally end this highly exploitative system. While she talked, Thakur saheb's poise was looking strained, but even then it did not buckle under pressure.

Instead, at the end of Amma's speech to me, he also addressed me, saying jovially that a young girl like me must find these issues complicated and boring. Then, changing the subject, he asked if I would like to see the local museum the next day. We then drove back to the mansion for an elaborate feast in the dining hall. Amma was pleased to learn that the family was as strictly vegetarian as she, although their reasons were as far removed from Gandhian values as hers were from religious taboos.

The food was plentiful and beautifully presented, but in some ways I found the meal strange, even disappointing. Jayanti ben's polite hospitality was in stark contrast to the enthusiastically insistent serving I was used to in Jaipur and Bhagalpur. I also noticed that most of the dishes had a tangy flavour with just a hint of sweetness. Thakur saheb apologized to Amma for the mild flavours that Malwi cuisine shared with neighbouring Maharashtra and asked the server to add some hot pickles and chutneys to the spread; Amma, of course, protested and declared the meal delightful. I was indeed missing the bold heat of Bihari cuisine and the spicy richness of Marwari cuisine, which were part of most of our meals, but Amma's watchful gaze made me hold my tongue. Didi, I thought, would have a lot to learn.

Our last day in Dhar was a Sunday, when I got to go to the Officers' Club to watch Hamir Chandji play tennis while Thakur saheb took Amma back to the Kalika temple to meet the priest. The Officers' Club of Dhar was originally meant for local nobility and British officers posted in Dhar state, now a district, but it had recently opened its doors to the families of the new Indian elite—senior government bureaucrats. Liveried orderlies ran the club with unwavering attention and unchanging old-world manners. I had the option of watching tennis in one of the pavilions or joining the ladies in one of its many lofty halls.

With fashionably coiffed long hair, bright lipstick, and expensive jewellery glinting through their sheer silk saris, a small group of ladies was sitting at a round table, playing a game of cards. Hamir Chandji introduced me to these ladies, most of whom were wives of senior bureaucrats and local nobility. They reminded me of the ladies in Lucknow whose daughters I had gone to school with, but they were graciously curious and invited me to join them at the table.

Among them, however, I felt acutely aware of my outsider status, what with my unfashionable khadi clothing, simple braid, lack of makeup and ignorance of card games. So I politely declined the invitation, choosing instead to sit under the awning to watch the tennis match, where I sipped from a glass of cool rose sherbet while the rules were explained to me.

It did not take me long to learn how to follow the game, and I soon came to admire the dance-like grace of the foot movements that accompanied each powerful shot. Hamir Chandji ended the spectacle triumphantly after winning three matches in a row, thanking his opponent for a good game. The other player, a senior public works official who was somewhat older than Hamir Chandji and slightly out of breath, shook hands with him and complimented him on his elegant game style.

As our time with the intriguing father-son duo came to an end, Amma told Thakur saheb that although she could not predict Didi's decision, they were welcome to visit our family whenever they happened to be in Jaipur. On the train back to Jaipur, I chirped away excitedly. "Amma, everyone was so nice!... Do you remember that time...?" "And did you see when...?" Amma smiled at me distractedly, as usual.

Back in Jaipur, she filled Babu in on the details of our fact-finding mission. After his most recent pangs of fatherly duty, Babu was once again eager to be left undisturbed in the world of his books. Without any sarcasm, he expressed his total confidence in Amma's ability to make the right decision. I took my job of reporting back to Didi very seriously, delivering with great animation every single detail of what I had seen and heard in Dhar. Amma impatiently interrupted my enthusiastic narration to add that all this great wealth and urbane sophistication were confined within a feudal structure, religious ritual, and purdah.

Didi looked up slowly. "Have you already refused them?"

It was not up to her to accept or refuse, Amma said, but it was her duty to present all the facts to Didi so that she could make an informed choice for the right reasons.

Suddenly, the placid Didi became very emotional. "I know what you want from me. You want me to suffer in life like you do. What did your idealism get you in life except misery and struggle? You and Babu threw away your lives and think it makes you saints. Don't expect the same from me."

Didi's tears flowed furiously now, as she bitterly condemned Babu's irresponsible behaviour toward his family. Amma tried to calm her down by reminding her that Babu's mysterious disappearances were nothing new and did not affect the normal functioning of our lives.

This made Didi furious. "What is normal? Your life away from your family was normal? The constant uprooting of our childhood was normal? An absent father and husband is normal? Your quiet tolerance of his verbal abuse is normal? Do you even know anymore what is normal? Does anyone in this family know what normal is?"

The stunned silence enveloping the house was broken only by Didi's sobs, until she calmed herself finally and folded her hands in front of Amma. "Please, Amma, I am suffocating in this prison. I don't have the strength for a lifetime of struggle like you."

Amma sat motionless for several moments as Didi cried and I sat stunned. Finally, Amma caressed Didi's lowered head. "I hope you know what you want. It is hard for me to put myself in your shoes. I just hope you are not choosing to go from one prison to another."

Amma sent Didi's date of birth to Thakur saheb, since their pandit needed to prepare her horoscope to compare with that of his son. The two horoscopes were a good match, and the wedding date was chosen for 13 May of the following year—four days after Didi's final exam.

7

Departures

I loved every visit that my future brother-in-law, whom I now called Jijaji, made to Jaipur. Every few weeks he used the pretext of a tennis match or a business meeting to drive hundreds of miles just to spend a short visit with his wife-to-be. I thought it was incredibly romantic, but Amma was not impressed. She made sure that Didi had a constant chaperone—me.

Didi pretended to be ambivalent about these frequent unplanned visits, but I could see her glow under the undivided attention of her handsome fiancé. He introduced us to the Beatles, and we nearly swooned when he played the guitar for us. He took us for joy rides, on picnics, even to movies. Amma kept her disapproval contained, though she regularly voiced her concerns about our final exams. But Didi and I understood that this was an important year for both of us, and in between Jijaji's visits we really did study hard.

Babu was back in his solitary cocoon, and the gaps between Kamala mausi's visits were lengthening. It was now Amma's turn to pester Kamala mausi to look after her health. Her tall frame was often bent under recurring spells of fever and coughing. When she failed to show up two Sundays in a row, Amma decided to pay her a visit, and she took me along.

We crossed to the other side of the imposing Ghat Gate, leaving the broad avenues of the city behind to enter the haphazard crisscross of narrow streets behind the central jail. The lanes were irregular in every way, and the houses ranged from old shacks to newly built mansions. We came to one of the dusty bazaars, where narrow multi-storey buildings stood cheek-by-jowl in a shabby cluster. After some enquiries we were shown to one of the dark and narrow staircases that led from those dark and narrow streets. We climbed it to the top of the house, where it opened onto a rectangular cement terrace. A brick room with a tin roof stood at one end, a small pile of unwashed dishes outside the closed door.

Amma stood outside for a moment, listening and looking around, holding my arm to keep me from knocking. Then she quietly pushed open the door. Late morning sunshine rushed into the room, stirring a sluggish wave of strong odour. On a thin mattress on the floor, Kamala mausi's long body lay, curled up like a question mark. The lumpy pillow and thin cotton sheet were stained with phlegm and streaks of blood. Amma took her handkerchief from her shoulder bag and tied it around her nose and mouth, instructing me to do the same with mine. Then, gently, she spoke Kamala mausi's name, talking to her as one does to a sick child. A feeble groan acknowledged our presence, though the sick woman's eyes remained shut. In the same soft voice Amma asked me to go to the bazaar and find the nearest phone to call an ambulance. While I did that, she set about straightening the room and packing a bag.

We rode with Kamala mausi in the ambulance to the SMS Medical College hospital, the largest public hospital in the region. Although samples would need to be sent for testing, the doctors suspected that she was suffering from tuberculosis, and so she was admitted to the TB ward. Amma and I were given instructions about how to protect ourselves against this highly contagious disease.

Amma's routine now included daily visits to the hospital. Didi and I visited much less frequently, partly because we were dismayed at the dramatic decline in Kamala mausi's health and partly because we were trying hard to remain focused on our impending exams. Before many days had passed, we learned that the tests were indeed positive. At this news, despite her dear friend's feeble protests, Amma wrote a long letter to Kamala mausi's son-in-law, Pratap bhaiya, apprising him of her illness and of the doctor's assurances that, although the infection was chronic, with proper medication and care her health could be restored. A week later, Pratap bhaiya arrived with Kanti bhabhi, determined to take Kamala mausi back to Wardha.

Kanti bhabhi was angry rather than sad, at least at first. Over the past few years, her only contact with her stubborn mother had been through letters. She complained to Amma that Kamala mausi had repeatedly declined Pratap bhaiya's requests that she come to live with them in Wardha, on the grounds that doing so would violate traditional customs. And yet, Kanti bhabhi pointed out rather acidly, when it came to the customs by which widows were supposed to abide, her mother had shown no such concerns—nor had she raised her daughter to defer to traditional ways. She and Pratap bhaiya had been prepared to defy tradition by taking her mother in after she fled the oppressive atmosphere of her family home, but, instead of trusting her daughter's judgment in the matter, Kamala mausi had conveniently used the excuse of traditions to live far away from the only family members who would have her.

Amma agreed with the need to challenge traditional customs that were designed to deprive daughters of a source of support and solace by weakening their ties to their parents. But, she asked, could Kanti bhabhi not appreciate Kamala mausi's point of view? Her refusal to live in her daughter's home had more to do with an ingrained sense of self-respect than with any faith in antiquated traditions. She just didn't want to be dependent on her daughter if she could possibly help it.

Kanti bhabhi's anger was not assuaged. "In other words, my mother didn't trust me to understand her or be able to help her."

Amma tried again to explain. "She knew you genuinely cared about her. And she also wanted to protect you." Amma went on: "Think about your own daily struggles as a wife, mother, and daughter-in-law, and add to these the loneliness of a widow, the travails of a single mother, and the strains of reinventing your life multiple times in unfamiliar places. What do you think kept your mother going? It was her unshakable belief that she deserved dignity, and, to your mother, that came from self-reliance."

It was hard to see the tall, dark Kamala mausi as the mother of this petite young woman with the pale complexion. But if you closed your eyes sometimes it was hard to tell whether it was the mother or the daughter who was speaking. Fortunately, in addition to her determination, Kanti bhabhi had also inherited her mother's generosity, which allowed her, with a little time and effort, to look past her own hurt.

Over the next few days, Kamala mausi's health began to stabilize, much to everyone's relief. But when the suggestion she move to Wardha was made, her protests were only half-hearted. The fire in her spirit had been dimmed, if perhaps not entirely doused.

With Kamala mausi's care safely entrusted to her family, Amma turned her full attention to the other pressing matter—planning Didi's wedding. Thakur saheb had completely won over Amma by agreeing to every one of her conditions. As a gesture from her side, Amma was willing to hold a traditional wedding, although the ceremonies—which could continue for as long as two weeks—would in this case last for only four days.

While Didi and I were busy with our exams, Amma bought twenty-one khadi-silk saris, some dyed in the most vibrant colours and others covered with silk brocade. Thakur saheb expected no dowry, so Amma bought lengths of khadi-silk fabric as gifts for the groom and his immediate family. I was not sure whether Babu disapproved or was just uninterested, but he was noticeable through all this mostly by his limited presence. The busiest person in the household was Shafiji, who joyfully lent Amma his reliable shoulder to lean on, jetting about on his bicycle, running endless errands all day, taking as much of the burden from her as he could.

My last exam paper was a week before Didi's, and as soon as it was done I plunged into the fun of preparations. I was thrilled to see our relatives from Bhagalpur and our freedom-fighter-family from different parts of the country arriving to participate in the ceremonies. The furniture in the house was stacked away to make way for rows of overstuffed cotton mattresses in every room, to maximize the sleeping area. The kitchen and the dining room were hubs of constant activity. Mangi bai and her helpers served endless rounds of snacks and meals throughout the day. Two days before the wedding, the groom and his family and friends arrived. Several rooms had been booked for them at Jaipur's elegant LMB Hotel, but, as a mark of extreme respect, Thakur saheb and his eldest daughter, Jayanti ben, insisted on staying in our house, thus adding to the general chaos.

For the wedding itself, Amma had rented the premises of the Maharaja School, which was closed for the summer. Those days the school was housed in an imposing building just a few streets from us. A high, arched doorway led to a large courtyard open to the sky, surrounded by scores of rooms on three levels. We moved into the building the day Didi wrote her last paper. From that point on, a whirlwind of festive customs and preliminary rituals, live *shehnai* music, singing, dancing, dressing up, and lavish meals filled our days and nights. Still, by the standards of the wealthy business community that surrounded us, the arrangements were decidedly humble.

On the second day of the ceremonies, the bride's gifts from the groom's family arrived. In addition to a trunk filled with a dazzling array of silk saris, two men carried in a round silver tray, easily a yard wide, piled high with gold jewellery studded with precious stones. I looked excitedly through the pile of ornaments, at times unsure which part of the body they were intended to adorn. The aunties laughed at my bewilderment, reminding me that Didi would have help from her sisters-in-law in figuring it all out. Such gifts were to be delivered to the bride before the wedding but only worn afterwards, at the reception organized by the groom's family.

A third day passed in a blur of noise, perfume, flowers, food, dancing, singing, ceremonies, and laughter, mixed with the sad knowledge that my sister would soon be going far away. But then, just a few hours before the main event, an unseasonal downpour flooded the courtyard where the holy fire was to be lit. Amma was stunned to see this punishing rain in the middle of summer, at least two months ahead of the monsoon season. It seemed bent on wiping away all of the wedding preparations. The rain only lasted a couple of hours, but it left the streets ankle-deep in runoff and the sunken courtyard under several inches of water.

However, while Shafiji and Amma were still trying to come up with a plan, scores of men who were expected as guests for that evening's event descended on the school with pails, buckets, and brooms and set to work emptying and drying the courtyard. Among them were several members of the state legislative assembly, municipal councillors, presidents of unions, and patriarchs of some of the largest business families in the city. Amma was moved beyond words. She stood near the entrance with her hands folded and tears in her eyes, silently radiating her gratitude.

A few hours later, the groom arrived, riding on an elephant mounted with a silver howdah covered in gold brocade. Dinner was served soon after the bride and groom exchanged heavy floral garlands. The marriage was sanctified in front of the holy fire, accompanied by Sanskrit hymns in a ceremony that extended into the wee hours of the morning. Most of the guests departed at some point during the night, but Amma and Babu sat through the whole ceremony, as did Shafiji, his family, and nearly one hundred of the guests.

Early morning marked an abrupt end to the merriment of the past several days, as friends and relatives bade the bride an emotional farewell. Traditional songs, sung by the older women, conveyed blessings for a peaceful and prosperous new life. The songs reminded the bride that today she ceased to be a daughter and stepped into a new life as the daughter-in-law of another family. They exhorted her to keep her husband's family happy at all costs, to bring them luck and many sons, to love her new family more than her old, and not to leave her husband's home except on her funeral bier.

A procession of the remaining guests followed the bride and groom to the exit, with the women singing the heart-rending songs bringing up the rear. Amma and I embraced Didi, standing on either side of her as she cried her heart out. Everyone was moved to tears except for Amma, who almost seemed angry. Her stony face was focused on the waiting car, barely visible under the rows of floral garlands decorating it.

At the last moment, she kissed Didi's forehead in blessing. "Remember, none of these songs applies to you. You will always be my daughter. You do not have to wait for pallbearers to rescue you from a life you do not want. Just one phone call to your mother, and she will come running to protect you." Only then did Amma's tears begin to flow, as she asked Thakur saheb and Jijaji to look after themselves and her precious daughter.

Didi did not let go of my hand as she got in the car. She wanted Babu, whom nobody had seen since the end of the fire ceremony. I wiped away my tears and ran into the building, calling out for him; I ran up and down the three storeys of the school and even checked the terrace. But Babu had vanished.

All I could do was run back down to the car and tell them that Babu was nowhere to be found. Shafiji suggested that maybe he had stepped away for something important and offered to go looking for him, but Thakur saheb's pandit was getting impatient with the delay, which could make them miss the auspicious hour of departure. Amma knew how important it was for Thakur saheb to follow the rigid cycles of planetary movements. So she caressed Didi's brocade-covered head one last time and told Thakur saheb not to wait.

We returned home to be greeted by the sound of Babu's harmonium. I sat at the foot of his bed, Amma leaned against the door frame, and we watched Babu's tear-streaked face, his eyes closed, as he sang like the sound of a breaking heart—*Giridhari lala, chakar raakho ji, mhane chakar rakho ji,* "O Lord, mover of mighty mountains, make me your servant, please. Take me to your abode, I beg of you."

The mood of chaotic joyfulness sank without a trace into the void left by Didi's departure. I was thankful for the many guests who had stayed after the wedding to tour the city, as this provided me with a welcome distraction. But Amma's gruelling routine was back with a vengeance, especially after Babu failed to return home from his morning walk one day soon after the wedding.

Thakur saheb had expressly told Amma that he did not expect her to observe the numerous customary obligations traditionally borne by the daughter-in-law's family several times a year. His only request was that someone be sent to accompany Didi back to Jaipur within a fortnight of the wedding, as was the custom in his family. This short absence from her new family, needing to last only a couple of days, was considered auspicious. It would also be a welcome break for the new bride from the long stream of house guests and visitors, from the constant exposure to unfamiliar customs and surroundings.

Traditionally this duty of accompanying the bride back to her parents' home fell to a brother or her father. But Didi had no brother, and now our father had disappeared again. So Amma and I bought boxes of Didi's favourite sweets and boarded a train, this time travelling by a different route, to Indore, the rail link closest to Dhar.

Didi and Jijaji were there to meet us. As we drove away from the station, I asked about their honeymoon in Bombay. It was Jijaji's favorite city, and they had spent three days there, away from the hubbub of post-wedding ceremonies and visitors. Didi had brought along pictures of the two of them in the luxurious Taj Mahaj Hotel, by the Arabian Sea, and at the Bombay Presidency Radio Club, of which Jijaji was a long-time member.

I was eagerly looking through the pictures, but Amma was peering out the window, distracted by what she was seeing. "Bhaiya," she said to Jijaji, "it looks like something is wrong." The street down which we were driving looked deserted except for a few large groups of people crowding around certain storefronts. Jijaji laughed that the famously contented Malwi way of life was on display for our benefit, since little work was done in the middle of a summer afternoon. He suggested that the crowds packing the storefronts were most likely listening to a new show tune or a radio drama.

However, we crossed two small towns on the way to Dhar and noticed the same deserted streets in each. As we entered Dhar, it became apparent that something momentous had happened, for there were many sombre crowds gathered around radios in the bazaar, and we saw police everywhere we looked.

Once at the house, we found Thakur saheb sitting in the drawing room, a large radio on the centre table, surrounded by nearly all the inhabitants of the household, serving and served alike. In a voice clearly choked with emotion, the newscaster was speaking about the death of Prime Minister Nehru.

Thakur saheb rose from his peacock throne to greet us, but Amma almost ignored him as she pushed past the people near the door to get closer to the radio and listen to the live description of the mourning enveloping the country. The newscaster confirmed the news one more time: Nehruji was dead. Only then did Amma sit down, as other listeners slowly started filing out of the room, many wiping away tears.

Thakur saheb listened sympathetically when Amma told him about how she had first met Nehruji during the civil disobedience movement. She was saddened by the news of his death and worried for the country, which had barely recovered from its defeat in the war with China. Thakur saheb asked Amma's opinion about Indira Gandhi, whom he referred to as Nehruji's obvious heir, but Amma bristled at the suggestion that family pedigree could have any place in a democratic society.

More than once, I had heard Amma and Babu discussing their concerns over the political rise of Indira Gandhi. Babu had denounced her growing influence as yet further evidence of Nehruji's dynastic ambitions. Amma had argued that Nehruji's refusal to offer his daughter a cabinet position was proof of his commitment to democratic values. Yet her confidence had been shaken in 1959, when Nehruji used his constitutional powers to dismiss the Communist government of E. M. S. Namboodiripad in Kerala, which had been democratically elected two years earlier. Nehruji had initially seemed prepared to accept the results of the election, and it was widely suspected that his subsequent decision reflected the influence of his daughter—who had, in 1959, spent a year as president of the Congress Party.

With Nehru's death, I reflected, Amma had lost another link to her past. Her visits to Delhi had become infrequent since 1962, when President Rajendra Prasadji had retired in the middle of his third term. His death less than a year later had been very hard on Amma, who had travelled all the way to Patna to offer her condolences to his family. Babu, too, had been affected, despite himself. He wrote a moving poem about the loss of a generous, unassuming mentor, although he firmly rejected Amma's suggestion that he send it to Prasadji's family.

Now, only fifteen months after Prasadji's passing, here we were, sitting in this ostentatious drawing room, mourning the loss of yet another great leader of our still young and vulnerable nation. Looking at Amma, I remembered her telling us about Kamla Nehru's kindness to her in the Lucknow jail, so many years ago.

As I was aware, Amma had not always agreed with Nehruji's choices. During the struggle for freedom, she had not considered herself objective enough to judge the merits of Nehruji's pragmatic critique of Gandhian ideals, since she herself was committed to those ideals. Over time, however, her own understanding of satyagraha had gradually evolved, and she had begun to view Nehruji as the commander of an army of dedicated foot soldiers who could together transform a divided and impoverished nation into a place of equality and prosperity. While she continued to lead her own life in accordance with Gandhian principles of service and social reform at the local level, Amma had come to respect Nehruji's brand of socialism, with its emphasis on economic development at the national level, and had publicly supported the industrialization policy adopted by his government in 1948. Her increasing disenchantment with the Congress Party had stemmed less from Nehruji's policies than from seeing corruption, nepotism, and dirty politics become the order of the day at so many levels of government. She was also worried, now more than ever, for the vast rural populations who were still waiting to reap the benefits of independence.

Still digesting the momentous news, we spent a very anxious day in Dhar before returning to Jaipur with Didi. Jijaji planned to drive up to Jaipur at the end of the week to take Didi back to Dhar, so I had little time to waste. I glued myself to Didi, talking into the wee hours of the night, asking her a hundred questions, telling her a thousand things that had happened since she left. Didi listened, looking happy in her usual quiet way.

At one point, Amma joined us on the divan in our guest room, where we had settled in to talk. "You're happy, aren't you?" she asked Didi. Although she tried to sound confident, her anxiety spoke through her words.

Didi nodded her head and smiled, before turning away from us slightly. "It's just that I miss you two a lot. It's such a different world. I have so much to learn."

We each sat for a few moments in our individual pools of sadness, until Amma rose to leave. "Every stage in our lives has its challenges and opportunities," she said simply, and then, walking stiffly, she moved toward the door. I watched as she left the room, then turned back to Didi, hoping she might want to confide in me. I was hurt by her reluctance to share her burdens with me, not wanting to admit that we now led separate lives.

We had barely returned to Jaipur before Amma left again, this time travelling to Delhi to pay her last respects to Nehruji. She returned from her day there looking more tired than ever before. She threw herself back into her work right away, but her eating habits remained erratic, and we noticed that the swelling in her ankles had spread to her legs. She still refused to rest or see a doctor.

Much to our collective relief, the day before Jijaji was due to arrive in Jaipur, Babu miraculously returned. There he was, in his office at the press as though he had never left. We knew better than to ask him any questions. Shafiji and the staff were as unperturbed by his reappearance as they had been by his disappearance.

Amma's faith in the Congress Party was somewhat restored when Home Minister Lal Bahadur Shastriji was appointed the new prime minister, banishing the spectre of an inexperienced Indira Gandhi or the conservative Morarji Desai filling the post. Since independence, Shastriji had had a stellar political career as a state and then cabinet minister, unsullied by scandal or corruption. He was respected for his humane and efficient management of the refugee crisis after partition and of the agitation that had followed the imposition of Hindi. Even Babu could not find fault with the appointment of Shastriji.

JAIPUR, 1965

Jijaji was my ideal of urbane sophistication rooted in the confidence of an ancient heritage. Although I was more than a decade younger than he was, he called me "Rekhaji," combining affection and respect in that effortless way of his that I admired so much. We saw Didi and Jijaji often that first year. They came to visit every few months, and when they did they would arrive with gifts and take me to fashionable restaurants in the city and to the latest movies. During their visits, Amma tried very hard to conceal her disapproval of what she viewed as the immoderate indulgences of the affluent. After they left, I knew better than to chatter on too much about these luxuries, unless I was in the mood for a long lecture.

I missed Didi a lot and had trouble adjusting to the reality of being the responsible one. Without the buffer of my organized and efficient elder sister, my carefree world was evaporating in front of my eyes, disappearing at a frightening rate. No more spending hours talking to Karuna in the stairwell of her house, until it was so dark that we could no longer tell the time. No more hanging out for hours in Bai ki ma's kitchen as a delectable lunch blended imperceptibly into a tantalizing dinner. No more sheepish phone calls to Amma seeking her reluctant permission to go out with Karuna and her cousins, just because the weather after the first rains was practically begging us to ride our bikes to the edge of the hills for a picnic. No more losing myself in the treasure of the written word in the room on the terrace until I could barely see in the fading daylight.

I was finally beginning to realize just how much work and planning was required to run Amma's overlapping domestic, social, and political lives. Unlike Didi, I was totally unused to the idea of planning days and weeks ahead, and I felt very unsure with my new responsibilities, despite Mangi bai's experienced dependability and Bai ki ma's frequent help. It did not help that my master's degree was not in the subject of my first choice.

Much to my surprise, as an undergraduate, I had excelled in ths study of painting. I was drawn to the seamless blending of history and artistry in painting, which I enjoyed much more than the dryness of history courses or the relentless practice required by music. But the University of Rajasthan did not yet offer a master's degree in painting, and I was loath to continue studying history. That left music, which did offer one advantage. The music department conducted its classes at nearby Maharani College, so I wouldn't have to ride all the way to the university's growing campus at the edge of the town.

Babu had been dismissive of my dilemma. "The in-depth study of any subject is fulfilling and rewarding," he declared. "What difference does it make whether you are studying painting or music? They are both art forms, repositories of history and culture, and you'll still have to find your own niche in either of them." Amma had been more sympathetic and had offered to find out more about art schools in big cities like Bombay or Delhi, if that was where my passion lay. Her only condition was that I had to stick to one field and not be a disciplinary nomad like Babu. All three of his degrees were in unrelated fields. However, I was not prepared to live away from home, which I knew would double the void in Amma's life since Didi's marriage, so I chose to remain at home and pursue a master's degree in vocal music, with a focus on the history of Hindustani classical music.

As I began to realize, Didi had served as a buffer for me. Not only was she the older daughter, but her graceful manners and physical beauty attracted attention away from me, leaving me free to be myself. Now, however, with her gone, the social spotlight turned toward me, and it did so in a way that made me angry and uncomfortable. Although I'd never been shy to perform in public, I found myself unnerved by all the attention I was suddenly getting from women who were apparently concerned about my future. Every time I turned around, it seemed another woman was making comments on my age, my appearance, my suitability for marriage—and, most frequently, on my disappointingly dark skin. It was as if all the many aunties in my life, related and unrelated, were vying with each other to see who could persuade me to take the problem seriously. They gave me gifts of various herbal or dairy-based products that promised to lighten my bronze skin to a "wheatish" complexion.

I felt such meddling to be an insult not only to me but to my mother. I had never thought of short, dark Amma as an object of beauty. But she had an arresting way of speaking, as though she were addressing your very soul. Invariably, her speech made people lower their eyes, and that, to me, was beautiful. I also admired how tidy and professional she always looked: it made her austere dress seem elegant.

One evening, Amma sat down on the edge of the divan to brush my long hair. It was not often that we found time just to be together. I sat at her feet, looking down at my hands, painfully aware that all my friends had much paler skin.

"You have beautiful hair," Amma said, smoothing a long lock of it. "It is strange for me to say this to you, since I do not think of beauty in terms of a physical features but as something reflected in a person's thoughts and actions. A snake protecting its nest of newly laid eggs is beautiful to me, but a peacock torturing a snake before killing it is ugly. But then, when I was growing up, my senses were my guide to survival, not to degrees of beauty. You, on the other hand, are living in a world where everything is judged by its capacity to please the senses."

"What do you mean, Amma?" I was a little shaken that she had read my thoughts. But Amma often managed to make me feel like my skull was transparent.

"Think about it. Among the privileged, food is no longer simply nourishment; it has to be a visual and olfactory indulgence. Music is no longer a lifelong practice that speaks to the soul; it merely has to please the ear. Clothes no longer protect one's body from the elements; they have become the very measure of a person. Are these not examples of our greed for sensory pleasure?"

I turned around to look at her. "But what's wrong in wanting food to look nice and taste good?" I retorted. "What's wrong with humming a forgettable tune? What's wrong in wanting to look good?"

Amma was thoughtful. "There is nothing wrong with any of it, until you consider the source of these wants and the outcome of this emphasis on sensory pleasure." She looked at me intently. "When you stand in front of the mirror, what do you see?"

"I see a dark-skinned girl with long hair." I braced myself for the usual lecture about the range of human diversity on earth and the sociopolitical reasons for the continued privileging of light skin, followed by the usual reassurance that I was beautiful in her eyes. But this time Amma did not repeat any of those things. "What you are describing is how a stranger's eyes would see you. When you look in the mirror, what are *you* seeing? Skin and bones do not make you. Who are you?"

I searched for a reply, but Amma stopped me before I could speak. "Don't answer that. But this is a question that you need to ask yourself, repeatedly. As you grow, the answers will keep changing, and that is also something to think about."

I felt confused. I wasn't sure what I supposed to say. "What do *you* see when you look at me, Amma?"

Amma smiled broadly. "Aha—you want me to do the hard work. But there are no shortcuts, my dear daughter, in defining yourself. What anyone else sees in you is extremely subjective, ever changing with time. What matters is what you discover and rediscover within yourself. But I *will* tell you what I see when I look at you," she added, as she put a soothing hand on my head. "I see a curious and confident young person, affectionate to the point of being indulgent, generous to the point of being selfless, and gregarious to the extent of being distracted."

I put my head on her lap, savouring this rare moment of communion. "I see a very beautiful person when I look at you," she continued. "I know that all those who know you can see how beautiful you are, inside and out. There will always be those who are intimidated by your personality or jealous of your talent or your successes. But if they choose not to see your beauty, that does not lessen it."

Unexpected tears stung my eyes and dropped onto the crisp folds of my mother's sari. I wanted desperately to tell her about the most recent humiliation I had endured. I had been returning home from class, walking with my bike and chatting with friends. A middle-aged man had started following us closely, too closely. A hush fell upon us, and our pace quickened.

I had reminded myself of Amma's definition of bravery: it is not the absence of fear, but the ability to rise above fear by confronting it. I thought, *We are four girls walking on the quiet sidewalk by a major school, only a few yards from the walls of the city.* So I held the handlebars of my bicycle tight and shouted at the man to leave us alone.

He had obviously not expected one of us to confront him. He stopped and stood for a moment, blinking, looking from my face to the bike and back. I was ready to charge him if he came any closer to me or my friends. Then, with a leer, he began to scold me for daring to imagine that I might be the object of his attention. I was *ulta tawa,* black as the bottom of a griddle. I was shaking, but I stared him down until he finally crossed the street to walk away from us. I'm not sure which of my friends finally unglued my clammy hand from the bicycle handle and pulled me along to catch up with the rest of the girls, who were already hurrying toward the safety of the gated wall ahead.

Outside the walls of the old city, such encounters had become sickeningly routine. Inside the city walls, people knew me: I was Amma's daughter—Amma, the former freedom fighter and disciple of Gandhi, the social activist who stood by her principles, the woman who had taught the daughters of some of Jaipur's most prominent families. I lived in the shelter of her aura. Once I moved beyond those walls, I was a stranger, not a neighbour. It was another world, where families lived in colonies of newly constructed, single-storey homes that could have been almost anywhere. There, I was merely a dark-skinned girl, and I was vulnerable.

Even as a child, I had heard older girls talk in hushed whispers about lecherous glances, about having their bottoms pinched or their breasts grabbed as they passed a stranger in a stairwell, or about receiving secret letters from unknown admirers. No one thought to complain to parents or other elders, as the burden of blame would almost certainly fall on the victim. Such harassment was simply part and parcel of a woman's life, something to be endured and then passed over in silence.

Didi, I knew, had had her fair share of letters and phone calls from secret admirers, but she always seemed to know what to do in public. She moved with confident purposefulness and regarded every unfamiliar man with suspicion when we walked together within the walls of the old city. When Didi had to venture outside the city walls, however, even just to go to her daily classes at the university, she would summon our regular rickshaw driver.

Rather than having to wait on our rickshaw-walaji, I preferred the freedom of riding my bike wherever I needed or wanted to go, even outside the old city. But I paid for this freedom. Catcalls and whistles, vulgar lines from movies, and outright propositions were flung at me on quieter streets. A few times, particularly aggressive men tried to push me off the road, and one even drove his scooter into my bike to make me fall.

I knew I was not alone in facing these things. The Jaipur newspapers were full of stories about scarves being pulled, about groping, and about other forms of verbal and physical harassment that women experienced on their way to school or work. Amma was livid about the way the reporting trivialized sexual harassment as "teasing," as well as about the frequent implication that the fault for this harassment lay in the way modern women dressed or in their audacious insistence on appearing in public unaccompanied by a man. Amma would lecture the newspaper over her cup of tea, sometimes lowering it to vent her anger: "The freedom movement would not have been possible if women had stayed behind walls and veils. Now these *naradhama,* the lowest of human beings, want to push women back behind walls."

I had never told Amma about a single one of my numerous encounters or about the lingering pain I carried from all the callous comments. I just hoped that Amma could read my transparent head, as always.

All of my physical and emotional strength and organizational abilities were put to the severest test one Sunday afternoon at the beginning of the monsoon season when I came home to find Amma lying on the cold stone floor. I had spent the morning at Karuna's house after a long absence. We had lots of catching up to do that day, a project that was aided by the delicious sweet and savoury snacks supplied by her indulgent mother and aunts. We had planned this day weeks ago—a chat session at Karuna's home, followed by a picnic with her cousins out at the Amer palace.

I had gotten up really early that morning, excited to be spending the day with my closest friends for the first time in a long while. Early as it was, I was not surprised to see Amma already working at her desk. Mangi bai had not been feeling good the day before, and Amma had told her not to come in that day, so she asked me to make her a cup of tea before I left. She looked like she had been working all night, but when I asked her about getting some rest, she promised she would lie down after finishing her tea. I brought her the tea and then happily rushed out of the house on my bike, promising to return before my curfew.

And yet, even as I peddled away from the house, an uneasy feeling made me want to turn around. For a moment I actually slowed down, but then I considered the difficulty of organizing another day like today when all conditions were perfect—the mild weather, the alignment of our often-incompatible schedules. Babu's current absence even added to the perfection of the day, since it meant not having to maintain his rigid schedule in Mangi bai's absence. I told myself that Amma was fine; she was just working from home, and Mangi bai would probably show up later.

The first few hours of the morning at Karuna's house were, as usual for that family, filled with laughter, food, music, and incessant talking. The uneasy feeling lurked in the pit of my stomach, but I kept it in check by throwing myself into the spontaneous singing and eating that was going on around me. Around noon, everything was packed for the picnic, everyone raring to peddle away to the beautiful fortress on the hill. But the knot in my stomach was still there, so I decided to call home to see if Mangi bai was with Amma. Nobody answered, and my sense of impending doom increased. Everyone was surprised at my sudden, irrational, anxiety after my exuberance up to that point. However, seeing me close to tears, Karuna's father offered to escort me home.

I thanked him, but that would mean having to walk, and it was over a mile. Instead, I jumped on my bike and peddled furiously the whole way. At long last, I reached the closed doors of our house. When I pushed them open, I saw my mother lying on the floor, not far away. My heart began to pound. My chest felt like it would explode. I threw down my bike and knelt beside my mother's motionless body. *Is she dead? What did I learn in my emergency first aid training? Think, you stupid fool, think, and do something!*

The house was deathly quiet. Babu's big desk, piled high with papers, stood desolate next to the doors. The giant presses were quietly celebrating their Sunday rest. I grabbed a roll of paper from the cutting room and put it under Amma's head. She groaned without opening her eyes, her face contorted in pain. I ran to the phone on Babu's desk and, my hands shaking, called for an ambulance. Then I dialed Dr. Vohra's number. He wasn't there, so I left an urgent message with his son. Then I dialed Bai ki ma's house. Jain saheb picked up the phone. "I think Amma is having a heart attack," I said, in a voice I did not recognize. "Please come right away."

"Rekha, is that you?" Jain saheb's shout hurt my ear.

"Heart attack," I repeated. "No one is home. Amma is dying. I need help! I have to hang up now."

Amma was wincing and gasping. I tried awkwardly to loosen the clothing around her chest. The CPR steps that I had learned a few years ago—my mind raced as I tried to remember them, realizing to my horror the great difference between practicing on a plastic dummy and knowing what to do when your mother is lying in front of you, gasping for air. At last Dr. Vohra and Jain saheb burst through the door, almost simultaneously. Dr. Vohra bent over Amma, and Jain saheb pulled me away and tried to lead me upstairs.

But it was no use. The volcano inside me erupted in uncontrollable sobs, which stopped only when I heard the sound of an ambulance siren. Then men were lifting Amma onto a stretcher. I asked Dr. Vohra if I could go in the ambulance with her, but in his characteristically clinical way, which seemed very cruel at the time, he told me to come to the hospital later and took Jain saheb with him instead.

At least I had helped Amma enough to know the running around that was required to complete tests, get medicines, and do the many other tasks associated with a hospital stay. Now, with unsteady hands, I packed a bag of supplies, which included flasks, towels, water bottle, and chequebook. Bai ki ma had arrived by that point, and I knew that the house would be in safe hands with her. I knew that there would be people willing to help. I just had to focus on getting Amma better.

Once the doctors had completed their assessment I learned that she had, indeed, suffered a heart attack. Doctors suspected that she had been ignoring her elevated blood pressure for some time already. Her kidneys showed damage, but she was fortunate not to have suffered a stroke, perhaps because she was only in her late forties. Nevertheless, she had to stay in the hospital for over a week before she was considered stable enough to be sent home to convalesce. I stayed there with her the whole time.

We returned home from the hospital weary and overwhelmed by the doctors' grave warnings about the regimen of medicines and lifestyle changes that Amma would have to follow. Didi came for a time to help us, and she administered a severe tongue-lashing to Babu when he finally returned home, shortly after Amma was released from hospital. He did not quarrel with the rebuke. That evening, he sang *bhajans* for longer than usual.

By August 1965, India was fighting yet another war, this time with its estranged sibling, Pakistan. Border skirmishes along the disputed Line of Control in Kashmir had escalated into a full-scale war, and, in contrast to the war with China in 1962, fought in the distant reaches of the Himalayas, this time the battleground was our own backyard. Intense battles were reported along the border regions of Kashmir, Punjab, and Rajasthan. By September, air raids into civilian border areas brought the war even closer. All India Radio regularly broadcast updates, in an effort to dispel the persistent rumours of Pakistani paratroopers landing on the outskirts of major Indian cities, and both radio and newspapers issued instructions on how to observe a blackout.

The border between Rajasthan and West Pakistan stretches for more than six hundred miles, passing mostly through the parched landscape of the Thar Desert. Early in September, the fighting spread to Pakistan's southernmost province, Sindh, with Pakistani forces capturing nearby towns in western Rajasthan. Although Jaipur was well over three hundred miles from the boundary area, we all feared that Pakistan would send air raids to destroy the only two airfields in Rajasthan—one in Jaipur, the other further west, in Jodhpur.

Amma and I spent most of the months of August and September going door-to-door handing out paper, cloth, and homemade glue to residents so that they could cover every single window and latticed screen in their homes. Despite her recent health scare, Amma was back on her feet and working hard, although she was also, for a change, taking her medication regularly. She and Babu joined many others in the city in organizing *prabhat pheri* rallies, held shortly after daybreak. Their aim was to encourage people to donate money, time, and goods for war relief and, most importantly, to appeal for peace and harmony.

The Muslim minority in the city was feeling the pressure of public hostility, as people questioned their loyalty. Shafiji still came to work as usual, but Amma insisted that he leave before dusk to avoid trouble on his way home. Babu often walked with him to Ramganj Bazaar, where Shafiji lived with several generations of his extended family among the largest concentration of Muslim families within the walled city.

To supplement the limited news available from All India Radio's restricted reporting, we listened to international radio stations on shortwave. It was horrific to hear the numbers of casualties reported by both countries. Pakistani leaders spewed vitriol toward "Hindu India." Indian leaders made chilling boasts about Indian forces advancing into Pakistani territory as far as Lahore. The air raid sirens went off several times a night, constantly testing the preparedness of the city. This more than anything made the dread of a violent war that hung over our city almost palpable.

We lived in this way for the better part of two months until, under pressure from the Soviet Union and the United States, both sides agreed to an official ceasefire on 23 September. Dread was replaced by jubilation in the streets, with drums, brass bands, and loud chants of Prime Minister Shastriji's slogan, *Jai jawan, jai kisan,* "Victory to the soldier, victory to the farmer." But international commentators were calling it an inconclusive war, not a victory. Both countries were still claiming parts of each other's territories. Meanwhile, China was threatening military action on the eastern border once again, although this had only led to political posturing on both sides—so far.

Nehruji's foreign policy lay in shambles. The friendly Soviet Union had remained neutral during the war. Pakistan and China had formed a military entente against India, and the United States had become an ally of Pakistan in response to India's socialist leanings. Within two decades of independence, India found itself with hostile neighbours on its eastern, northern, and western fronts. Even relations between India and its southern neighbour, Ceylon, were marked by tensions surrounding the large population of ethnic Tamils left stateless by the Ceylon Citizenship Act of 1948, whom the Sinhalese government wanted to deport back to India.

The brief but bloody war meant that the second year of my two-year master's program had been shortened, as classes were often suspended. Now I was forced to double up my study and practice hours in order to graduate on schedule. But the need to concentrate on my work distracted me from other concerns, including lingering worries about my mother's health.

JAIPUR, 1966

The year started with yet another national trauma: Prime Minister Lal Bahadur Shastri died in Tashkent on 11 January. He had gone to the Soviet city to sign the agreement with Pakistan that officially settled the conflict of the previous year and had died there of a heart attack the day after the signing. Rumours of foul play abounded, with his family alleging that he had been poisoned. Amma remembered Shastriji fondly from her freedom movement days; she had known him as an earthly man of humble beginnings, with an extremely progressive social and political vision. Even Babu, who had no love for Congress leaders, attended the public meeting of mourning to express his sorrow at the country's loss.

Having wielded considerable unofficial influence in government during her father's long term in office, Indira Gandhi was keenly aware of her unpopularity within the Congress Party. She had wisely declined the offer to take office after her father's death, keeping a relatively low profile instead as Minister of Information and Broadcasting in Shastriji's cabinet. Now, however, with the sudden death of Shastriji, her ascendance to the office of prime minister was being opposed only by the conservative faction within the Congress Party, which was led by Morarji Desai. And once again, Babu was directing verbal venom at the Congress Party for not allowing the country to emerge from the grip of hereditary rulers.

Amma, however, was torn between her earlier doubts about Mrs. Gandhi and her delight at the appointment of a woman. In 1960, with the election of Sirimavo Bhandaranaike, neighbouring Ceylon had laid claim to the world's first female prime minister. Now India was next! So Amma put aside her misgivings about Mrs. Gandhi and reminded Babu of Mahatma Gandhi's vision of women's equality in society. Babu looked unconvinced but chose to retreat into sullen silence rather than argue any further. On my part, I was grateful for Amma's interpretation of these dramatic political events. It helped to replace the anxiety I was feeling in such uncertain times with a sense of hope.

These were indeed very uncertain times for India, but they were uncertain for me as well. I was almost twenty, still unmarried, and thinking about leaving home to continue my studies. Especially in this final year of my master's degree in Hindustani classical music, I had begun to enjoy that discipline as much as I had painting. Amma and Babu were thrilled by my decision to pursue a doctorate, but I needed to do well in my exams.

Despite Amma-Babu's dislike of show tunes on the radio, music permeated our lives. Shafiji's jasmine tree was a magnet for song birds, sun birds, sparrows, robins, bulbuls, hoopoes, swallows, and others, which filled the courtyard with avian notes every morning. The sound of music from the blaring radios in the stores in the bazaar blended with morning and evening prayers from the neighbouring temples, mosques, and houses. Closer by, Mangi bai often sang while working in the kitchen; she had a repertoire of Marwari songs for every occasion and emotion. Babu's hour-long *bhajan* sessions in the evenings, sung to the accompaniment of his harmonium, were always followed by my practice sessions with the *tanpura*. At night, I put my little transistor radio under my pillow to muffle its sound so that I could listen to show tunes, old and new, without incurring Babu's wrath.

In many ways I wanted desperately to leave home, even if it meant living an austere, regimented life in the dusty bowl of a village, about fifty miles south of Jaipur, where Banasthali Vidyapith was situated. The University of Rajasthan presently offered only a master's degree in music, despite constant rumours that the music department here was on the verge of introducing a PhD program. Recently, however, Banasthali Vidyapith—a women's college affiliated with the University of Rajasthan—had announced the imminent arrival of Professor B. R. Deodhar to head the music department. A highly respected musicologist and vocalist, who was nearing the end of a long and luminous career, Professor Deodhar came to Banasthali from Banaras Hindu University, where he had spent a number of years as the principal of the program in vocal music. With Deodhar on board, Banasthali Vidyapith had been authorized by the University of Rajasthan to launch a doctoral program in music—the first in Rajasthan. This was exciting news. All the same, my lifelong habit of deferring to the wishes and needs of others inclined me to stay on in Jaipur, dutifully remaining with my parents until the inevitable matrimonial alliance plucked me away from home.

In an astonishingly short time, Didi had put her days of sitar concerts, classical dance recitals, and public rallies behind her and had become a keen card player and an avid clubber, just like Jijaji. Amma's horror at her transformation was held in check by Didi's sadness at being childless, despite trying numerous medical and non-medical fertility treatments. Thakur saheb attributed it to an ancient curse, which had predicted an end to his lineage. Meanwhile, Jijaji's days of driving around the country had been replaced by periodic trips to Jaipur and the development of his factory for agricultural machinery.

I wanted a life unlike either Amma's or Didi's. I was not sure what that would look like, but I knew I needed time, which I was running out of rapidly. A twenty-year-old unmarried girl was an uncommon entity in my world. She was the focus of criticism and suspicion, considered well on her way to being an old maid. Although I felt guilty for abandoning Amma and Babu, I enjoyed the prospect of being away from home to pursue my doctorate. It might help alleviate the criticism, and at the very least it would take me away from the disenchanted Babu and long-suffering Amma. As for the educational qualification, it might be my only ticket to a new life.

Amma had been consciously taking care of her health, perhaps trying to ease my anxiety about leaving home. My bike gathered dust in a corner of the house as I retreated into my room to study for my final exams. Only one thing, at first, could tempt me from my seclusion: Karuna's wedding that summer. But then, in the midst of the singing, dancing, and merriment of the wedding festivities, Karuna introduced me to an aunt who was looking for homes for newborn Briard pups.

The number of animals needing care in our own home was by then down to one resident cat and two talkative parrots in a large cage. Shafiji's young family had been enthusiastically taking in his tiny rescues, thus thankfully reducing our own menagerie, but that didn't mean I would be allowed to take one of these puppies. I had fed and loved a number of stray dogs in our neighbourhood, but until now had never been allowed to bring one home: Amma and Babu were opposed to the idea of human ownership of animals, except when necessary to relieve the animal's distress.

Once the wedding festivities and the exams were all over, I tentatively broached the subject. To my surprise, instead of launching into a diatribe on the difference between owning an animal and loving all creatures, Amma smiled indulgently. "I know how lonely you have been since your Didi left home. But soon you will leave this house too, no?" I suggested that a dog would fill not only my present loneliness but also the eventual void that the journey of my life would create in Amma's and Babu's lives. Banasthali wasn't very far away, I argued, and it was well connected to Jaipur both by rail and bus. I would be visiting Jaipur frequently, and I could help train the puppy. Amma surprised me again by agreeing to visit Karuna's aunt.

A bigger battle lay ahead in convincing Babu, so I spent the night honing my arguments to counter his moral objections to adopting the puppy. Early the next morning, while I was still steeling myself to face him, I heard Amma's voice in his room, informing him of my plan to adopt a dog. I could imagine his sepia-brown eyes glinting in anger as he growled, "So you think it's all right to separate a baby from its mother because it's a dog? Rekha is a child, so her irrational desire is understandable. Isn't it our duty to point out the difference between love and cruelty?"

Amma interrupted him, "Rekha is not a child. She is a twenty-year-old woman who does everything to please her demanding parents. She will soon leave this house, only to return as an occasional visitor. While she is still at home, I would like her to feel less lonely and not like a sacrificial victim on the altar of duty."

I wasn't sure how to interpret the stunned silence from the other side of the wall. But I hurtled out the door the second Amma summoned me to accompany her to Nitaji's house. We took a tonga to the large new house by the university where Nitaji's family lived with their pair of Briards and the one pup that still remained from the recent litter, a male. Armed with a square wicker basket lined with towels, I spent our journey there excitedly describing to Amma all that I had learned from Nitaji about this breed's characteristics and how to train it. When the tonga arrived I leapt out of it, but Amma did not move. Instead, she handed me the basket and asked me if I had thought this through.

I tried to assure her, and myself, that the pup would have to be separated from his mother, whether by us or some other family. He was two months old, the right age to start training. I would take care of him. At my assurances, Amma asked me to fetch the pup. But she did not move from her seat in the tonga. It was clear that, although I had her support, I would have to own the decision to separate a puppy from its mother.

I had a long list of names for the puppy in my head—heroes from various classic novels, mythological figures, historical characters, and names of trees, mountains, and rivers. But when a broad, beige, furry puppy with captivating indigo-blue eyes began licking my face, I knew from the colour of his eyes that he could only be called "Neelu."

Amma and I took Neelu to our vet, Dr. Ramchandani, who had been a young boy when his family fled their ancestral home in Sindh during the partition of the subcontinent. As a child he had often accompanied his feisty mother on her visits to the refugee camps, and so he had known Amma-Babu since those days. Today he looked amused at the spunky little bundle of fur that we had brought to him. He drew up a chart of inoculations and declared Neelu to be in perfect health. He reassured me that the puppy would grow into his chubby paws quite well. He also lent me a few books from the shelf in his office on dog training and breeds.

Then he turned to Amma. "A dog this big will need appropriate food to lead a healthy life," he said, a delicate allusion to Amma and Babu's strict vegetarianism.

Amma did not hesitate for a moment. "As the newest member of our family, he will eat whatever we eat."

Dr. Ramchandani chuckled. "So you plan to raise a grass-fed lion."

Amma caressed the pudgy puppy cradled comfortably in my arms. "This lion cub will do just fine on roti and dal." And he did.

It would be at least three months before my exam results were out and the verdict on my application to the doctoral program announced, and the long lazy summer months lay ahead like an endless delirium. The scorching sun forced people to stay indoors until the desert sand cooled, late in the evening. Unlike other summers, however, this time I was occupied with the task of raising a bouncy puppy, training him to socialize amicably with the human and non-human residents of our home, and teaching him the rules of the open-door setup of the house. For once, I needed no motivation to stay indoors.

Our normally quiet house came alive with the sweet excitement that only a frolicking puppy can bring. Even Babu could not resist the cuddly ball of fur. I was relieved by this at first, but then Neelu found the best way to escape my discipline—an alliance with Babu. I was trying hard to train Neelu so that he would grow into a well-behaved dog, but—to my utter dismay—Neela soon discovered that he could use Babu as his refuge whenever he grew tired of my training sessions or my scoldings. Whenever Babu saw Neelu slinking under his desk or onto the bed, he would invite him to sit on his lap, where he would address him as "Shyam Sundar"—a name for Krishna alluding to his dusky beauty. For this boisterous blonde pup it seemed highly inappropriate. Neelu was rapidly growing into a large dog, but he continued to climb onto Babu's lap, where he radiated an air of invincibility.

When the monsoon clouds appeared on the eastern horizon, heralding the end of a joyous summer, they also brought news of my acceptance into the doctoral research program at Banasthali Vidyapith. I could not wait to start the new chapter of my life, sad though I was to leave Neelu behind.

8

Crossing Thresholds

Banasthali Vidyapith was the tribute of a grieving mother and father to the memory of a daughter who had died too young, at the age of only twelve. From its humble beginnings in 1935, as a school for village girls, it had grown into a residential institute for women, offering education from primary school through to the graduate level. Amma had known the founders, Pandit Hiralal Shastri and his wife, Ratan Shastri, since before her Wardha years. In 1927, under the influence of Gandhiji's philosophy of social uplift, Shastriji had given up a senior government position in the princely state of Jaipur to dedicate himself to rural advancement, advocating for peasants' rights and for women's empowerment in the region, and had later become a leading member of the Praja Mandal, a nationalist organization. When, in 1949, the various princely states of Rajputana were incorporated into the Dominion of India, Shastriji became the first chief minister of the newly formed state of Rajasthan, but he resigned in 1951, soon after the death of his mentor, Sardar Patel, and returned to Banasthali. Many considered the university his most enduring legacy.

An hour-long train ride took me to the dusty town of Niwai, which surrounded the campus of this women's university—a cluster of modest buildings situated in a serene oasis of shady groves, trees-lined paths, and lush green sports fields, home to multitudes of majestic peacocks. This self-contained community had a library, a bank, and a hospital, as well as housing for the students, staff, and faculty of the institution. In its regimented daily routine, the requirement that we all wear khadi, and the focus on community work, campus life preserved a sliver of Gandhiji's dream. We were regularly reminded of the privilege it was to be on these hallowed grounds in pursuit of knowledge, and we were exhorted to give back to our communities and country in any way possible.

My supervisor was the recently arrived Professor B. R. Deodhar, the new head of the Music and Dance Department at Banasthali. I was excited to learn that he had studied with the illustrious singer and musician Vishnu Digambar Paluskar, an iconic figure in modern music history. Touring Gujarat around the turn of the century, Paluskar had taken the unprecedented step of giving a public concert—a shocking event at a time when musical performances were still confined to the homes of wealthy patrons or, alternatively, to temples. Then, in 1901, he had established the first classical music school to be funded by public donations—the Gandharva Mahavidyalaya. This was where Professor Deodhar had studied, before going on to earn his own distinguished reputation. He was greatly respected for his work on vocal training and for his deep knowledge of both Western and Hindustani musical traditions, and he was also one of the country's foremost advocates of the introduction of music into university curricula. His crowning credential, though, at least in the eyes of Amma and Babu, was that he had led a satyagraha of artists during the struggle for independence.

I was beginning to understand why Babu always insisted that music is the ultimate science—*Ekam sangeet vigyanam,* he often said—as I learned about the impact of music on human psychology and the formal complexity of the system of ragas on which Indian classical music is based. The origins of this system can be traced back more than three thousand years, to the *Samaveda,* a collection of melodies to which verses from the *Rigveda* were intended to be sung, attesting to the integral role of music in rituals of worship. But music also occupied a central place in classical Indian drama, as is clear from the *Natyashastra,* a Sanskrit treatise on the performance arts compiled from about 200 BC to 200 AD.

For many centuries, knowledge of music theory and practice was passed down orally, from *guru* to *shishya,* in an ongoing chain of transmission, and music remained closely associated with temples. During the medieval period, however, the music of northern India began to diverge, at least to some degree, from that of the south, largely owing to the influence of Muslim rule. Islamic tradition strictly prohibits the worship of idols, and early Muslim rulers often set about destroying Hindu temples and disbanding their retinue. Yet many of these rulers—the Mughal emperors, especially—were generous and enthusiastic patrons of the arts, including music. As a result, music became more secularized in the north, moving out of temples and into royal courts, where Hindu and Sufi musicians often mingled in a musical dialogue that enriched Hindustani classical music in many ways. At the same time, this system of patronage contributed to a weakening of musical traditions that had been kept alive in temples by *devadasi*s and that continued to flourish in the wealthy temple-towns of southern India.

Only in the early twentieth century, however, were efforts finally made to develop a comprehensive theory of classical Hindustani music, one capable of knitting together a patchwork of local traditions. Credit for this accomplishment belongs largely to the Marathi scholar Pandit Vishnu Narayan Bhatkhande—a gifted musicologist, as well as a sitar player and vocalist, and author of the four-volume *Hindustani Sangeet Paddhati.* Bhatkhande, who was well versed in both northern and southern classical music, undertook a detailed comparative study of the ragas presently popular in northern India and, drawing on the southern Indian system of *melakarta*s, devised a system of classification based on the concept of a *thaat*—an ascending scale of seven notes on which musicians then elaborate to produce new ragas. He also developed a standardized system of musical notation and wrote a series of school texts that I knew well.

One of the consequences of the oral transmission of music, in the absence of any standard system of musical notation, was, of course, that melodies could easily be transformed or lost, even when lyrics survived. I was thus beginning to appreciate the musical legacy of the *bhakti* poets, whose devotional songs Babu sang every evening. Emerging in northern India during the fifteenth century, the *bhakti* movement marked a turn away from asceticism toward a more emotionally charged form of worship that found expression in poetry and music. One of the most celebrated of the early devotional poets and singers was Surdas, who, according to legend, was blind from birth. Born in the late fifteenth century, Surdas is revered as one of the *ashtasakha,* the eight poets credited with creating most of the lyrical repertoire of the Pushtimarg sect, which is also known as the Vallabh Sampradaya after its founder, Vallabhacharya. Followers of the Pushtimarg worship Krishna, and the sect developed a well-preserved musical tradition.

Central to the Pushtimarg is the daily worship of an icon of Krishna, often as Shrinathji, one of the god's many manifestations. I was somewhat familiar with the Pushtimarg tradition, not only because of Babu's singing of *bhajan*s but also because, even though the sect originated in Vrindavan, one of its most famous temples was in Rajasthan. The one notorious iconoclast among the otherwise temperate Mughal emperors was Aurangzeb, who ruled in the second half of the seventeenth century. So, in 1672, fearful for the safety of their venerable icon of Krishna, the Pushtimarg faithful undertook to move it some four hundred miles southwest, where it was installed in the now famous Shrinathji temple at Nathdwara, not far from Udaipur.

The Pushtimarg was known for its custom of *nitya kirtan,* or endless chanting, referring to the continuous daily round of worship, or *seva,* service to god, with devotional songs accompanying every ritual observance. Drawing on both local folk and classical forms, the adherents of this sect developed a rich musical tradition called the Haveli Sangeet, partially preserving an ancient musical form, the *dhrupad,* in the process. Since the time of Surdas, the uninterrupted transmission of the Haveli Sangeet had ensured the survival of a medieval musical tradition. Before the end of my first year at Banasthali, with my supervisor's approval, I was developing a research proposal to explore the role of the *ashtasakha* poet-singers in preserving the musical traditions of the day.

Summer break took me home to news of the latest violence in the Naxalbari region of West Bengal, where a peasant uprising had been in progress for several months. Poor sharecroppers, backed by Communist Party workers, had seized land and had repeatedly clashed with wealthy landlords protected by armed police. A village inspector had been murdered, and now police had opened fire on a group of peasants, killing nine adults and two children.

In the meanwhile, Zakir Husain had been sworn in as India's third president, and Amma wanted Babu to write an editorial for *Praja Sandesh* about the appointment of a Muslim as a boost to Indian secularism. But Babu's focus was firmly on the uprising in Naxalbari. "This is what happens," he declared, "when political independence stops short of social revolution. Colonial masters are eliminated only to be replaced by a homegrown set of rulers, whose goal is to preserve their own privilege. The result is a bunch of half-hearted land reforms that serve to create a new class of absentee landlords who find ways to evict tenant farmers."

Amma agreed that land reform had been a slow process, especially in the eastern parts of the country, where feudal traditions ran deep. But she could not condone the violence. Babu argued that, in this case, such reservations merely denied the dispossessed the only real source of power available to them. "Can you blame the poor for resorting to violence? For not wanting to wait another century for genuine reform?"

Amma quoted Gandhiji: "There are many causes I am prepared to die for. There is not a single cause I would kill for."

Babu countered, "Gandhiji also said that if the choice is between cowardice and violence, 'I would advise violence.'"

I disliked listening to my parents argue, so I decided I'd rather go play with Neelu. He had grown into a handsome and rather large dog, weighing just over 30 kilograms and spoiled rotten. With a long, bushy tail and his indigo eyes hidden behind a tawny veil of coarse fur, Neelu needed regular brushing, but he wouldn't allow anyone near him with a brush except me. He had been trained not to go into the kitchen, much to Mangi bai's relief, but he stood like a vicious sentinel at Babu's doorway once Babu's food was served. He was equally fierce when it came to his own food bowl, which nobody other than Amma, Babu, or me could approach.

Neelu seemed to me like protector and destroyer rolled into one. He was a boisterous, playful, overgrown puppy who let me do anything to him and often sat on Babu's lap, however uncomfortable for man or dog. When Amma was at home, he rarely let her out of his sight, trailing after her like a bodyguard. He understood that the ground floor was Shafiji's domain and was prepared to be totally submissive, but this tolerance ended the moment that Shafiji came upstairs. And if Neelu ever wandered out of the house, he would aggressively chase after anything that moved, completely stopping traffic in our narrow street. Aside from the three of us, no one could touch him without eliciting a deep, threatening growl followed by a warning snap of his powerful jaws. Neelu had not yet bitten anyone, but I was terrified that one day he would.

All the same, I adored Neelu, and I loved playing with him on the terrace. His loud, joyous barks echoed throughout the house, when his strong jaws weren't tugging at a toy in my hands. A few nicks and scratches seemed a small price to pay.

After I returned to school in the fall, I began my field research, which Professor Deodhar and I had agreed would be conducted primarily at the Shrinathji temple in Nathdwara. Amma had already spoken on my behalf to people she knew who had some connection with the town, including Rajasthan's chief minister of state, Mohan Lal Sukhadia, whose family home was in Nathdwara. Amma also accompanied me on my first trip there, armed with letters of introduction. After meeting a number of politicians, as well as temple priests, I was eventually allowed to see original palm-leaf manuscripts containing song lyrics and early Pichhwai paintings depicting musical performances.

I felt deeply grateful, as I knew I might be the first outsider ever to see these manuscripts, which had been preserved by the same priestly family for generations. Although my access to the manuscripts was initially somewhat restricted, I was given unlimited permission to attend temple ceremonies. These were different for each of the eight subdivisions of a day, and the songs that accompanied them were supplemented by an additional musical repertoire that marked the numerous festivals associated with events in Krishna's life.

My first task was to transcribe the verses sung in the Shrinathji temple. My research seemed to be off to an aupicious start when the head priest invited me to lead the singing of a *kirtan* one evening—a call-and-response form of devotional song common in the Pushtimarg tradition. He confirmed that I was indeed the first woman, and a non-Brahman at that, to have received such an honour, at least in his lifetime. It would take more than a few trips to Nathdwara over the course of the next several months, however, before I could correlate my collection with the available scholarly literature on the topic and complete my analysis. I was especially interested in the association of ragas with specific emotional states, and I hoped to explore the relationship between the performers' reverence for music and their devotion to Krishna.

JAIPUR, 1968

Kamala mausi was dead. Pratap bhaiya and Kanti bhabhi's regular letters had been conveying reassuring news of Kamala mausi's health, which seemed to remain steady. Her own long, erratic letters told a different story, however, of the stifling, self-imposed silence of a caged spirit. The opinionated and independent Kamala mausi was a poor fit in the socially compliant life of her daughter—a young mother of three children who kept the peace at all costs, even if it meant sacrificing her own career, her personal comfort, and even her principles. Kanti bhabhi's conformist choices were a constant reminder to Kamala mausi of her own willfulness and rebellion, and she felt the contrast acutely.

Kamala mausi wrote long letters addressed to both Amma and Babu, in which she expressed doubts about the wisdom of her audacity in going against the flow. Amma and Babu discussed these letters and wrote equally long replies, reminding her that audacity leads to creativity, without which the individual and the society stop evolving. Again and again, Kamala mausi would lament her decision to break from tradition—refusing to accept her fate as a young widow, charting her own course, and ultimately finding a lonely, uncertain future. Babu would remind her that we learn making from breaking, and Amma would ask what would remain to define us if we never veered from the expected path.

Now there would be no more letters. I was home on a visit, and Amma, Babu, and I were sitting around the desk in Babu's office, reliving these conversations, rereading the telegram that had so bluntly announced the death of a woman whose life had been part of our own, and then waiting for the long-distance call to Wardha to connect. When the call went through, Kanti bhabhi was in shock, but Pratap bhaiya was at least able to speak. He haltingly explained that Kamala mausi had disappeared a few nights before. They had searched and searched for her and had finally found her unconscious in the forest of teak trees a few kilometres outside the town, not far from the Dham River. She had died within hours of being brought home. He could not understand why Kamala mausi would do such a thing. Physically, she had been stable, but she was fragile. She must have known that she was courting death by wandering so far in the chilly night. They were not even sure how she had managed to walk such a distance.

Babu could not bear the thought of facing the grieving family. It was pointless, he argued, to go all the way to Wardha when the funeral rites were already over. But Amma began making preparations to go. She was determined to make the trip, even if it meant changing trains several times and travelling in unreserved coaches.

After Amma returned from Wardha, her blood pressure was high again. I was worried about her, so I brought my research notes home to Jaipur, where I hoped to continue my work by focusing on the secondary literature that I needed to read, temporarily suspending my field trips to Nathdwara. Thus it was that I returned home from one particularly long day at the University of Rajasthan library to be startled by the sight of a bearded old man asleep on the divan in the drawing room. He sat up with a cat-like fluidity of movement as I entered the room and then smiled impishly. "Years of living in prison does this to you. How are you, Rekha?"

Babu joined us in the drawing room. "Rekhu, this is Pandit Parmanandji of Jhansi, my *param mitra*."

I had never heard Babu refer to anyone as his "dearest friend." Babu then explained that Parmanandji had been arrested in Lahore for his role in the 1914–15 Ghadar Conspiracy and had been imprisoned for a total of nearly thirty years, seven of which he spent in one of the tiny cells of the Kala Pani jail in the faraway Andaman Islands. I had read about the dreaded prison complex in my history books. The British had been exiling allegedly dangerous political prisoners to the Andamans since the time of the Indian Rebellion of 1857 and had constructed the so-called cellular jail at the turn of the century. Its seven three-storey wings radiated out in straight lines from a watchtower, a design based on Jeremy Bentham's concept of the panopticon. It had almost seven hundred cells, in which prisoners were kept in solitary confinement—when they were not forced to labour in conditions so harsh that some of them died.

His years in Kala Pani had not broken Parmanandji's spirit, however. Pandit Parmanandji was freed in 1937, but his incendiary public speeches continued to land him back in jail all the way up to the eve of independence.

He now divided his time between Jhansi and Delhi, when he wasn't travelling across the country connecting with old comrades. Babu reminded me that Parmanandji had been a guest at Didi's wedding, but I had little memory of the hundreds of guests who attended, given the chaos of hosting, organizing, laughing, and crying that had accompanied the several days of festivities.

Parmanandji's eyes beamed bright in his gaunt face as he smiled from Babu to me. I was intrigued. "How do you know each other?" They exchanged a meaningful look before Babu continued his story.

"We met in 1940. I had just moved to Wardha and returned one evening to find this dishevelled man lying on my bed in my straw hut. I was about to scold him for appropriating the bed without my permission, but then realized that it was Pandit Parmanandji. We have been friends ever since."

"But how did you know who he was? Did you know him from before?" I wanted to know more. Unlike the detailed descriptions of Amma's eventful life that had filtered through her writings and other people's recountings, glimpses of Babu's past were extremely rare, and rather opaque.

But Babu was not prepared to give up any more information. "Are you going to keep interrogating me or make sure that our guest has something to eat?"

I returned from the kitchen with a tray full of snacks and hot tea for everyone. Parmanandji asked me what I did and took great interest in my research topic. Amma was not home yet, which was not unusual. At the mention of Amma, Parmanandji smiled and said something startling: "If I had known that Prakashwati would change her mind about marriage, I would have waited. And you, sweet girl, would have been my own daughter."

His remark made me deeply uncomfortable, but it also sparked the memory of a train ride many years ago, when Amma had mentioned a persistent admirer who inundated her with ardent letters entreating her to marry him. Could this be the same man? I was offended by his depiction of my Amma as the object of carnal desire, but Babu merely sat unperturbed, sipping his tea. The two soon struck up a spirited conversation about the Vietnam War and the recent assassination of the American civil rights leader, Martin Luther King, Jr., both men evidently oblivious to my discomfort.

As he did every year on 21 August, Professor Deodhar marked the anniversary of the death of his illustrious teacher, Pandit Paluskar, with a concert that drew an impressive gathering of musicians and scholars whom the two teachers had mentored over the years. It was on this occasion, as I savoured the opportunity to hear some of my favourite classical ragas performed with exquisite emotional depth and technical mastery, that I learned about my research supervisor's plans to retire. He would be turning sixty-seven in the coming year and intended to move back to Bombay. I was upset, since his impending departure meant that Banasthali would no longer be in a position to offer a doctorate, unless someone could be found to replace him. My anxiety subsided a bit when he told me that by the time I was ready to submit my thesis, the department of music at the University of Rajasthan would no doubt have introduced its long-awaited doctoral program, and I would be able to finish my degree there. He also agreed to continue to supervise my research to completion, but I was left to wonder about the cost of repeated excursions to Bombay.

There was a nominal tuition fee at Banasthali, which covered the simple accommodations and meals. But my frequent field trips, numerous extracurricular activities, and recurrent trips to Jaipur added up to a substantial figure each month. I thought it might be more than half my mother's monthly salary, but I didn't know for sure since Amma refused to discuss the cost of my education or the financial health of our household. Whenever I tried to ask, Amma just told me to focus on my studies and enjoy the privileges of being a student.

Now, however, faced with the prospect of this additional travel expense, I asked Amma's permission to find some part-time employment, perhaps offering private tutoring to junior students. Amma looked hurt at my suggestion. "Do you no longer trust your mother to look after your needs?"

"How can you say that?" I countered. "I think I'm old enough to lend a helping hand."

This time Amma raised an eyebrow with a smile. "Ah, you must have grown up overnight. Suddenly I am discussing family finances with my younger daughter!"

I was embarrassed to realize that I had never before wondered how Amma was able to afford the expense of raising Didi and me, as well as helping Babu set up the press, to say nothing of paying for Didi's wedding and continuing to support my education. The sporadic income from the press was mostly managed by Shafiji, but I knew that it was often absorbed by the press's running costs, if not sucked dry by Babu's charity. I had only seen Amma make out cheques for repairs to the press and other such unforeseen needs; never had I seen any money travelling in the other direction.

Feeling somewhat guilty, I asked Amma to reconsider, but she determinedly rejected the idea. "I do not want anything to distract you from completing your degree. Finish your doctorate, and then use it for the advancement of knowledge. You can find employment at any point in your life. But the opportunity to inhabit the abode of Saraswati comes once in a lifetime. I don't want you to squander it by worrying about trivial concerns such as money—not as long as your mother is alive."

I was not convinced that money actually was inconsequential in our household, but the hurt in Amma's eyes and the resolve in her voice stopped me from arguing any further. Instead, I began mentally to review ways I might be able to cut back on my extracurricular activities, reduce my trips between Banasthali and Jaipur, and use my field trips more efficiently.

Didi's visits to Jaipur had been growing shorter and fewer as the year went on. Jijaji's beloved project had suffered a major setback: his project manager has absconded with a large amount of cash that was meant for the construction of the factory. Unbeknownst to Jijaji, the manager had also incurred huge debts on the company account. Now creditors were contacting Thakur saheb, which offended him deeply, and he was preparing to sell a section of their farmland to settle the various debts.

Amma was grateful that Jijaji's family was not holding Didi responsible for their ill luck or for not producing an heir yet. Thakur saheb continued to blame the ancient curse for Didi's infertility and the evil eye of enemies for their financial misfortunes. He sought the help of a variety of priests and ascetics, who performed prayers and ceremonies of appeasement on his behalf.

In the meanwhile, there appeared to be little outward change in Didi and Jijaji's routine of clubbing, marathon card games, and parties. But, in her phone calls and letters, Didi increasingly mentioned social causes. She was becoming more involved in local charitable trusts and boards that ran orphanages and educational institutions in Dhar. Amma was pleased, but she was much less comfortable with the recurring references to the performance of rituals designed to placate troublesome planets.

On her brief and hurried visits to Jaipur, Didi said nothing about her situation. But I noticed the way she avoided other people's children and the longing in her eyes at the mention of anything related to a baby, and I heard the hushed whispers at social gatherings referring to her as *baanjh,* sterile. I wished I could hug away her sadness. It seemed to me so very unfair.

JAIPUR, 1969–70

By the time the new year began, I had resumed my field trips to Nathd-wara, although I returned from them to Jaipur rather than to Banasthali. I was, as ever, concerned about Amma's health, and, as I explained to her, the books I needed to consult were more readily available in Jaipur's numerous libraries than at the college. My former regime of picnics in the parks and walks through nearby woodlands had thus been replaced by transcribing, reading, writing, and organizing copious amounts of notes, with an older and more sedate Neelu by my side.

My labours were briefly broken by a visit from someone Amma had known since her Wardha days. At the time that Didi was born, Maitreyi didi—our visitor—was a little girl living with her parents at Gandhiji's ashram. After India's independence, Maitreyi didi's family moved back to their ancestral house in Jharia, in southeastern Bihar. Amma had a special place in her heart for Maitreyi didi and her departed parents, whom she regarded as among her many teachers and mentors, and they had kept in touch all these years.

On this particular visit, Maitreyi didi was on a mission. She had recently been introduced to a young man, now in his early thirties, who was, she told Amma, *absolutely* the ideal match for her bookworm of a daughter. He was the chief liaison officer at one of the mining operations in Dhanbad, and she had met him through a common acquaintance. She was terribly impressed by his exquisite manners and by the fact that he had an MBA from the Xavier Labour Relations Institute, one of the premier business management schools in the country. *And* he was very handsome.

Maitreyi didi always talked in a tone somewhere between bullying and imploring; her voice rose urgently when she got excited. This time, Amma listened to her rousing description in apparently indifferent silence until Maitreyi didi mentioned that the young man hailed from a zamindar family in Lahana, a small village in western Bihar. This piece of information sparked a comment about the persistence of feudalism in India, which escalated into a heated discussion. Amma pointed out that, despite the formal abolition of the *zamindari* system, large tracts of farmland remained under the control of landlords, especially in the eastern states of Bihar, Orissa, and West Bengal, where feudalism was deeply entrenched—a situation that was already fuelling outbreaks of violence. Witness the violence in Naxalbari two years earlier, with angry peasants forcibly seizing land. As for Bihar, she argued, the entire state remained stubbornly immured in paternalistic attitudes that had not budged in centuries. Maitreyi didi retorted that, when it came to clinging to outmoded traditions, Rajasthan was no better. Not only was purdah still quite a common practice there, but widows were occasionally coerced into committing sati.

Maitreyi didi continued to press her case for the young man, pointing out that his family's caste matched our own—hastening to add that this was merely a lucky coincidence—and noting that the family had at one time enjoyed the patronage of the local Maharaja. Finally, fed up with her relentless badgering, Amma snapped, "I would rather push my daughter into a well than consider a marriage proposal from a zamindar family in Bihar." Not one to back down, Maitreyi didi angrily pointed out that Amma was herself married to someone from a landholding family in Bihar. Then she chided Amma for judging the young man without even having bothered to meet him. He was not, she said, what his family background might suggest.

I sat in the dining room trying to concentrate on my notes while noise of this wrangling continued to rise and fall from Amma's room. I was almost certain that this proposal could not be serious. These days, I was far more concerned about the departure of Professor Deodhar from Banasthali than I was about finding a husband—not least because, as I was painfully well aware, in the absence of a hefty dowry I was hardly the ideal bridal candidate. Despite myself, when I looked in the mirror, I still saw someone who was dark-skinned and too thin and wore glasses to read and paint.

True, I had had some suitors, mainly brothers or cousins of past and current girlfriends, who had sent messengers or notes to declare their admiration. Their interest had surprised me, and sometimes it made me feel flattered, but, rather than take it to heart, I had mostly felt annoyed by their attention.

Cinematic romance, I had come to understand, was a lie. Parks and gardens were spaces to cross quickly if you were alone, not places in which enraptured lovers break into song and dance. The movie paramour promises the sun and the moon, but I knew why movies always ended with the glorious wedding. I saw how the married lives of my friends consisted of the heat of cooking fires and the coldness of unrelenting domestic routine. Didi and Jijaji's sweet courtship had lasted only until the marriage, before solidifying into what seemed like a well-oiled business relationship between two partners working on different projects. If there was any love in the joylessness of Amma and Babu's relationship, it was very well hidden.

I often thought of Amma's conversation with Gandhiji about the need for marriage. If she had not given into the pressure of those she idolized, there would be no husband to insult her in front of her colleagues. No family obligations would have prevented her from pursuing her calling—her desire to fight for justice and equality and to stand up for ordinary people in the corridors of power. There would have been no daughters to worry about. Amma could have actually been happy.

Instead, although her high blood pressure seemed to be under control, I wistfully noticed the exhaustion set permanently in Amma's eyes. When Babu hadn't temporarily vanished, he clung to his regimented routine. The two of them continued on, like parallel tracks of a lumbering long-distance train, never meeting, never arriving, forever condemned to each other's company.

Much as part of me still longed to believe in romance, what I saw around me always brought me back to earth. Yet there I was, just a few months later, living out a scene from a movie. Although it hadn't been easy, Maitreyi didi had finally persuaded Amma to consider the match, and now I was talking to a charming young man in my parents' drawing room. His wide forehead, I noticed, was furrowed with gentle lines as he made hesitant small talk about the beauty of the walled city. He remarked on how close our home was to the LMB Hotel, where he was staying. His name was Bir Bahadur Prasad Sinha, but, with a boyish grin, he said that I could call him B.P.

This suggestion caught me off guard. I bent down to stroke Neelu's relaxed but attentive head, leaning against my leg, and to consider this delicate question. Although Amma was an exception in this regard, very rarely did wives address their husbands by name. To do so would be to acknowledge the existence of intimacy. Nor could I imagine using someone's name without adding *ji* or some other honorific. Even Amma appended *saheb* to Babu's surname—which, by coincidence, was also Sinha. After struggling for several long moments to balance the force of tradition with my urge to challenge convention, I decided simply to follow her example, despite the odd parallel. And so I explained that, in view of the ten-year age gap between us, the informality of "B.P." made me somewhat uncomfortable, and I would prefer to address him as "Sinha saheb." I tried hard to sound nonchalant, but my stomach was in knots and my throat drier than the Thar Desert.

Sinha saheb seemed to me even more attractive in person than in the photograph left behind by Maitreyi didi. He peppered his schoolbook Hindi with English words, which made him seem quite cosmopolitan. I gathered that, especially with the land reforms of the post-independence era, his formerly powerful zamindar family no longer had much land to lord over. An illustrious ancestor, Dewan Rai Bahadur Jai Prakash Lal, was once the chief minister of the Maharaja of Dumraon and was credited with establishing several public institutions in the Maharaja's name in the late nineteenth century. But, after the Maharaja died, the family fell out of favour with the royals. Their fortunes slowly dwindled, and their estate in Lahana was now limited to an orchard and a one-hundred-year-old mansion with a doorway big enough to allow an elephant to pass through.

Sinha saheb explained that he had three brothers, two older and one younger, as well as an older sister and a younger sister. Their father, Bindeshwari Prasad, had been his parents' eldest son and so claimed first rights to the ancestral property, but he was a rigid, domineering man and had managed the estate poorly. Sinha saheb's uncle, Gupteshwar Prasad—the first in the family to leave the ancestral home—had encouraged Sinha saheb to emerge from the circle of shadow in which his highly traditional father lived and had supported his education, first in Varanasi, then in Patna, and finally in Jamshedpur, at the Xavier Labour Relations Institute. Much to his father's disapproval, Sinha saheb had charted his own course, joining a major coal mining company in Dhanbad as a liaison officer. For the past several years, he had been successfully dodging the marital alliances proposed by concerned family members.

I wanted to ask why he was interested in me. Instead, my mouth formed a question about his views on women who aspire to professional careers. Sinha saheb did not miss a beat, reassuring me that the accident of his birth had not tied him to any antiquated social ideas about a woman's place. His family had yet to accept his quest for an equal partner rather than a compliant wife with a big dowry. That was one of the reasons why he would not let anyone else represent him. Maitreyi didi, I thought, had prepared him well.

Throughout our conversation, I was perched on the edge of my wicker chair, never comfortable leaning against its broad, rounded back. Neelu had parked himself protectively between me and the stranger. Sinha saheb sat on the adjacent divan, knees crossed, fingers interlocked above his top knee, a picture of poise. In order not to appear insolent, I made eye contact only when I spoke. As Sinha saheb talked in his deliberate way, my eyes mostly fixed on the fulcrum of his lean fingers. I compared their much lighter skin tone to the dark skin of my long fingers, half-hidden in my lap. I averted my eyes from this reminder of my darkness, glancing to his black penny loafers and his narrow pant leg with its sharp crease.

When he spoke of how much he enjoyed travelling, making new connections with people and places, rather than bearing the tedious burden of family obligations and social expectations, I looked up briefly, to agree with a quick nod. That was when I noticed the slight curve in his otherwise straight nose—from a football injury long ago, he explained, as a glint of pride made his eyes sparkle. His deep-set eyes were almond-shaped, so unlike my slightly hooded eyelids. His gentle reassuring gaze made my heart pound oddly faster. I dared not look at his lips.

For this awkward mutual interview, we had been left alone in the drawing room. Yet we were surrounded on all sides by human activity—the sound of people talking and walking, the muffled clatter of elaborate preparations in the kitchen, the clanking of the busy press on the floor below.

When I asked him about his university studies, Sinha saheb's response was short and matter-of-fact, but when he asked about my research topic I became animated, passionate, articulate, and confident. I was at home in this territory. Sinha saheb genuinely appeared to enjoy my verbosity, interrupting only briefly to acknowledge his recognition of a musical tradition or composer's name. I was pleasantly surprised by the extent of his familiarity with classical musical traditions.

Amma's footfall sounded particularly loud as she paused on the other side of the drawing room curtain before entering the room and asking us to join everyone in the dining room for some snacks.

Milky tea, infused with spices, accompanied my favourite winter sweets—almond *barfi,* sesame *gajak, gwarpatha laddu*—and spicy savouries freshly made by Mangi bai, including dal *kachori* and *moong pakori.* Didi, who had come to Jaipur especially for the occasion, graciously helped to serve food. This was the first marriage proposal for me that arrived at the stage of a face-to-face meeting. I wasn't sure whether anybody had expected things to progress this far, least of all me.

Babu had joined us in the dining room, but he sat quietly in a corner with his eyes closed, his back ramrod straight and his long arms resting in his lap. Maitreyi didi's husband, who had accompanied Sinha saheb from Dhanbad to make formal introductions, ate with admirable gusto, clearly enjoying the hospitality. Sinha saheb politely attempted to refuse endless offers of more food, while I self-consciously toyed with the lone sweet on my plate. Amma was not eating at all, just watching the proceedings with slightly furrowed brows.

When it was clear that no more food could be piled onto our guest's plate, Amma picked up her cup of tea. "Bhaiya, in my experience, marriage is the end of the aspirations of many gifted and educated girls in our society. My *bitiya* here has been working very hard to leave the prison of her parent's home. But I am not sure she knows what that freedom will look like."

I squirmed uncomfortably, embarrassed by Amma's frankness, and was thankful for Didi's interjection. "Our Rekha will be the first in the family to earn a doctorate. Our Amma is worried about any break in her education."

Sinha saheb assured us that travelling to Bombay from Dhanbad would be even easier than getting there from Jaipur, as the train service was better.

"My worry is not for the means," said Amma, "but for the will to continue."

Sinha saheb's next words made me stare at him. "If your daughter has the will, I will find a way." His face wore an earnest expression, unperturbed under Amma's gaze.

My heart jumped into my mouth. *Slow down you fool. Keep your head clear. Don't get so taken by this total stranger so quickly.*

Amma sounded unsure. "I raised my daughters to be self-reliant individuals and nurtured their many talents. But I must warn you, Rekha's knowledge of cooking and housekeeping is largely theoretical."

"I am looking for a life partner," Sinha saheb responded, "not a cook."

Didi hastily added a word about how quickly she had learned to supervise the bustling kitchen in her husband's home. I could attest to Didi's swift and thorough transformation into a domestic goddess. But I could not see that happening to me.

Amma looked equally unconvinced. "It is easy to be idealistic when you are young and independent. What about your family's expectations from a daughter-in-law?"

Sinha saheb solemnly declared his well-established status as the renegade son who lived his life on his own terms.

There were no more direct questions and answers. Curious and concerned, Jain saheb had joined the little party in the dining room. He had struck up an easy conversation with Maitreyi didi's husband, even drawing in Babu by asking him to explain the history of this or that in Jaipur. The inherent awkwardness of such a visit was gradually overtaken by an easy bonhomie, accompanied by rounds of tea until it was time for supper. I held back on my own involvement in the conversations, my heart intent on the moments when Sinha saheb spoke a few short, polite sentences.

Following this visit, Maitreyi didi and her husband went to Dhanbad to inspect Sinha saheb's house and to meet his uncle Gupteshwar and his family. When she phoned us afterwards, she could not stop talking about the warmth and courteousness with which they had been received. After hearing an account of his nephew's meeting with me, accompanied by photographs of the prospective bride, Gupteshwar chacha had approved the match. He had also promised to speak to his older brother, Sinha saheb's father, about the wedding.

It thus came as no surprise to us when, within two weeks of Maitreyi didi's phone call, a letter arrived for Babu from Sinha saheb's father. However, the contents of the letter were utterly unexpected: the writer formally introduced himself as the groom's father, described the family's high social standing and Sinha saheb's advanced qualifications, and then included a long list of goods that he, as the head of the family, considered worthy of the proposed matrimonial alliance. Of course, no mention was made of the word "dowry." Rather, the quantities of jewellery and other valuables intended for the groom and his family were merely gifts that would earn honour for the bride and the family of her birth.

"*What were you thinking?*" Babu angrily threw the letter toward Amma and stormed out of the house. Amma did not resist when I took the letter from her. As I read it, I became more livid with each line.

Amma looked puzzled. "I have never been such a poor judge of character. The young man sounded so earnest and honest about his progressive views. How could he possibly think that gold and silver can measure a person's worth?"

A short while later, she was on the phone with Maitreyi didi, reading the letter aloud to her. Maitreyi didi was convinced that Sinha saheb could not possibly know anything about the letter, but Amma dismissed her protests and told her to call the whole thing off.

I fixed my eyes on the floor, trying to contain a burning mixture of incandescent anger and inconsolable grief. With a deep sigh, Amma put a calming hand on my head. "He seemed so perfect for my bright little girl."

I did not want Amma to see my angry tears. "Maybe it's for the best, Amma."

"Maybe," Amma said uncertainly. Not knowing what else to do, we retreated into our lonely rooms, hoping to find sanctuary of some sort in a world of books—inanimate objects, incapable of wounding us.

I jumped out of bed as the shrill ringing of the phone reverberated through the silent house. It was five in the morning. A phone call at such a time surely meant bad news.

"Mr. Sinha, calling from Patna," the operator announced. My anger pumped blood into my ears. I was preparing to give him a furious lecture before slamming the phone down on him. But all I could manage was a throaty "Hello."

My pulse quickened at the sound of his voice. "Surekhaji, please listen—give me a moment to explain. Maitreyi didi phoned me about the letter your parents received from my father. I had no idea he had sent it. I drove all night to see him. I wrote him a blank cheque, and I told him he could use it to buy whatever he wants. I can promise you that this will be the end of it. There will be no demands for dowry from my family."

Amma was standing in the doorway of her room looking at me quizzically. Now she took the phone out of my unsteady hand with a stern "Who's this?" She listened to Sinha saheb intently for the next few minutes, then ended the call with a brief but pointed account of the pain his father's letter had caused, especially to me. It had, she said, revealed an unpleasant truth about the family into which her daughter would be marrying.

She stared at the phone for a while after the call was disconnected, then said to no one in particular, "We will see how this goes."

It took several more phone calls, both from Sinha saheb and from Gupteshwar chacha, to convince Amma that Sinha saheb was as pained by his father's attitudes as we were and that he would do everything in his power to shield me from any further distress. Her confidence more than restored, Amma happily declared that Sinha saheb was indeed "solid gold." And I was happy to agree. Babu did not object to the proposed marriage. Tears filled my eyes when he proclaimed his faith in his daughter's ability to handle whatever came her way.

Our wedding date was set for the day after my twenty-fourth birthday, less than five months away.

I was discovering new meanings in songs from old movies. Verses woven around the sweet pangs of separation and longing felt like they were written for me. A doting man drove well over seven hundred miles just to see me briefly. Sinha saheb brought a Philips reel-to-reel tape recorder as a gift on his visit in the New Year. It had state-of-the-art controls to improve the quality of recording; the sound quality was better than I had ever heard from such a small machine. He taught me to operate the tape recorder by asking me to sing. He said he wanted to keep a recording of my songs to fill his lonely evenings with, until we were together.

In deference to Amma's wishes we spent most of his short visit in the drawing room, where he asked me to sing or to tell him about the progress I was making with my research. He was a man of few words, so I happily did most of the talking, trying with my lively chatter to drown my thudding heart. Sinha saheb had won over every member of the household except for pouty Neelu. He stopped growling at Sinha saheb after I scolded him, but he physically wedged himself between us whenever we are alone.

I was the last one of my friends to be engaged to be married. Most had been married long since; some were already rearing multiple children. Our lives barely intersected except for boisterous social occasions where we met warmly, briefly. The only exception was my friend Karuna, who was also enrolled in a doctoral program.

Since her own marriage, Karuna had been dividing her time between her parental house in Jaipur and her husband's house in Delhi. Our long visits had been replaced by long phone calls and letters, but our bond remained the same. Since she was spending more time in Jaipur at present, trying to finish her dissertation during her first pregnancy, Amma enlisted her to chaperone us should Sinha saheb wish to plan a movie or dinner date some evening.

But Sinha saheb had other ideas. He asked my permission and help to plan an excursion, affectionately insisting that Amma and Babu accompany us. Babu's outings were never social events, so he refused our request resolutely and rather rudely, as I thought he would. Amma, however, gave in to my entreaties with mild amusement. So we went for a picnic in the Nahargarh Fort Hills, with Amma, Karuna, Jain saheb, Mangi bai, and Shafiji.

After a vigorous walk around in the sprawling fort, we settled in the mild winter sun near the edge of the massive *baoli,* or stepwell. Amma asked me to sing a *bhajan.* Then Karuna and Sinha saheb took turns asking me to sing songs from Hindi films. Sinha saheb made appropriately sedate requests for classical songs, but, with a mischievous twinkle in her eye, Karuna chose romantic songs laced with seductive innuendo.

I was spared further embarrassment by the appearance of Mangi bai's potato-stuffed parathas and spicy mango pickle, complemented by hot tea in flasks and sweets from the market. After our delicious meal, Jain saheb and Shafiji animatedly acquainted Sinha saheb with the landmarks of Jaipur, visible from the lofty heights of our picnic spot. Amma was watching Sinha saheb with an approving smile. Karuna tugged at my braid playfully. "You are actually enjoying this family-friendly style of romance!"

I stuck my tongue out at her, but my heart did not stop singing.

My last field trip to Nathdwara felt like an auspicious ending. It was spring, and the most colourful festival of the Hindu calendar, Holi, was celebrated for a whole month in the temple town. The white marble temples, with statues clad in white silk and many attendees in snowy-white clothing, bore unmistakable marks of the celebration of Krishna's mischievous side. Clouds of colourful *gulal,* a powder made from fragrant dried flowers, sandalwood, and ground roots, were flung at devotees during the festival, speckling everything in joyful shades of pink, yellow, and green. I recorded two full days of narrative songs and *kirtans* rendered in classical ragas, celebrating the various moods and activities of Krishna, eight times a day.

Armed with these treasures, I then returned to Jaipur to work on the draft of my dissertation. I locked my room to shut out the world, but the distraction was within. It was hard to stay focused on my work, to not give in to daydreaming. I would wait for Sinha saheb's phone calls, and then I would think about our conversations long after we had stopped talking. These sometimes scratchy long-distance calls came frequently, and our conversations were often filled with long companionable silences and sighs. I protested sometimes that he need not make these expensive calls so regularly, while secretly wishing that he would call every day.

Meanwhile, Amma and Shafiji embarked on the wedding preparations. As expected, Babu remained disinterested. Sinha saheb had requested a small and simple celebration without any dowry. Since final exams would be finished by mid-April, the trustees of Amma's school had given her permission to use the school building for the wedding and for guest accommodations as well. The catering, decorations, and music arrangements were the same as for Didi's wedding, but my trousseau was larger, since both Amma and Didi were contributing to it.

Despite all these distractions, I managed to finish writing the first complete draft of my dissertation: three hundred pages of description and analysis in eight chapters. After I posted the bulky tome to Professor Deodhar's address in Bombay, it hit me hard that the life I had known so far was about to change irrevocably. I had not yet completed my doctorate. I still had to navigate the process of transferring my degree program to the University of Rajasthan and finding a new supervisor there. But Professor Deodhar had made good on his promise to oversee my fieldwork, and that was the heart of my dissertation, which was now awaiting his feedback. It could take several months, he had said on the phone. I was disappointed at first, but then I realized that it might be for the best. I was leaving my whole world behind for a total stranger, and I would need time to adjust to living with a husband.

That was when Amma found me sitting in the dusty library on the terrace, crying. She kissed my forehead, her tears mingling with mine.

"You will be fine," she kept repeating, as the dusk gave way to darkness. "We will be fine."

The stars were exceptionally bright on this moonless night. Amma pointed to the *saptarsi* constellation, the seven sages in the sky, guardians of eternal knowledge. "Whenever I will see them in the sky, I will believe that my sweet daughter is watching the same corner of the sky at that very moment." I held my mother's hand and promised to return to Jaipur as soon as I could.

Amma regained her pragmatic composure. "Of course not! You need to build your new life, a new home with a loving and wise man. I can see that he sees you for who you are, adores you for who you are. I am so proud of you both. I have never been happier."

We stared into the dark bowl of stars that blinked away above our heads. Amma mused, "What's seven hundred miles? They are sending missions to the moon and to Mars. Surely we can manage this short distance."

My heart had two halves, one as sad as the other one was happy.

DHANBAD, 1970

I have few clear memories of the days just before the wedding. All I remember is being tired, exuberant, poised, nervous, happy, and sad, all at the same time. Once again, out-of-town guests started arriving days in advance, but Didi and Jijaji were there to take over much of Amma's burden of welcoming and looking after visitors. Two days before the wedding we moved to the school building, for complete immersion in elaborate rituals and raucous celebrations.

My body was painted with turmeric paste, and my hands and feet were adorned with henna. I had not slept much over the past several days, uncomfortable with all this attention being directed at me. The piercing music of the *shehnai* floated above a constant buzz of noise—men and women talking, laughing, singing, children running around. The fragrance of essential oils that permeated people's clothing mingled with the sweet scent of the floral canopy over the wedding fires, both dizzily competing with heady aromas that wafted in from the kitchen.

I vaguely remember being dressed up from head to toe, the arrival of the small procession of Sinha saheb's family and a few of their friends that was preceded by a brass band, the long parade of wedding guests to bless the bride and groom, the lengthy wedding ceremony in front of the sacred fire, the teary farewell from Amma and Didi, getting whisked away in a white Ambassador that was heavily laden with floral garlands and a canopy of suitcases on its roof, and the absence of Babu toward the end.

Two of Sinha saheb's oldest nephews—Kunwar and Anil—sat in the front seat next to the driver. Sinha saheb sat in the back, between his younger sister and me. I held his hand and battled with sleep most of the way to Agra, our first night's stop. There we were received with much warmth by Hari mama and Suman mami. The affectionate attention of everyone ruled out any possibility of privacy, but I was not complaining. I was happy with stolen glances, meaningful smiles, and spine-tingling accidental contact.

We made the obligatory trip to the Taj Mahal, with the whole entourage. The blistering heat of the white marble flooring made me ever so thankful that Didi, who had taken charge of my packing, had thought to include lightweight *kota-doria* and chiffon saris along with the heavy silk and brocade ones that I was expected to wear for the next several weeks.

By virtue of my marriage, I had earned a new series of relational epithets: one nephew called me *mami,* the other called me *chachi,* and my sister-in-law—Sinha saheb's younger sister—called me *bhabhi.* She was youngest of the six children, but she was a couple of years older than me and already a mother of four.

With an endearing intimacy, Sinha saheb addressed me as "Rekhuji," but I still couldn't find an adequate equivalent for him. Some of his family called him "Munmun," but this seemed too childish for a grown man. I tried out a number of variations on his name, but my tongue insisted on stumbling over any term that did not contain a respectful suffix. So, in the end, I decided that I would just continue to call him "Sinha saheb," even when we were speaking to each other privately.

We drove from Agra to Kanpur the next day. A journey of well under two hundred miles took nearly the whole day, our progress slowed by narrow roads that shrank into rugged paths through the twisting ravines of the Chambal badlands, home to notorious bands of dacoits. Our otherwise alert driver did his best not to be distracted by the the two nephews in the front seat, who promptly invented a new game: spotting possible dacoit dens.

Finally, just before suppertime, we arrived in Kanpur, where Sinha saheb's second eldest brother lived. He and his wife, Prabha didi, had been at the wedding but had returned to Kanpur ahead of us by train. Now she lovingly welcomed me into their home and on the next day replaced Anil, their son, in the car. Sinha saheb moved to the front seat to sit with his older sister's son, Kunwar, while I shared the back with his youngest sister and Prabha didi, who liked to talk and giggle all the time, telling us jokes, asking us riddles, and generally being happy.

We reached Varanasi the next evening, just in time to witness the reverberation of hundreds of temple bells and conch shells in prayer along the mighty Ganga River. One of Sinha saheb's college friends, Vijay bhaiya, was our host for the night. He lived with his wife and two young children in a brand new house, still surrounded by construction. Aside from my own, this was one of the few non-multi-generational households that I had encountered, and their home seemed remarkably spacious. There was no need to convert the drawing room into a dormitory-style guest bedroom or to hastily empty out a room for the newlyweds; instead, there were three whole spare rooms for our travelling party.

After supper, as everyone was getting ready to retire for the night, Vijay bhaiya broke out a celebratory bottle of scotch, fixed a drink for Sinha saheb, and teasingly invited me to join them. I suddenly realized that I had neglected to inquire about this particular detail. I turned to my husband and asked, "You drink?"

"Only socially," said Sinha saheb.

Vijay bhaiya tried to make light of the situation. "Come on, *bhabhi*, my brother here is a modern man. We need to move with the times."

"All right then," I replied, as I reached for the drink he had made for Sinha saheb.

Vijay bhaiya was startled. "Actually," he said, "I was just joking."

"But why?" I asked. "Do you have different standards for modern men and women?"

Sinha saheb laughed. "What did I tell you, Vijay? Don't just stand there. Mix her a drink."

Vijay bhaiya handed me a tall glass of soda with a shot of whisky in it and did not take his eyes off me until I took a sip of the foul-smelling concoction, which I managed to do without sputtering. I could feel the cool liquid trace a warm path down my throat as I sat sedately next to Sinha saheb. He looked triumphant but whispered in my ear, "I promise—I hardly ever drink, and only to keep a friend company."

Sinha saheb emptied his glass slowly. But when Vijay bhaiya filled it a second time, he nursed his drink for the remainder of the evening. A few sips of my own drink later, I was self-consciously checking to see whether my hands were steady—so far, so good. I could not bear to think what Amma or Babu would have to say about our intemperate ways.

The two friends had been reminiscing about their college days, and soon the conversation turned to music. Sinha saheb asked me to sing his favourite *khyal*. I protested that it was too late, and half the people in the house were already in bed. In response, Vijay bhaiya gathered the half of the household who were not yet in bed and also pulled out a set of tabla to accompany my singing. After the classical song that Sinha saheb had requested, I chose popular movie songs that everyone could join in on—except my dear husband. He could not hold a tune in a bucket; even his clapping was arrhythmic. But his eyes were fixed on me, and he did not stop smiling, which made me blush, especially when I sang *Baiyan na dharo o balma,* "Let go of my arm, my darling," in which, as darkness gathers, a woman rather feebly protests when the man she loves tries to prevent her from returning home. As I sang, the room fell still. The music went on until far into the night, and we got only a few hours of sleep before continuing our journey east.

Leaving the bustling banks of Varanasi, we crossed an unbroken series of fertile farms that framed small clusters of straw huts or, sometimes, brick houses. It was lush and green with fields and orchards as far as you could see. I realized how much I had missed these tall, dense, and ancient trees of the east. The next leg of our journey took us to Lahana, Sinha saheb's ancestral village, a little southwest of the point where the graceful Ganga meets the temperamental Son River.

Despite my familiarity with Maithili, I struggled to understand Bhojpuri, the language spoken in western Bihar. The only thing I knew about Bhojpuri was the legend of Lorik and Chanda, a popular folk story about an Ahir warrior, Lorik, who leaves his first wife to elope with a wealthy landlord's beautiful daughter, Chanda. I had read the Hindavi version, *Chandayan*, written by the fourteenth-century Sufi poet Mulla Da'ud, which I had found in Amma and Babu's eclectic collection of books. In Mulla Da'ud's telling, the erotic entanglement of a man and two women was interpreted to represent the mystical relationship between God, the Sufi, and the world. But my literary knowledge was of no use when it came to deciphering Bhojpuri itself.

After driving several miles along what was essentially a path for bullock carts and foot traffic, our bumpy journey finally ended in front of a long wall broken by an imposing gateway. Sinha saheb's ancestral home sat haughtily on a height of land amidst a sea of farms and orchards dotted with straw huts. Various members of his family had gathered there to welcome the newlyweds, and an even larger group of curious onlookers crowded around the entranceway.

Before we had set out from Varanasi, Prabha didi had ensured that I was wearing an appropriately heavy silk sari and had warned me to keep my head and face demurely covered when I met the elders of the family for the first time. Now, as I tried to pull the *pallu* of the sari away from my eyes so that I could take in the place and the people I was here to meet, Prabha didi kept yanking it forward to cover my face. I whispered to her, "How will I see?"

Guiding me by hand, Prabha didi whispered back, "You can see all you want after the welcoming rituals are over."

A group of women, led by Sinha saheb's mother, took turns blessing Sinha saheb and me by placing pinches of *sindoor* in my hair parting and sandalwood *tilaka* markings on his forehead. Before I crossed the threshold, a young woman asked me to knock little pots of grain inward, to ensure that the new addition to the family would bring Lakshmi's blessings of prosperity on the household. Then we passed through the gateway into a large courtyard. A group of women from the nearby village, young and old, sat in a corner of the courtyard, playing the *dholak* drum and singing songs that—as far as I could tell—described Sita's wedding to Ram.

I was led to a dimly lit room to sit in front of idols of the family deities. A silver container of *sindoor* was thrust into my hands, and my mother-in-law said to me, "Start with a *chutki* and *pranam* to Prabha. She is the eldest of your sisters-in-law present." I wondered for a moment what the significance might be of pinching an elder sister-in-law before touching her feet in respect. Prabha didi sat in front of me with her head slightly bent and her hands folded in her lap. An impatient female voice from behind urged me, "Do *chutki*." So I dutifully but delicately pinched the flesh on Prabha didi's arm before touching her feet, making her burst into a laughter that brought tears to her eyes.

I was confused and a bit alarmed at the note of grumbling disapproval I heard from the crowd behind me. It took a long minute for Prabha didi's laughter to give way to a sentence. "The new *bahuria* does not understand Bhojpuri."

"But I spoke to her in Hindi, didn't I?" My mother-in-law replied rather indignantly.

"Yes, ma, but *chutki* means 'pinching' in Hindi, not a dab of *sindoor* as you meant."

A stately woman pushed her way to the front of the crowd. "Let's get this done with. Welcome to the family, Rekha. I am Munmun's *chachiji*. Munmun has told me all about you and your family. You can put *sindoor* on my head or pinch my arm, I don't mind. But do be sure not to pinch the rest of the women waiting here." I was grateful for her good humour, but my hand trembled when I heard a disembodied female voice from the rear of the room complain: "Has her mother taught her nothing?"

I fought the urge to unleash a rousing defence of my upbringing without religious rituals, in this alien world of unfamiliar people. It helped to feel the protective pressure of my mother-in-law's arm on my shoulder and to hear Chachiji's scolding. "*Chup karo!* We are also her mothers and sisters now. She will learn with time." Resentfully, I listened to a wise voice in my head telling me to keep quiet as well, for now.

Several *chutki*s and *pranam*s later, I was led back into the courtyard to sit on a divan next to Sinha saheb. We played a series of ritual games that were supposed to predict our future, the dominant one in the relationship, and the number of children we were likely to have.

Most of my numerous cousins-in-law and sisters-in-laws were older than I was; many had teenage children. The teenagers were all solidly on my team, encouraging me to win the little games and cheering loudly when I did. Sinha saheb was not even competing, letting me win game after game.

Switching to Bhojpuri appeared to transform Sinha saheb into a talkative person, full of sass, reveling in his popularity among his siblings and cousins, flirting with me openly. I was thankful for the privacy offered by my *pallu* in these awkward moments.

The singing ladies and their drums went at it for hours. An elaborate feast had been organized for the family as well as for visiting villagers, who would keep arriving in small waves until halfway through the night. There was a huge array of vegetable dishes, variously sautéed, fried, gravied, and mashed, served with fragrant basmati rice and enormous flaky puris. But there were also many meat dishes.

Chachiji assured me that the main kitchen was strictly vegetarian and that meat was cooked in a separate outdoor kitchen. As she explained, many of the family members refused to eat meat on specific days each month, in honour of various deities. With this assurance, I was handed a plate laden with more food than I could possibly hope to eat, a display of bounty that reminded me of my Bhagalpur visits.

This time Sinha saheb came to my rescue, waving off his own heaped-up plate, choosing to share the food on mine, and forgoing the meat dishes. He was also very effective in warding off the pressure to accept additional servings, as his word appeared to carry a lot of weight in this household.

After supper, the young nieces and nephews brought out the *dholak* and harmonium for a session of *antakshari*, the same singing game I had enjoyed with my cousin Suresh so many years ago. Two teams were formed, and nearly all the young ones joined my team. Each team had to sing a full verse of a song. The last syllable in the verse had be the same as the first syllable in the next song, and the team that could not come up with a song beginning with the right syllable lost points. The game went on and on, in the light of kerosene lamps, our voices rising into the starry night.

It was hardly a fair fight. The other team, made up of older women and a few men, could not hope to match the extensive repertoire of film songs that a group of young people jointly possessed. Even after our team allowed them to include songs that none of us could recognize, some of which we suspected they made up on the spot, they lost so many points that we stopped counting after a while. Their resounding defeat did not weaken their enjoyment of the game, nor did it deter the young ones from teasing them incessantly. The game ended only when some of the non-playing older relatives started to snore on distant cots in the courtyard.

In the morning, before we left on the final leg of our journey to Dhanbad, I finally had a chance to see my husband's ancestral home. It was majestic, at least twice the size of the house in Bhagalpur, but in a sorry state of disrepair. For the occasion of our visit, nearly fifty members of family had gathered at the house, but only one of Sinha saheb's four uncles actually lived there, and only intermittently, to ensure minimal upkeep. There was a well in one of the courtyards but no running water or reliable supply of electricity in this remote rural area. The main courtyard was surrounded by several large rooms with vaulted ceilings, on two floors. But this was the only part of the house that still stood strong. Two additional courtyards attached to the building were in various stages of crumbling decay.

Even in the morning, the heat was intense, and I inwardly groaned at the prospect of draping myself in yards of heavy silk brocade. Sensing my plight, Sinha saheb suggested that I choose between my usual *salwar-kamiz* or a chiffon sari. Under the circumstances, a sari seemed more appropriate, and, in any case, I wanted to get more comfortable with wearing one. So, for our departure, I chose an olive green georgette

sari with a thin gold border running its length, one of Didi's many taste-
ful gifts.

Sinha saheb made me pose for pictures all around the house, leaning
against an elaborately carved door frame, sitting on a step in the courtyard against a lotus pillar, and standing in a large window on the second
floor adjacent to the imposing elephant gate. One of the young nieces
complimented me on my poise, comparing me to the film star Vaijayanti
Mala. I was not sure how to react, unused as I was to such compliments.

There was another round of farewell rituals to send us off, and then
Sinha saheb and I were the first to leave the ancestral house. The driver
had to fight off a milling crowd of onlookers from the village, stick-thin
children in raggedy clothes, shrivelled old men and women, the occasional
young woman with a baby on her hip. Most able-bodied people were
already working in the fields that spread as far as the eye could see. As we
drove away, the moss-covered house gradually dissolved into the expanse
of surrounding greenery.

Crossing through paddy fields and over rivers, we entered the heart
of the great coal belt of eastern India. The rich coal reserves had brought
major railway lines to the area, followed by large-scale industry, including coal processing plants and steelworks. Dhanbad had grown rapidly
from a mining town into the coal capital of the region, a modern city
bustling with commerical activity. Outside the city lay vast swathes of
lacerated landscape, occasionally interrupted by swift rivers, placid lakes,
and clumps of deciduous forest. All this destruction, I thought, in the
name of industrial progress.

Our house was a modern bungalow surrounded by a neat little garden. It
was situated in one of the newer "Officers' Colonies," a cluster of similar
bungalows huddled together, edging out lush farms and thickets of tall
trees. A burly older man guarded our front gate, a rifle on his shoulder.
Sinha saheb assured me that Man Singhji, the sentry, had the softest heart
and that the rifle was just a deterrent.

"Deterrent against what?" I asked in alarm. But we were interrupted by an eager young man with a perpetual grin jostling with the gardener to unload the suitcases tied on the roof of the car. Nandkishor was the domestic helper, about sixteen years old—who, I was pleased to discover, spoke Maithili, a language more familiar to me than Bhojpuri. While he ran about to serve us tea and snacks, Sinha saheb tried to explain the lay of the land to me.

I learned that a network of trade unions, labour contractors, and moneylenders ran the many legal and illegal coal mining operations in the area. As liaison officer, Sinha saheb's job was to mediate among the miners employed by his company, the brutal moneylenders to whom they were indebted, and various trade union leaders and politicians who were vying for control and intent on expanding their power. His day started late, he explained, just before the first shift of miners returned from work, their bodies tired and their ragged pockets warmed by the day's pay. Between the thugs hired by the moneylenders, who forcibly extracted exorbitant interest rates, and the toddy sellers who set up shop at strategic locations, little money stayed in the hands of the mineworkers for even the most basic necessities. This led to more indebtedness, much drunkenness, and sporadic violence. In addition, there were often violent clashes between ambitious union leaders, in which the mineworkers served as cannon fodder.

"But unions are meant to protect worker's rights," I protested.

Sinha saheb shook his head. In the coal belt, many union leaders were thugs, in the pay of political masters. To retain their control, they would kill, maim, kidnap, or torture. But, he reassured me, they left you alone if they thought you were a bigger scoundrel or had a larger gun.

I was appalled. "So are you a bigger scoundrel?" I asked, not certain I wanted to know.

Sinha saheb smiled mischievously. "The day they find out the answer to that question will likely be my last. As for you, my nightingale, I'll let you decide for yourself."

Then he went on to explain that, in this very traditional society, respect was born of fear. In order to do his job, he needed to make it crystal clear to company mineworkers that he was their superior, and this meant treating them at all times as his inferiors—even, if need be, as scum. He could not afford to allow that hard line of separation to soften: doing so would place him in an impossible position. The truth was irrelevant, he said. If he expected to have any authority, he had no choice but to behave like a heartless brute.

I was reeling from these revelations when a troupe of about a dozen women abruptly descended on the house. These were wives of colliery executives, bearing gifts to welcome me to the neighbourhood. A woman called Mrs. Rai made introductions. Everyone was "Mrs. So-and-so," but I insisted that they call me Surekha.

A woman wearing bright red lipstick teased Sinha saheb about losing his most-eligible-bachelor-of-the-company status. A fleshy arm covered in gold bracelets helpfully handed me a roster of card parties, club parties, *chaat* parties, and picnic parties. A bouffant-haired head leaned close to my ear, instructing me to keep my jewellery in a bank locker and never to go out alone with only the driver in the car.

I was feeling sick to my stomach. Sinha saheb noticed my discomfort and rather rudely dismissed the gaggle of ladies. They dispersed as noisily as they had arrived, their sudden departure accentuating the quietness of the house. Sinha saheb held my hand to guide me to a large but sparsely furnished bedroom and suggested that I get some rest while Nandkishor made supper and he went to his office to check on some work.

I woke up with a start just as the high ceiling above the bed started to cave in on me. I had barely finished feeling grateful to be released from my nightmare when the entire bed shuddered. I jumped out of it and cleared the several yards to the door in two leaps. Nandkishor's startled face peered out from the kitchen door, "Memsaheb, did you feel the *bhuchaal*—the faltering step of mother earth?"

I sighed with relief. Sinha saheb had warned me to expect periodic tremors, caused by the depth of the mining activity in the region. My composure returning, I gave Nandkishor a smile and asked him to call me "didi." Then I entered the kitchen to inspect his supper preparations. I liked the small but tidy kitchen with counters and cupboards, although I noted the absence of anything other than a gas fire for cooking—no earthy charcoal or smoky wood to add additional flavours to the food.

Proudly, Nandkishor displayed the variety of dishes lined up on the kitchen counter. He had made a curry of peas and paneer with gravy and a platter of fried okra. My favourite yellow *moong* lentil was flavoured with fresh coriander from the garden, and the fragrance of basmati rice was barely contained by the steel lid on the brass pot. Another pot held a cluster of *gulab jamun* floating delectably in saffron-infused syrup. Sinha saheb had remembered my favourite foods and had instructed Nandkishor not to cook any meat. I was impressed, but I also felt a touch of guilt for obliging my husband to abstain from meat.

The dough was kneaded and covered, and Nandkishor was ready to make piping hot rotis as soon as we were seated at the table. But it was past seven and Sinha saheb was not yet home. Although I told him that he could return to his quarters in the back of the house, Nandkishor insisted on sitting in a corner of the kitchen to wait so that he would be ready to serve hot food whenever Sinha saheb arrived.

I walked around the quiet house, gazing at the clean but bare walls along the passageway, the bare stone floors everywhere, and the two empty bedrooms. The living room and main bedroom were the only furnished parts of the house, obviously the abode of a bachelor who came home only to rest. I tried to shake off a sense of isolation and loneliness by reminding myself of the impending visits of Maitreyi didi and sundry relatives. I had a harder time trying to referee the battle between hunger and fatigue.

A gentle caress on my head woke me up with a fright. Then I smelled his musk cologne. He had returned from the office after nine o'clock to find me sleeping in a chair at the dining table and Nandkishor curled up on the kitchen floor. We did not talk much over the meal. I pointed out that we needed a lot of things for the house to host the many guests we are expecting. Sinha saheb told me to make a list but also said that the guests would have to wait. We were going to Nepal for our own holiday, just the two of us.

I was shocked by this announcement. There was so much to do—unpacking, setting up the house. And what of all the people who had already made plans to visit us? "*Sab ho jayega*," Sinha saheb replied. "All will get done." I just didn't know how. But my anxieties were swiftly overtaken by the sweet excitement of visiting a new place with my new husband.

The next morning we were on the train to Calcutta and then aboard a flight to Kathmandu. It was the first time I had ever flown, as well as my first trip to another country. Sinha saheb said that most of his trips to Nepal were made by road, through Raxaul, often to spend a weekend away from work, but this had to be a special trip.

We spent an entire week in Kathmandu—the city named for the wooden temple, built without using any metal nails or supports. Philosophically, it is sometimes hard to tell where Hinduism ends and Buddhism begins, and in Nepal this overlap was especially evident. We devoted a day to exploring Durbar Square, with its numerous stupas, temples, and palaces, some of which dated back to rule of the Licchavi dynasty in Nepal. On a balmy morning, we visited the sprawling Pasupatinath temple complex, my unbelieving self thanking the gods for these new beginnings and silently praying that their outcome would be happy. We spent an afternoon among the throngs of visitors to the towering Boudhanath stupa, collectively inhaling the fragrant blessings of incense and prayer flowers.

Early one morning, we left for the long trek to the Swayambhunath complex of stupas and shrines. Climbing 365 steep steps led to to a large white dome that represents the world, being watched over by the compassionate eyes of the Buddha. The stupa sat on a green hill overlooking the Kathmandu valley below, surrounded by the Himalayan range in the distance. We spent most of the day exploring the otherworldly beauty of this place, absorbing the unbroken history and sacredness of the space, and being entertained by the pert monkeys that abound in the area.

Every evening we returned to our hotel by the river to recharge for the next adventure. Our room had a gorgeous view of the snowy peaks of the Himalayas, which were never too far from us in Kathmandu. I was touched by Sinha saheb's thoughtfulness in finding this hotel. The family-run establishment was superbly located and tastefully appointed, and it also specialized in incredible vegetarian food. Most evenings, we had supper overlooking the river or on sunset boat cruises.

One exceptionally lazy morning we had breakfast on the cruise boat. We had made friends with another newlywed couple from Calcutta who joined our table on the upper deck. The other new bride was appropriately clad in an ornate silk sari and a small ton of jewellery, the bright red bangles on her wrists nicely complementing the flame-red *sindoor* in her hair parting and her scarlet lipstick. In my case, the only signs of my newlywed status were the burgundy henna patterns still staining the palms of my hands, a vermillion *bindi* on my forehead, and a gold *mangala sutra* around my neck. Perhaps I seemed underdressed in my simple khadi *salwar-kamiz* outfit, but, if so, it didn't bother me.

The Bengali man suggested that, as the only vegetarian in the group, I needed to start to widen the horizon of my palate, perhaps beginning with eggs for breakfast. My polite declining invited his scornful reminder of the vast array of tastes and textures I was missing out on. So I gave the table a lecture on the variety of vegetarian cuisine that I had encountered in my travels around the country. The young man dismissed my spirited sermon and ordered poached eggs for the table. His rudeness drove me to channel Amma, expounding on the Gandhian reasons for vegetarianism.

Before long, the waiter approached our table with a tray perched precariously above his shoulder. He tried to wedge himself in a corner behind the young woman, but just as he began to serve us the boat made the slightest of lurches, and a plate of toast and poached egg flew off his tray into the fast-flowing river. Stopping mid-sentence, I witnessed the scene with wide-mouthed wonder as Sinha saheb let out a guffaw. Sinha saheb merrily accepted his plate and asked the waiter to get me a menu.

Our new friend was no longer very friendly, pouting through the remainder of breakfast. His timid wife tried desperately to placate him. I ignored him over my spicy potato-stuffed paratha and freshly churned butter. Sinha saheb's adoring gaze hardly ever left my face, making me squirm and beam simultaneously.

I hadn't been feeling very well for the past couple of days. I thought our incessant travelling in the humid heat was taking its toll, making me weak and nauseated. Nevertheless, within two days of returning from Kathmandu, we were expecting our first guests. I had very little time to furnish the two empty rooms in the house to convert them into comfortable guest bedrooms.

The young driver, Mauji Singh, was a very polite Nepali, who spoke halting Hindi interspersed with words from too many dialects that I did not understand. His open face betrayed no impatience as I tried to decipher the message that he had returned after dropping Sinha saheb at his office to take me and Nandkishor to the market. We spent the better part of the day buying fabric, furniture, and provisions for the house, Mauji Singh and Nandkishor watchfully not letting me out of their sight.

I was impressed with the variety of goods available in this small town, some from faraway Europe and America. Still recovering from its colonial experiences, India restricted imports from other countries; however, landlocked Nepal had far fewer restrictions on imports of all kinds. So it was not surprising to see some of those imported goods illegally making their way into India, particularly in areas relatively close to the border with Nepal.

Mining also made Dhanbad very cosmopolitan for its size. The numerous private coal mining companies were owned and operated by people from all over the country, while the mineworkers themselves hailed from various tribes and villages in the region. This diversity was reflected in the assortment of foods and textiles. To my delight, I found the most exquisite rolls of fine *jamdani* muslin, from Bengal, a weave that uses an extra weft of thicker cotton yarn to produce floral and geometric patterns.

The next day, while Nandkishor was setting things up and making sweet and savoury snacks that could easily be stored, I sewed curtains for the whole house. Despite Sinha saheb's protests about my working so hard, I kept at it until I finished, late at night.

Maitreyi didi was our first guest, accompanied by her husband and their young daughter and son. Armed with baskets of Nandkishor's sumptuous sweet and savoury dry dishes, we had a lovely picnic at the nearby Bhatinda Falls. While the children frolicked in the water and her husband struck up a conversation with Mauji Singh about the politics of the day, Maitreyi didi and I reminisced about the few holidays we had spent together growing up and the prospect of being able to see each other more often.

Maitreyi didi was very proud to be the mediator for our marriage and had nothing but high praise for Sinha saheb. Even when, two days in a row, word arrived to go ahead with our supper as he would be late getting home from the office, Maitreyi didi used his absence as an opportunity to expound on the importance of his work and on what a good job he was doing. Long after everyone else had eaten, Sinha saheb returned home to his very hungry wife and dutiful cook. Maitreyi didi stayed up to keep us company, inadvertently becoming a buffer against my rising annoyance with Sinha saheb's long office hours.

Sensing my displeasure, Sinha saheb came home for an early supper not long after Maitreyi didi and her family left. That same night, we were woken up around two by a group of men who were arguing loudly with Man Singhji at the front gate. From the window of our darkened room, I could see their well-oiled lances gleaming in the flame of torches.

Sinha saheb dressed in a flash, giving me strict instructions not to step outside the house or even to switch on the lights. My heart in my mouth, I watched through the window as he walked to the gate and stepped outside, while Man Singhji trained his rifle on the group. By then, Mauji Singh and Nandkishor had also arrived at the gate and were standing close behind Sinha saheb, both armed with equally menacing lances.

A chilling awareness of my impotence suddenly washed over me. I still had the folding knife that Amma had given me years ago, which I had never actually used. It was safely tucked away among my clothes, but now I ran over to the bureau and pulled it out. Hurrying back to the window, I tried a practice stab or two on the wooden windowsill, acutely aware that wood was not the same as living flesh, feverishly trying to think—*What would Amma do? Surely she wouldn't just stand behind a window and watch.*

As I searched hopelessly for an answer, I saw Sinha saheb walking away from the gate toward the house, with the bare-chested leader of the group following a few steps behind him. I rushed into the living room but then hesitated about opening the screen door that connected onto the patio, where they had stopped. Sinha saheb sat down on one of the wicker chairs, and the other man squatted near his feet. The man was clearly agitated, but he kept his voice low. Even at this hour, I noticed, Sinha saheb had taken care to dress in his office clothing—an immaculate button-up shirt and neatly pressed trousers. The only thing out of place was a pair of sandals rather than his formal shoes.

The man seemed to be both complaining and pleading, but he spoke in a language I did not understand, and all I could catch was the name Singh. What he said was followed by a mixture of threats and commands from Sinha saheb, delivered in Bhojpuri. I could not make out precisely what he was saying, but there was something about an injured man and his family, about the need to avoid any further trouble, and about breaking the man's arm if he failed to comply. He spoke quietly, in short, crisp sentences, but his tone was cold and stern. When he finally raised his voice, to summon Nandkishor, the squatting man quickly wiped his brow with the end of his dhoti. I could see that he was trembling.

I stood frozen behind the screen door as Sinha saheb pushed it open, instructing Nandkishor to give the man some tea. The door narrowly missed hitting my face, but it hardly mattered: I already felt as if I'd been slapped. Sinha saheb was momentarily startled by my ghostly appearance, although he assumed that I was simply scared. I stared at him in disbelief, struggling to transform him back into someone I could recognize. Then I held out my hand to show him the knife I was clutching. Puzzled, he reached out gently to touch my arm, but I involuntarily recoiled. Coming closer, he read my face with dawning comprehension. "It's just a way of talking, you know—it isn't anything serious."

"So you've never broken the arm of one of your workers?" I gasped, nearly choking on the words.

By way of a reply, he took me by the shoulders and steered me to the sofa, where I sat stiffly while he explained the situation. A brawl between two groups of miners had gotten out of hand, nearly killing one of the workers from Sinha saheb's mine. Both sides were eager for a final bloodletting, and the friends and family of the injured man were clamouring for revenge. But the leader of the group had ordered them to hold off temporarily. The miners from other colliery had the protection of the much-feared mafia leader S. P. Singh, and, as it was, if the workers from

Sinha saheb's mine were to retaliate, Singh would bring in his goons to punish them, violently. Sinha saheb's workers needed level ground on which to settle the score, and the leader of the group was convinced that Sinha saheb had a direct line to Singh and could persuade him not to intervene in the dispute.

"Do you? Can you?" I sputtered.

Sinha saheb looked squarely at me. "My job is to avert bloodbaths, not to ensure that the fight is an even one. I am able to do that because I know how to talk to these people in a way that will get the message across." He paused. "So do you still think I'm a monster, or are you ready to go back to sleep?"

With that, he led me by the hand back to our bedroom. I did not resist, but the grip of my other hand around my knife remained tight.

Sinha saheb's parents, Gupteshwar chacha, and chachiji arrived at the same time for a visit. I was very grateful for the effort that everyone was making, especially my mother-in-law, Ma, to shield me from the discontentment and disdain of my father-in-law, Babuji. Sinha saheb thought he was a man impossible to please, but I did everything I could think of. I dared not cook on my own, for fear that the result would be less than perfect, but I spent a lot of time in the kitchen planning, supervising, and tasting. Sinha saheb chided me gently for spending too much time in the hot kitchen, and the heat did seem to be getting to me, making me feel sick and dizzy, Chachiji laughed that I was trying too hard, but Ma took a long look at me and asked me to go to the doctor with her.

It was confirmed: I was pregnant. But it was not supposed to happen. How much did I know this man or this place? I was supposed to travel the country and the world. I was supposed to finish my doctorate and be a professional woman first. A truly independent woman who could choose her own path and who went wherever it took her. Not a woman old before her age, who joylessly bore the double burden of family and professional responsibilities. I was inconsolable. Sinha saheb looked miserable.

Amma's voice was not very clear on the scratchy trunk call. She still sounded amused. "Why are you so surprised?" she asked. I tried to tell her what this meant for my dreams, but I could barely speak. Amma tried to listen to my silence and then announced that she would be taking the first train available to make the three-day journey to Dhanbad.

Professor Deodhar had not replied to any of my letters of enquiry. When we finally connected on the phone, all he could tell me was that he was busier in retirement than he ever had been. His priority was the research of doctoral candidates whose future employment or chances of promotion hinged on their degree. In his opinion, my situation was not urgent. I was married, and I was not employed. I just had to be patient. Had I known that it would be six years before I would be able to return to my dissertation and complete my doctorate, I might have pointed out that even patience has its limits.

Sinha saheb pulled out all the stops to make me happy—picnics by the rivers and lakes, long drives to nowhere through emerald greenery, the latest Hindi movies, records of music from everywhere, even a pair of shoes that cost as much as what I suspected was half of Amma's salary. He tried to make pragmatic future plans to help me finish my degree, promising me that everything would work out the way I wanted. I was not sure what I wanted, except that I did not want to be nauseated all the time, or battle with debilitating headaches or achy swollen feet.

Mrs. Rai from the neighbourhood took it upon herself to bring a cup of spinach juice tempered with lemon and rock salt every morning. Another neighbour argued that spinach would make the baby dark-skinned, and insisted that I eat lots of coconut and drink lots of milk with saffron to ensure a fair-skinned baby boy. Ma and Chachiji regularly sent homemade sweet and savoury *laddu*s so that the baby would be born satiated and not drool. It was also suggested that I take special care during the pregnancy, given that my sister had borne no children, as though it may be a family trait that I needed to or could avoid. All this attention surrounded me like a sugary web. I struggled to feel grateful for it or find any comfort in it.

When Amma arrived after her long train journey with three connections, I rested my throbbing head in her lap and sobbed. I wasn't sure if she understood the cause of my misery; I could hardly put it in words within my own head. I felt partially erased—the only part that seemed to matter was my body as the vessel of a birth. Amma nourished my soul by holding my hand quietly, allowing me to not explain anything. Her visit made me feel more settled than I had ever been in Dhanbad.

Near the end of Amma's two-week-long sojourn, Sinha saheb encouraged me to accept Didi and Jijaji's invitation to spend part of the summer in mild Dhar rather than hot and humid Dhanbad. He promised to drive up to bring me back in two weeks. Amma and I travelled two days by train to cover the eight hundred miles to Indore. I was ashamed of my misery in front of Didi, her enthusiasm at the news of my pregnancy only making me feel worse.

Didi organized a musical evening to announce and celebrate the pregnancy. She dragged me and Amma along to all the shrines and temples in Dhar to pray for a safe delivery. Her kitchen staff worked long hours preparing special foods for me to eat and take back with me to Dhanbad, while Jijaji treated us to day-trips to all my favourite sites—the palatial ruins of Mandu, the impressive ghats and palaces of Maheshwar, the island temple of Omkareshwar, dedicated to Shiva. As Thakur saheb and Amma discussed the American incursions in Cambodia and the ongoing secessionist movement in East Pakistan, I realized with embarrassment how quickly my own world was shrinking.

9

Letting Go

Amma hired a brass band to play in front of the house to welcome the arrival of a healthy baby. Neighbourhood ladies arrived at the house to sing traditional songs as *hijras* and beggars gathered outside to sing and dance and to receive gifts. Amma proudly carried the tiny, squealing creature to seek their blessings, horrifying them by announcing that the child was not a boy, as they expected from the musical celebrations. The *hijras* refused to accept any money, but when Amma insisted, they sang one song and gave their blessings, even though the baby was a girl.

I had come home, as was customary, to give birth to this tiny being, for whom every family member had a different name. Amma called her Bittu, a variant of *bitiya,* daughter. Didi called her Guddu, and Babu called her Guddan, both meaning a doll. Sinha saheb called her Meenu, a precious gem, but was hilariously awkward in holding her in his arms.

I felt the love that radiated from Didi when she held the baby close to her. Her love felt stronger, less tangled, than my own mixed emotions. "She is yours too, Didi," I said softly.

Didi's large almond eyes were brimming over, "She is a girl. How long will she be ours, Rekha? Look at our Amma—raised two daughters with her blood and sweat. For what, to find herself sick before she is old? To find herself alone again."

But Didi did hold on to the baby a bit tighter when I embraced her to bring them closer. We comforted each other until the incessant cries of my colicky baby completely took over. Didi, Amma, and I took turns rocking her throughout the night. Sometimes, I cried with her, and Amma cried with me.

Sinha saheb had arrived in Jaipur, just in time for the delivery of our daughter, in a shiny new Standard Herald car. "A private chariot for my queen and princess," he had said. Amma suggested that I stay in Jaipur for a few more weeks to recuperate. But I did not want to spend any longer than absolutely necessary away from Sinha saheb, even if it meant braving the long road trip back to Dhanbad within a month of giving birth. Amma promised to visit us during the summer vacation, and before too long she was with us again.

Amma loved the garden in Dhanbad and made sure that breakfast was always served at the covered swing next to the fragrant bush of *kaner*—the yellow oleander. As long as her aching knees allowed, she liked to tend to the numerous plants and incessantly quizzed the company gardener on his visits. Amma also added western Indian recipes to Nandkishor's repertoire of dishes.

Sinha saheb took a few days off to drive us to nearby attractions, for walks along Maithon Lake, boat rides on the Damodar River, excursions to bird and deer sanctuaries, and explorations of centuries-old temples. One morning he suggested a road trip to the Chhinnamastika temple, one of the region's most important sites of Tantric Shakti worship. The temple was dedicated to the goddess Devi, in her terrifying aspect as Chhinnamastika, a name that means "severed head." The goddess is often depicted holding a knife in one hand and, in the other, her own head, which drinks from the fountain of blood shooting up from her neck.

Perhaps ironically, the temple sat at the confluence of two rivers, which formed a spectacular waterfall. Amma asked whether, as at other such shrines, they still practiced animal sacrifice to appease the fearsome goddess. Realizing that his suggestion had landed him in trouble, Sinha saheb delicately noted that, on certain days of the week, there were no sacrifices. Amma said that she would go if he insisted on it, but that she couldn't promise not to protest animal sacrifice in the temple.

"But Amma, who are we to judge the matter of someone else's faith?" I sounded more irritated than I felt.

"You are right—so I'd rather not go at all," Amma replied. "But you know me well enough to know I will never be a bystander to any act of violence." Her tone made it clear that she was not backing down.

To prevent our debate from escalating, Sinha saheb suggested that we go to Panchet Dam instead. Nestled in the hills bordering West Bengal, the dam was surrounded by the ruins of forts and temples. We managed to have a lovely trip despite the baby, who cried every time the car stopped.

Only a few days after Amma returned to Jaipur, Jain saheb called to say that she was experiencing heart palpitations but was refusing to go to the hospital. Sinha saheb wasted no time in piling us into the car for the long trek to Jaipur.

These lengthy road trips were no longer fun, but Sinha saheb insisted on driving rather than taking the train. Instead of the thrill I once felt at discovering new sights and exploring unfamiliar terrain, I now winced at dangerous curves, worried about the narrow, shoulderless roads, and dreaded the crossing of dacoit-infested areas.

My worst fears came alive when the engine spluttered and died a few miles past Mainpuri, two-thirds of the way into our journey. It was already dusk when we reached Mainpuri, where we should have stopped for the night. But Sinha saheb decided to keep driving toward Firozabad, which was only about forty miles away and had the only decent hotels along this route until Agra.

Now here we were with an infant wailing her lungs out, a terrified Nandkishor shivering in the warm night, and a sullen Sinha saheb trying to negotiate with the engine. A beam of light from his electric torch revealed an unbroken thin line of petrol under the car, which explained why the tank was empty when it should have been at least half full. He guessed that a flying stone must have hit a seam somewhere in the under-carriage.

At that hour, there were few vehicles on the road. We tried to flag each one down, but they just swerved and sped past us. Sinha saheb explained that gangs of highway robbers were known to employ many tricks to stop vehicles at night to rob them.

Several long minutes passed with not a single vehicle in sight. Finally, as the blanket of the dark night tucked tighter around us, I spotted the high beam of a bus in the distance. I waited until it was close enough that the driver could see us clearly and then took the wailing baby out of Nandkishor's cold hands. Before Sinha saheb could stop me, I planted myself squarely in the middle of the road, baby in one arm, the other arm raised above my shoulder, in a frantic wave. The bus driver could swerve to the left into our parked car or over to the right and into the ditch, or he could run me down. Thankfully, he chose to bring the bus to a screeching halt, just inches away.

The bus conductor leaned out of the window screaming profanities, pausing only long enough to catch the sound of a baby wailing. At that, he hurriedly opened the door to pull us into the bus, and the driver stepped on the accelerator hard the instant the door shut. Some of the passengers moved around to make room for the newcomers. Once we had all had a chance to catch our breath, I noticed that the baby's wailing had, miracu-lously, stopped. The old man sitting next to me said the real miracle was that we had survived being stranded in those parts, where two nights ago they had driven past the bleeding body of a dead or dying man.

Forget about the car and your belongings, the driver told us. This was a long-distance bus bound for Agra and did not normally make stops along the route, but we just needed a ride out of the jungle to somewhere we could spend the night safely and then find a mechanic who would return with us in the morning—with the hope of finding the car where we left it. Twenty minutes later, the bus dropped us off at a roadside *dhaba* in Shikohabad, the only place in town that still had its lights on in the dead of the night.

The Sikh owner of this trucker's food-stop was incredibly hospitable. Sardarji made us fresh tea, paratha, and *paneer-bhurji,* despite our vehement protests. He especially insisted that I eat. "For the little one. My granddaughter was born a few months ago in the village. I have not seen her yet. I'm sure she is just as little," he said.

The roadside *dhaba* was just an enclosure of three brick and mud walls supporting a metal sheet roof. Leafy trees surrounded the front of the enclosure, where the clay tandoor sat next to a low brick counter lined with large steel pots. Against the back wall of the enclosure were shelves for storing ingredients in clay jars and tin boxes, as well as a jute *charpai* piled high with onions, garlic, potatoes, and other root vegetables, to keep them dry. Sardarji tipped the load out of the cot and offered it to me as a place to rest with the baby. Then he joined Sinha saheb and Nandkishor on one of the many other rickety jute cots that were scattered under the trees, to keep vigil and wait for the morning light.

Lying on the smelly cot, I dared not close my eyes, wondering about scorpions and snakes lurking in the muddy recesses of the *dhaba*. Thankfully, eardrum-piercing wails from the baby were not one of my concerns that night—*of course now she is comfortable*. I could focus just on keeping my bladder and bowels shut tight until we could get to a hotel.

At the first light of morning, Sardarji brought a car mechanic on a motorbike. Nandkishor and the mechanic left with a can of petrol to find the car, while Sardarji hailed the first passing truck, which agreed to give us a ride as far as Firozabad. Sardarji refused to accept any money from us, so I took off my baby's silver anklets. He could not refuse them when I said that they were a gift from one little one to another.

As we had feared, Amma had had another heart attack. I had been in Jaipur for several months, unable to return to Dhanbad. Instead, with Mangi bai's dependable help, I was trying my best to run this bizarre household. Babu was concerned about Amma's health but did not know how to compromise his daily routine to help us. Amma remained dismissive about medicine, so I had to argue with her several times a day, trying to force her to take her heart medication and stick to her salt-free diet. Shafiji managed to keep the press afloat and continued to be Amma's rock in his strong quiet way.

Neelu was much more accepting of the baby in my life than he had been of Sinha saheb. He still contrived to steal Sinha saheb's shaving brush or his slippers and hide them in a corner on the terrace. Sinha saheb visited us as often as he could, but I fretted the whole time whenever he was on the road.

Babu's usually morose editorial associate, Viyogiji, was pumped up with the political developments in East Pakistan, excitedly discussing his ideas for special editions of *Praja Sandesh* that would resurrect the newspaper. West Pakistan and East Pakistan were separated by thousands of miles of Indian territory. Culturally, ethnically, and linguistically, the two were as dissimilar as Russia and China, sharing only a religion. Viyogiji called this odd political formation one of the many mistakes of partition by the British colonialists. Babu called it the deliberate dismemberment of the subcontinent to punish it for its freedom.

Since the beginning of the year, millions of Bengali-speaking refugees from East Pakistan had sought shelter in various parts of India, their presence visible not only in eastern cities such as Dhanbad, but as far west as Jaipur. All India Radio reported nearly 10 million refugees and nearly 30 million internally displaced since the West Pakistan–dominated military junta had annulled last year's election and arrested Sheikh Mujibur Rahman, the prime minister–elect. Newspapers had been reporting massacres of intelligentsia and university students to curb the Bengali nationalist movement.

Most of the news reports trickling into India focused on the ongoing genocide, placing the number of victims between several hundred thousand and three million. Instead of this, Viyogiji wanted to write about the civil disobedience movement and the resilience of Bengali nationalism in the face of the military-led pogrom. Babu, in support of this plan, asked him to find out more about the guerrilla tactics of civilians and the resistance offered by the Mukti Bahini forces since the declaration of independence earlier that year.

But my mind was preoccupied with a personal battle. The gynecologist had assured me that I had little chance of getting pregnant while I was breast-feeding. Yet here I was, with a baby just a few months old, pregnant again. Didi had accompanied me to the doctor when I received the news. She was irritated. "Are you two animals? Do you know nothing about family planning?" I sat there, unmoving and embarrassed.

Didi tried to make up for her outburst by breaking the news to Amma, so that I wouldn't have to do it. I told Amma that I wanted to talk to Sinha saheb about whether to terminate the pregnancy. But Amma said that a mistake cannot be righted by another mistake. She even suggested that I might think of it as "god's wish." She was trying to hand me an anchor, but this act of faith worked for me no more than it had ever worked for her.

I didn't know what to do. But there was little time to ponder, when all my waking hours were filled with looking after a colicky infant, a sick and stubborn mother, a man-child of a father, a sister and husband who showed up briefly as guests, an overprotective dog who frequently needed to be restrained, and the near-constant stream of visitors who came to the house every single day, despite Neelu's menacing presence.

Indira Gandhi was on the radio, addressing the nation, announcing Pakistani airstrikes on Indian bases, interpreting them as a declaration of war. Fifty Pakistani planes had struck as many as eleven targets, including Agra, which was some two hundred miles from the nearest border and even closer than that to Jaipur. Politically, India had supported East Pakistan's liberation movement, and had allowed the Bangladeshi government in exile to work out of Calcutta. Militarily, India was much more prepared than ever before.

Indira Gandhi had emerged as an astute politician, turning her expulsion from the Congress Party a few years before into a move to split the party and alienate her detractors. Redefining herself as the messiah of the poor had won her the last election by a landslide majority. Her swearing-in for a new term as India's prime minister had coincided with the revolt of the Bangladeshi military units against the genocide being carried out by the Pakistani army.

Indian military had offered protection and training to the Mukti Bahini of Bangladesh, so the war with Pakistan was inevitable. This time, though, it ended with a swift and decisive victory for India and for an independent Bangladesh. Indira Gandhi was being hailed as the Iron Lady and being compared to the goddess Durga.

Too tired to fight Babu's continuing objections to the political dynamics of the day, Amma had stayed away from the recent general election. This was most unlike her, and I was terribly worried. Her health was rapidly declining despite all precautions, and her blood pressure remained very high. Even her daily diary entries were brief and erratic now. Her palpitations returned when she heard of Sinha saheb's unanticipated arrival, just as the war came to its decisive end.

Sinha saheb went straight to Amma's room. "Ammaji, I have not come to take your daughter away. I have returned to bring you a son. I have resigned from my job."

I was not sure who was more stunned by this announcement, Amma or me.

Sinha saheb assured us that he had thought this through. Indira Gandhi's government had recently nationalized major banks, in a move to increase the credit available to agriculture and to expand banking in rural areas. Now, basking in the glow of her military victory and burgeoning popularity, she was planning to nationalize the massive coal mining sector. Nationalizing the mines might or might not ease the plight of mineworkers, but, in the coal belt, the mafia thugs and union bosses were already redrawing their boundaries. The mafia wars had intensified, and the pacifists were being forced out of the way—or eliminated.

"I can carry on as before. I know I will survive this turmoil. But it is not a place to raise a family," he said earnestly. "It is not worthy of your daughter's dreams."

Both Amma and I were speechless. So Sinha saheb continued talking, explaining that he had lined up a couple of interviews in Jaipur, as well as one in Sawai Madhopur, where a new cement plant was under construction.

Amma finally recovered enough to ask him to think carefully. She knew as well as I did that moving into his wife's family home would irreparably damage his honour and reputation. Perhaps he should consult his family before making such a drastic move, she suggested.

Sinha saheb shook his head. "My father has three other sons. Rekha is all you have. I will not take her away from you again."

JAIPUR, 1972

They said that when an old woman lay dying, my Amma held her hand and spoke the Mahamrityunjaya Mantra in her ear, easing her passage. They said that Amma could summon and banish spirits. They said Amma had fought fearlessly and won repeatedly against man and beast. They said Amma's past was a divine secret, the source of her infinite courage and wisdom, ever mysterious. They said Amma changed lives just by standing behind a person. They said they loved and worshipped my Amma.

I saw them everywhere through my blurred eyes. They were bathing Amma's body, anointing her head with sesame oil. They were covering Amma's lifeless body in one of her khadi saris. They were holding me by the shoulder as I walked numbly next to the *arthi,* the bier made from sticks of bamboo, which carried her body. They were arguing about whether women should accompany the body to the cremation grounds. They were filling the narrow streets, the broad bazaars, the cremation grounds.

Sinha saheb had the son's honour of introducing cleansing fire to Amma's funeral pyre. The smells of jasmine, sandalwood, and ghee mixed with the stench of immolating flesh. The mild spring sun hid its bloodshot pupil behind a murky cloud. Despite the interventions of a gusty wind and unseasonal showers, the wood pyre's leaping flames raged for hours, mercilessly reducing Amma's lifeless body to ashes and chunks of bones.

My tears broke the floodgates when I saw my sister. Didi and Jijaji reached Jaipur hours after the cremation. I heard Sinha saheb tell them how I had woken up at two in the morning the night before with a sense of foreboding, and rushed to Amma's room. She had been lying on her back on her pristine white bed, eyes bulging, barely breathing—waiting. My scream had brought Babu and Sinha saheb rushing into the room. Babu had sat on the bed and put her head in his lap, tears streaming down his cheeks. Amma had looked steadily into his eyes, without blinking. When Sinha saheb had said that he was going to call the doctor, Amma's grip on my hand had tightened. I asked Sinha saheb to stay. Babu put his hand on the crown of Amma's head. At his touch, a slight smile appeared on her face. The moment froze, and then the eyes, and then the smile.

Sinha saheb, Shafiji, and Jijaji were organizing the constant flow of mourners. Didi, Babu, and I sat next to a large picture of Amma on the floor of the drawing room, which had been emptied out in order to create space for people to pay their respects. Tears had not stopped rolling out of Babu's closed eyes.

Neelu had never been allowed in Amma's room, due to her low mattress-bed and its white coverings. Now the bedding was gone from the room, and Neelu lay on its cold hard floor for hours. For two days he refused to eat.

Jain saheb wanted to know if the big day of mourning would be the third or the seventh day after death, waking Babu from his mournful reverie with the question. Babu rose up to his full height and glared at him. "She lived to fight against meaningless rituals. We should not forget that in her death." With that he left the house and only returned the next morning, with a bunch of flowers plucked from Ram Niwas Gardens.

Babu had remembered that his granddaughter turned one year old that day. He laid the flowers beside the sleeping baby and told a surprised Mangi bai to make some celebratory halwa. Shafiji was aghast when Babu gave him money to buy sweets from the market. "Babuji, we have done no mourning rituals for the departed. Badi behenji died three days ago. It is too early to celebrate anything." So Babu said he would buy the sweets himself.

We were learning that eulogies for Amma had appeared in many news-papers, far and wide. Nobody could override Babu's injunction against any memorial gathering. But Amma's high school trustees, teachers, and students held a memorial without his participation, dedicating the death anniversary of their founder-principal as an annual day of remembrance for Veer Balika School. Amma had been fifty-four.

A stranger arrived from Ajmer. Dr. Mathur was a short and balding man whose thin frame was draped in a formal safari suit. He explained that when he read Amma's obituary in the newspaper, he immediately wished to pay his respects. He was, he said, a full-time physician and part-time historian, and he regretted that he had not paid us a visit earlier. We were used to encountering strangers who admired Amma. But Dr. Mathur had never met her.

Dr. Mathur had come across references to young Shanti in the course of his historical research. He had interviewed a number of former freedom fighters in Ajmer and Wardha and had traced significant steps of her jour-ney from prison to Gandhiji's ashram. Only recently, though, had he made the connection between Shanti and my Amma. He had been distracted from Amma's story, he explained, by his determination to unravel the mystery of Subhas Chandra Bose's death.

I thanked him for his condolences and took him to Babu's room to make introductions. Dr. Mathur regarded Babu's countenance with clin-ical interest and sought his permission to return the next day to talk about a historical research project he was working on. Babu curtly stated that he was as interested in discussing any research as he was in constructing a high bridge to jump off of. Dr. Mathur was undeterred. "Then I will come to talk," he replied, "and you can just listen."

Dr. Mathur arrived within moments of Babu's return from his mor-ning walk. Babu resignedly asked Mangi bai to serve breakfast to the eager talker. I decided to plant myself in Babu's room in case his temper got out of hand. Dr. Mathur explained that he was compiling a book about the freedom fighters of the region. Babu scornfully asked who would want to read such a book. Dr. Mathur said that people did not know the true history of the movement. Babu said it didn't matter.

They bantered and sparred until Dr. Mathur started to reveal the information he had collected about Amma's prison terms and her time in Ajmer and Wardha. He had brought along a large file of handwritten notes and photocopied documents. I was impressed, and even Babu stopped his snide commentary. Dr. Mathur asked a few questions about the gaps in his knowledge of Amma's political activities since independence. Babu warmed up and readily answered these questions.

Dr. Mathur wanted to know more about how the two of them met in Wardha and their wedding. Babu said earnestly, "Marriage ruined her life."

Dr. Mathur quickly apologized and asked whether Babu would be willing to talk about his life before arriving in Wardha. Babu's face hardened, and he closed his eyes without an answer. Dr. Mathur probed again, "I heard that you used to work with Subhas Chandra Bose. Is it true that Netaji used wireless telegraphy to communicate with his intelligence unit?"

Babu stood over the diminutive doctor and rumbled, "Netaji never used wireless telegraphy. Now get out of my room."

Babu was easily irritated, especially when people asked him questions about his time with Netaji. Dr. Mathur bowed and left the room but stood outside trembling, with an incongruous smile on his face. I asked him if he would like to sit down for a bit. He followed me to the dining room, the furthest room away from Babu's, and burst into tears. After a drink of water, he rummaged through his papers and showed me some letters. One of them described my father's physical appearance, right down to his nearly deaf left ear.

Dr. Mathur had been on a mission to uncover the truth about Subhas Chandra Bose's life and death. Like a number of people, he believed that Netaji did not die in the air crash in 1945. Rumours abounded of Netaji living in Russia, or in China, or in a reclusive ashram in India. Dr. Mathur was convinced that Netaji was indeed alive and that his close associates continued to get together periodically, and he had been trying to track down some of them.

As I well knew, there were many who had publicly proclaimed their association with Netaji, but also many who, for one reason or another, had kept it under wraps. Netaji had quarrelled openly with Gandhiji and Nehruji and had sought the help of Nazi Germany and fascist Japan against the British. The cryptic circumstances of his death in a fiery plane crash had sparked a number of conspiracy theories involving various people, both in India and abroad, who had reasons to want him dead, as well as rumours that he wasn't dead at all.

In Wardha, Dr. Mathur had heard the story of one of Netaji's intelligence officers who had joined Gandhiji's ashram after Netaji met with Hitler. One of the regulars at Gandhiji's ashram had sent a letter to Dr. Mathur describing what he remembered of the young deserter. I could certainly see my Babu in those scratchy lines on the faded blue envelope. It even mentioned his strength-building routines of hour-long headstands and his swims in the river.

Dr. Mathur quizzed me about Babu. Did he ever disappear without any explanation? Yes, periodically, for as long as I could remember.

Did he ever mention where he used to go? Never. Except that we sometimes received letters from him postmarked from distant places.

Does he know any Russian? Yes, along with French and German, and several other languages.

Tears rolled down Dr. Mathur's face. "Finally, I have met a living member of Netaji's inner circle!"

I was touched by his joy, but I also knew that Babu would never let him anywhere near him again. I gave him the only explanation Babu had ever offered for his unyielding refusal to divulge his past—that he had promised Gandhiji to keep it a secret in return for his protection.

Despite my efforts to spare him further trouble, Dr. Mathur left saying that he would return at some point and try to speak to Babu again. Indeed, every few years he would reappear, hoping to cajole Babu into revealing more about his mysterious past. Babu never obliged, but, nothing if not relentless in his quest for the truth, Dr. Mathur never gave up.

After a few days, Didi and Jijaji returned to Dhar. But, with Amma's death, we seemed to have lost the fulcrum in our lives. Babu could no longer sleep. He saw Amma staring at him wherever he went. He saw her waiting for him in dark corners. He saw her beckoning to him from behind tree trunks and electrical poles. He heard her curse him, calling him selfish and irresponsible. He heard her laugh at him maniacally when he tried to flee from the apparition.

Then Babu disappeared. Concerned about his mental stability, Sinha saheb and Shafiji roamed the city, looking for him. When the manager of an ashram in Vrindavan phoned to ask us to take a very sick Babu home, I was relieved but also annoyed.

Babu was indeed ill, but he recovered from his delirium and fever, and then he ran away again. It was becoming a strange cat and mouse game. Sinha saheb dutifully retrieved Babu from the various places he ended up on these escape attempts, all around the country, while I tried to keep the household together.

Sinha saheb had been offered the position in Sawai Madhopur, but the city was nearly a two-hour train trip from Jaipur. A family move was out of the question, so accepting the offer would mean that he would have to live there alone and come home as often as possible on weekends. But this arrangement seemed equally impossible: I had an infant who evidently specialized in being sick, a second baby due in a few weeks, and a very unstable father to look after.

In the meanwhile, Viyogiji was worrying about the future of Vaishali Press. With Amma gone, so was her income, and Babu was in no condition to run a business. There was a steady supply of printing jobs, which could potentially subsidize the publication of *Praja Sandesh,* at least as a weekly paper. But an initial investment would need to be made in modernizing the printing equipment. Seeing how reluctant Sinha saheb was to move away from Jaipur, Viyogiji was encouraging him to take over the press and invest his savings in the business. Sinha saheb agreed to this plan as a temporary measure, until our lives settled down, not realizing that this decision would mark the end of his former career.

One day, as I was sorting through Amma's things, I came across her shoulder bag, untouched since her death. As my fingers groped their way into its depths, I found myself holding a small bottle. It was a bottle full of salt. Buried with it were numerous vials of heart medicines, most of which had never been opened.

I stared at this evidence, not wanting to trust my eyes, caught in a whirlpool of grief, anger, and remorse.

But we were here, Amma. Why did you abandon us? Didn't you trust our love for you? Did you simply not love us?

Epilogue

Babu's ashes were scattered in the Ganga at the foothills of the Himalayas, without any priestly intervention, his release from life accompanied only by the chants of his favourite mantras floating up from the remains of his family—his two daughters, one surviving son-in-law, and three grand-children. Nearly a century of mysterious existence, several decades of angry disillusionment, his withdrawal into music and books, his stubborn refusal to compromise, his love of mangoes, the joy he found in the land's seasonal bounty, his strict yoga routines, his early morning recitation of Sanskrit *shloka*s in a voice that boomed throughout the house, the trans-formation of that voice into a silken murmur when he sang his evening *bhajan*s, his nightmares that would wake the whole household—all were reduced to a handful of lumpy white ash in an earthen container.

India was celebrating the forty-third anniversary of its independence. But for my tired, middle-aged self, it was just a much-needed holiday in the middle of the week. Although I was no longer anyone's daughter, I was still a wife, a mother, and a sister, as well as an academic and a perpetual hostess who might someday learn to be a good housekeeper.

Perhaps it was Babu's emotional disengagement, I reflected, that had allowed Didi to survive, with exemplary dignity, the dissolution of Thakur saheb's ancestral fortunes and the early death of Jijaji. But it must have been Amma's maternal devotion that had enabled her to raise, as a widowed mother, her adopted son—my third-born, a piece of my heart.

When, I wondered, did my life become the sum of my relationships? Was it when I agreed to marry a stranger and move hundreds of miles to an alien world? Was it when I first discovered, to my surprise, that I was pregnant? Or was it when Sinha saheb moved to Jaipur, forsaking a flourishing career to be tied instead to a steadily declining printing press? Or when Amma's death left me with the fragments of her legacy and a father who was also falling apart? Or when I could no longer endure my sister's sadness and bore a baby to give away to her? When did the demands of a busy household become more important than all the things I once thought would be at the centre of my life: vocal practice, public performances, research, and conferences? At what point did the need to be a good daughter, a good wife, a good sister, a good mother, a good teacher, and a good homemaker claim so much territory that no space remained for me? I wished I could say, "Enough. I cannot give any more. I am a person, not just a series of obligations." But I couldn't. Why was that? Had I learned too well the habit of self-sacrifice from Amma?

Amma made too many personal compromises—and yet her choices somehow expanded the space for freedom, for herself and for others. Amma's life continued to inspire people not to lose sight of a higher purpose, even in everyday decisions. The only purpose I seemed to serve was to ensure that all meals were ready on time and served perfectly. I was the nanny, the maid, the companion, the nurse, the hostess, the solid ground on which my family stood.

I wasn't sure that Amma would approve. Despite her unalloyed love for her family, she never wholly surrendered to domesticity: life was always something larger than that. But, even as I pondered my own choices, my thoughts were distracted by the many household tasks vying for my attention. The national holiday was my first opportunity in two months to turn to the long-neglected library on the terrace and survey the impact of an usually heavy rainy season.

At first glance, the library looked no worse than it had last year. The strong smell of damp paper and mouse droppings added an oppressive layer to the seasonal humidity at the edge of the desert. The ghosts of lives lived, of dreams dreamt and nightmares revisited, still lurked under heaps of paper silently disintegrating in this forsaken room. Nobody had ever fully counted, let alone catalogued, this eclectic collection of texts on history, philosophy, music and literature, ranging from ancient India to the unravelling Soviet Union. My guess was that there were at least twenty thousand books, along with endless letters, diaries, and other paper remains of my parents' lives.

Hundreds of volumes in French, German, and Russian—remnants of Babu's mysterious associations with various revolutionary groups—were lined up on haphazard shelves all along the south wall. An old, dusty tarp ineffectively sheltered them from the seasons that took turns pouring into the room through the gaps deliberately left in the wall. Huddled together in the most precarious part of the library, the volumes looked like immigrants in a crowded ghetto in some hostile land.

Yet the rest of the room was really no less perilous—rows and rows of makeshift shelves, crammed full of books in Hindi, English, Sanskrit, Bengali, Gujarati, Marwari, Marathi, Persian, and Urdu. All lay under layers of sandy dust, caked in places because of the recent rain, disturbed only by the trails of resident insects, geckos, and mice.

My unsure footprints left tracks in the soggy layers of dust on the cement floor. I made my way to the farthest corner of the north wall. I knew I needed to start from here, since I had ignored this section of the library for far too long. The top shelf was filled with the colourfully bound diaries of various vintages, arranged in no particular order, in which my mother had documented her life.

One diary jutted crookedly out of the uneven row, its cardboard binding covered in faded red cloth. I tugged gingerly at this thing, Amma's oldest diary, which had survived the constant movement of her restless childhood and then my own. It was the one diary that Amma had scolded me for reading when I could not contain the burning curiosity of my early teenage years.

The red diary slid out limply, followed by a puff of papery dust and a scurrying of tiny creatures at the back of the bookshelf. The binding was sagging and warped, punctured by silverfish, the volume's bottom corner chewed by mice. Between the fragile cardboard covers, a gaping hole ran through the entire thickness of the diary.

Faint words written in indelible indigo ink by a young girl seven decades before were still visible around the irregular edges of the cavity—a mouse nest, filled with soft shreds of paper and droppings, a urine-stained abode for the shiny silverfish that were scurrying and falling off the book in their rush to escape my intrusion.

I stared at this paper hole, this cavernous abyss, for a long, numb moment. Closing the covers, taking care not to spill any shreds of paper, I held the book close to my thumping heart. With my other hand, I started to pull out more diaries from the top shelf, raising more dust and more shredded paper, disturbing more droppings, mice, geckos, and silverfish.

Ignoring the swirling dust and the overpowering smell in this graveyard of books, I turned toward the visibly wet lowest shelf. Letters from comrades in the freedom movement, carbon copies of Amma's letters to various people, telegrams, and postcards that should have been preserved in an archive somewhere, all reduced to clumps of paper mush in the two decades of my wanton neglect. Words, textures, pen strokes, messages, stories, all irretrievably collapsed into each other, devoid of any meaning.

My chest tightening with panic, I began to tear about the library in search of something that had survived—some trace of Amma's life that remained legible. Amidst sodden, chewed-up, and brittle paper, I found one damaged copy of her autobiography, *Smriti ki shrinkhalayen,* and one green hardcover diary, damp but whole, that was filled with her handwriting.

I imagined Babu smiling mischievously, perhaps gratified by the destruction—a fitting end to his mysterious life of detachment. But Amma could not possibly have wanted it this way. Why else would she have written such detailed daily accounts, preserving her thoughts, recording her memories, amassing all the evidence? Why did I squander this treasure? In my determination to be there for others, why had I abandoned my own mother?

I sank down onto the dirty cement floor, surrounded by the rubble of my own creation, trying to grasp the enormity of despair.

How would I ever tell Amma's story? How could I even begin?

Writing Amma's Story

On 7 November 2010, the day after celebrating her last Diwali, my mother died, after a valiant six-year battle with cancer. She was sixty-four. Over the course of her life, Surekha Sinha had published eight books and had composed a total of more than a thousand pieces of verse, some of them stand-alone poems, some intended to be sung as classical *khyals*. Yet, despite her prolific writing, one story remained untold—that of her exceptional parents, Amma and Babu. During the last three months of her life, when the crystal clarity of her perception was occasionally clouded by extremely high doses of morphine, my mother often mused about her long-deferred task. With a breaking heart, I lied to her that we would work on a book-writing project together, when she felt a little stronger. That lie became my truth.

I began writing this book the year after her death, as I struggled to come to terms with her loss, as well as with the death of my father, five years earlier. As I tried, in fitful bursts, to put the voices in my head onto paper, my aunt Abha—my mother's sister, Didi—sent me a copy of Amma's autobiography, *Smriti ki shrinkhalayen*. Hastily put together to raise charitable funds after India's disastrous war with China in 1962, the book had little circulation and was never reprinted. Nearly half a century later, however, it became an invaluable point of departure for the writing of *Amma's Daughters*. Its 161 pages contain an assortment of stories from my grandmother's life, arranged in no apparent order and often told rather sketchily. As literature, it was not an autobiography worthy of straight-forward translation, and, in writing the present book, I borrowed from its text on only three occasions: the description of the young Shanti's experiences in jail, her conversation with Mahatma Gandhi about marriage and chastity, and the visit, many years later, of Amma and her two daughters with the writer Suryakant Tripathi Nirala.

This haphazard autobiography also became the starting point for further research. Over the years, I had heard stories about my grandmother not only from my mother and my aunt but also from the many family visitors who had known Amma, some of whom maintained a connection with Babu until his death in 1990. These included his good friend Pandit Parmanand and the ever-inquisitive Dr. B. L. Mathur, both of whom appear in the book, as well as the freedom fighter and journalist Dattatreya Tiwari. I also vividly recall conversations with Amma's long-standing friend Maitreyi Pathak, known to readers as Maitreyi didi, the woman who arranged my parents' marriage. This oral history enriched my understanding of Amma's life, filling in details missing in her autobiographical account as well as supplying information about events she had omitted. I had my mother's own writings to draw on as well—her diaries and her letters to me, as well as references to her family in some of her published works. All the same, gaps remained. So, in 2013, I travelled to London, New Delhi, and Patna, largely to conduct archival research, although, while I was in India, I also took the opportunity to interview people who had known Amma in one capacity or another.

My archival survey focused on the period of the civil disobedience movement (1930–33), in which my grandmother, then in her early teens, was caught up. I consulted microfilm copies of newspapers published in the United Provinces (later to become Uttar Pradesh), with special attention to the cities in which Shanti lived. Notable among these newspapers were *Aaj* (Varanasi), *The Leader* (Allahabad), *Sainik* (Agra), and *Sangharsh* and the *Indian Daily Telegraph* (both Lucknow), as well as Ganesh Shankar Vidyarthi's revolutionary weekly *Pratap* (Kanpur). I also examined a selection of All India Congress Committee bulletins, particularly those that supplied information about activities in Mathura, along with magazines from the period that published articles on social and political issues.

In addition, I sifted through confidential reports written by the governing officials in the British provinces of Ajmer-Merwara, the United Provinces, and Bihar and Orissa, who were responsible for exercising surveillance over the civil disobedience movement and relaying information to India's Governor General (the viceroy). In one of these reports, dating to the first half of August 1930, I found mention of my grandmother, then known by the name Shanti, whose public speeches were described as "intemperate." As we know, Shanti was subsequently arrested for sedition and sentenced to six months in jail. Born in 1918, she would have turned twelve that year.

This research allowed me to verify and contextualize much of the information that I already had. Beyond that, however, these archival materials revealed the scale and nature of women's participation in the independence movement, as well as some of the social mechanisms whereby women were routinely rendered faceless. The portrait that emerged—of women committed to the struggle for freedom while at the same time burdened by oppressive traditions founded on deeply patriarchal attitudes—corroborated the stories I had heard from my mother about a number of Amma's friends and confidants. While I knew only bits and pieces of their individual stories, their lives seemed to overlap. Most had a middle-class upbringing and at least some degree of education, and many had been widowed at an early age. They also shared the quality of strong-mindedness—women who, within their extended families, tended to be cast in the role of a willful relative who had lived a lonely life.

When I began to write about Amma, I found these women coalescing into the figure of Kamala mausi, the only "fictitious" person in the book. Although I worried that, by amalgamating their fragmentary stories into a composite character, I might be further contributing to the effacement of their identities, in the end it seemed that a single, more fully developed personality was the best way to convey a clear sense of the texture of their lives and to keep some parts of their memory alive. Growing up, I met only one of these women in person, and she is the source of my description of Kamala mausi's physical appearance and of her family history.

Writing about my own mother so soon after her death—trying to imagine the world through her eyes—seemed at times impossibly difficult.

Yet even as I was forced to confront emotions that I had perhaps never before acknowledged and grapple with insights that were not always welcome, telling her story was a powerful affirmation of her life. As I attempted to immerse myself in her experience, the closeness we shared when she was alive seemed to acquire a strange solidity and permanence, as if I was letting go of her by absorbing her, allowing her consciousness to merge with my own. Although the emotions were intense, the act of stepping into her perceptions was not as difficult as I had anticipated. She was, after all, my mother, and I knew her well.

What proved to be more challenging was the depiction of my mother's sister, Didi. It was not easy to suppress my own knowledge of and feelings for my *"badi mummy"*—my "older mother," as I was taught to call her—and imagine her instead as a daughter, albeit one whose experience is filtered through her sister's perceptions and voice. My mother and her sister were thrown together by their shared experience of two rather unusual and demanding parents, to whom they reacted very differently. My mother coped with her anomalous upbringing by putting her Amma and Babu on a pedestal, thereby making a virtue out of necessity, so to speak. Within the context of the family, her outspokenness and her embrace of the unconventional was, ironically, a gesture of obedience—while, with her impeccable manners, Didi politely rebelled, often questioning her parents' values. She was determined not to let her life be a sum of other people's choices, and she quietly insisted on the right to be "normal." As sisters, they were utterly loyal to each other, but their very closeness served to highlight their differences. I had to work hard to separate Didi from my aunt Abha Choudhary, and to capture the complex mix of devotion and tension that characterized both Didi's relationship to her parents and my mother's relationship to her.

Despite the mystery surrounding his past, I found it easiest to write about Babu, whom I remembered clearly, as he lived with us all the while I was growing up. My own memories of him dovetailed well with my mother's and aunt's stories about the father who intermittently presided over their childhood. Even as an old man, he remained somehow larger than life, ascetic and reclusive until an injustice, whether real or perceived, would produce a burst of temper, his deep voice rolling through the house like thunder. Despite his detachment, he was a devoted grandfather, the depth of his affection evident especially during my many spells of sickness as a child. I still recall him sitting by my bedside for hours on end, reciting Sanskrit mantras as he gently stroked my feet. Someday, I hope to write his own story—and may I not postpone this promise to myself until it is too late.

Early in 2014, just as I was finishing the first draft of *Amma's Daughters,* my brother Peeyush contacted me with the happy news that he had managed to locate Amma's sole surviving diary, which he subsequently scanned. The first entry is dated 24 August 1926, but, contrary to expectations, the diary does not proceed in neat chronological order. After the first few pages, it becomes a jumble of entries spanning more than three decades: an entry from 1936 could be followed by one dated 1958, followed by another from 1960, and then another from 1941. We know that Amma had multiple notebooks, and she must have reached for whichever one was at hand—writing entirely for herself, not for the convenience of a biographer. Some of the entries contain quite detailed accounts of specific incidents in her day-to-day life; others describe her emotions, although often with little explanation of what prompted them.

As I patiently deciphered the hasty handwriting on worn paper, Amma seemed to emerge from the pages. We experience our lives not as a coherent story but as a series of moments, and, after a while, the kaleidoscopic quality of the diary began to seem normal. Sometimes I was reading the words of a grown woman, absorbed in the events and cares of her day. More often, though, I was hearing the voice of the traumatized child who could never return home, the survivor intent on rejoining her sisters—the freedom fighter whose long struggle would eventually take her back to the river that had claimed their lives.

Despite extensive research, I was never able to fill in the two blank spots in Amma's story—her family history and her activities during the time she spent with revolutionaries after she ran away from her family home in Allahabad. It is possible that she met up with members of the Bengal Volunteers, a revolutionary group officially formed in 1928, under the leadership of Subhas Chandra Bose. Articles in Allahabad newspapers dating to 1928 and 1929 mention that the group included women and children and that it was active in the area at the time. Perhaps someday concrete evidence will come to light, but, if not, then the early years of her life were obviously destined to remain concealed.

In "The Body Under the Rug," Alexander Stille identifies two emotions that haunt the writer of a family memoir—"guilt about pillaging the lives of the dead and anxiety about harming the living." In writing Amma's story, I have tried not to pillage but to commemorate the lives of the dead and to respect the privacy and integrity of those still living. Knowing that my mother had long intended to write about her family did help to assuage the guilt. But I have no way of knowing how far I have strayed from what she would have written. I can only hope that I have divulged nothing that she would have kept hidden.

Acknowledgements

———

Although I bear sole responsibility for any errors and unintended omissions, this book is very much a collective achievement. I could not possibly have written it without the help of a great many people who contributed to its evolution in a myriad of ways. Numerous dear friends and extended family members were forced to read or listen to drafts of various sections of the manuscript. Their invaluable feedback pulled me out of bouts of self-doubt, offered me support on this difficult emotional journey, and helped me fill in gaps in the story. For their spirit of camaraderie and their wise guidance during the writing of this book, I am deeply indebted to the following individuals:

In India: Ghanshyam Agarwal, Sheela Agarwal, Shanti Bajpai, Kusum Bajpai, Rakesh Bhaiya, Prabha Bhaiya, Virendra Dangi, Prem Dave, Sona Godfrey, Kusum Jain, Indira Jena, T. J. Jitha, Anjum Joad, Anila Kothari, Khatija Khader, Vijay Kumar, Navin Lalji, Surbhi Manocha, Panchanan Misr, Mynoo Maryel, Anil Nauriya, Chandrabala Parnami, Apeksha Pendharkar, Kittu Reddy, Asharani Sahay, Sadhna Shrivastava, Ram Kumar Singh, Amita Sinha, Arun Sinha, Indra Kumar Sinha, Kamalapati Sinha, Kriti Sinha, Kusum Sinha, Niket Sinha, Prabha Sinha, Rajiv Ranjan Sinha, Suresh Kumar Sinha, Umapati Sinha, Aruna Srivastava, Jayati Srivastava, Prem Surana, Kusum Tai, D. D. Tiwari, Krishna Tiwari, Rashmi Tiwari, Vibhavasu Tiwari, and Hemchand Vaidya.

In Canada and the United States: Barbara Ballermann, Elisabeth Ballermann, Don Beacham, Janine Brodie, Rhiannon Bury, Eric Butterworth, Jean Crozier, Ann Marie Dewhurst, Dale Dewhurst, Chitra

Divakaruni, Rosie Dransfeld, Caterina Edwards, Alvin Finkel, Ann Goldblatt, Lorelei Hanson, Myrna Kostash, Darlene Lavender, Manijeh Mannani, Karen Nielsen, Kel Pero, Jay Smith, Malinda Smith, Lorna Stefanick, Anneli Twan, Wanja Twan, Karen Wall, and Janice Williams.

I am fortunate to have a large "family of the heart"—my *dilon ke rishte,* to borrow Amma's expression, so often quoted by my mother—scattered across several continents. It is impossible to name them all, but I especially wish to express my gratitude to my dear friends Valerie Luyckx and Thomas Mueller. Thank you, dear Valerie, for being the sister I never had—for your unstinted support, for our ardent discussions over the years, and for your infinite generosity of spirit. And thank you, dear Thomas, for your ability to combine the detachment of a clinician with unreserved affection and for sending me the piece by Alexander Stille to help me think through the dilemmas involved in writing about family.

I will be forever indebted to Abha Choudhary, my mother's sister, for her gracious support. My aunt patiently answered questions and forgave my frustration when she could not recall minute details such as the kind of printing press that Babu owned or the name of the movie that Amma screened in Jaipur to raise money for home repairs. She also surprised me many times by remembering, for example, that Babu wrote poems, which he kept but never published, or that we once received a letter from him that was postmarked Pondicherry, the site of Sri Aurobindo's ashram. As her knowledge of English is limited, she did not read the manuscript, and I am deeply grateful to her for trusting me to portray her fairly.

I am also indebted to the late Maitreyi Pathak (who appears in the narrative as Maitreyi didi) for sharing her memories of Amma and Babu—and for persuading Amma to consider a marriage proposal from a landowning family in Bihar. Without her, my mother and father would never have met, and neither I nor this book would exist! Special thanks to my brothers Peeyush Sinha and Amit Choudhary for being keepers of family history. I am especially grateful to Peeyush for his diligence in saving Amma's one surviving diary, and his capacity to pay attention to details often compensated for my lapses in memory.

Two archivists—Antonia Moon, at the British Library, in London, and Vijay Kumar, at the Bihar State Archives, in Patna—went beyond the call of duty in assisting with my research, often directing me to sources that I might otherwise never have found. In an era of shrinking budgets, heightened scrutiny of research activities, and challenges to academic freedom, researchers everywhere should be grateful for such exemplary dedication to ensuring that crucial archival documents are neither destroyed nor hidden away from view.

Thank you to the incredible team at Athabasca University Press for bringing this project to final fruition and, especially, for helping an academic author walk the wholly unfamiliar territory of creative writing. I am immensely grateful to Lesley Peterson for her transformative editing of the manuscript—for her uncanny ability to unclutter my characteristically wordy phrasing while carefully preserving individual voices, for her sensitivity to the overall arc of the narrative, and for her close attention to issues of chronology. I owe a special debt of thanks to Pamela Holway, senior editor at AU Press, whose scholarly background lies in Sanskrit literature and whose knowledge of Indian culture and history proved to be indispensable. This book is the richer for her thoughtful questions and comments and her willingness to enter into narrative, both intellectually and emotionally. I am grateful as well to Megan Hall for her faith in the project and for her help with images and with the book's companion website. Perhaps above all, I thank Athabasca University Press for its ongoing contributions to social justice and equity, not only through the books it publishes but also through its open access policy.

Finally, words are not enough to thank my dear husband, Sanjiv Shrivastava, the eternally patient physicist. He walked with me every step of this arduous but precious journey. His selfless generosity, boundless love, and incisive intellect have been my guide and anchors in times of crisis and uncertainties. No doubt he is as relieved as I am to see this writing project come to a conclusion. Breathe easy, my love, until the next one.

Interviews

———

Prabha Bhaiya, 2 and 3 September 2013, Nagpur

Rakesh Bhaiya (retired professor, S. K. Porwal College, Nagpur), telephone interview, 14 November 2012, face-to-face interview, 2 and 3 September 2013, Nagpur

Abha Choudhary (Dhar), telephone interviews, various dates

Virendra Dangi (lawyer, Jaipur), telephone interview, 15 January 2015

Prem Dave (retired professor, Department of Music, University of Rajasthan, Jaipur), telephone interview, 30 June 2012

Kusum Jain (principal, Maharani College, Jaipur), telephone interview, 2 October 2014

Indira Jena (director, Nirnaya: An Indian Women's Fund, Secunderabad), 13 September 2013, Patna

Vijay Kumar (director, Bihar State Archives, Patna), 13 September 2013, Patna

Navin Lalji (retired engineer, Jaipur), telephone interview, 16 October 2014

Panchanan Misr (retired professor, Department of History, Tilka Manjhi Bhagalpur University), 15 September 2013, Bhagalpur

Anil Nauriya (lawyer, Delhi), email exchanges, November 2014

Apeksha Pendharkar (retired professor, Department of Music, University of Rajasthan, Jaipur), telephone interview, 1 July 2012

Kittu Reddy (Sri Aurobindo International Centre of Education, Pondicherry), 22 September 2013, Pondicherry

Asharani Sahay (a.k.a. Bharti Choudhary) (former lieutenant colonel, Rani of Jhansi Regiment, Azad Hind Fauj), 16 September 2013, Bhagalpur

Sadhna Shrivastava, 12 October 2013, Gurgaon

Ramkumar Singh, 15 September 2013, Bhagalpur
Amita Sinha, 16 September 2013, Bhagalpur
Indra Kumar Sinha, 16 September 2013, Bhagalpur
Kamalapati Sinha, 16 September 2013, Bhagalpur
Kusum Sinha, 12 September 2013, Patna
Niket Sinha, 15 and 16 September 2013, Bhagalpur
Peeyush Sinha, phone and face-to-face interviews, various dates, Mumbai
Rajiv Ranjan Sinha, telephone interviews, 23 and 24 January 2013, face-to-face interview on 8 September 2013, New Delhi
Suresh Kumar Sinha (Mumbai), telephone interviews, 5 and 7 October 2013
Umapati Sinha, 16 September 2013, Bhagalpur
Aruna Srivastava (retired director, National Institute of Malaria Research, Delhi), telephone interview, 12 January 2013
Kusum Tai (oldest surviving resident of Sevagram), 3 September 2013, Wardha
Hemchand Vaidya (director, Rashtra Bhasha Prachar Samiti, Wardha), 3 September 2013, Wardha

Bibliography

Agent to the Governor-General in Rajputana and Chief Commissioner, Ajmer-Merwara. *Report for the First Half of August 1930*. 18 August 1930. 465-PC/30. India Office Records and Private Papers, British Library.

Agrawal, Lion M. G. *Freedom Fighters of India*. 4 vols. New Delhi: Isha Books, 2008.

Alam, Jawaid. *Government and Politics in Colonial Bihar, 1921–1937*. New Delhi: Mittal Publications, 2004.

Bakshi, S. R. *Simon Commission and Indian Nationalism*. New Delhi: Munshiram Manoharlal Publishers, 1977.

Bangladesh Genocide Archive. http://www.genocidebangladesh.org/.

Begum, Farida. "The Creation of Difference: Empire, Race, and the Discourse on Prostitution in Colonial Bengal, 1880–1940." Senior thesis, Barnard College, 2012. https://academiccommons.columbia.edu/catalog/ac:147843.

Bhandari, Rajika. *The Raj on the Move: Story of the Dak Bungalow*. New Delhi: Lotus Collection, Roli Books, 2012.

Bhandari, Sudhanshu. "Prostitution in Colonial India." *Mainstream Weekly* 48, no. 26 (19 June 2010). http://www.mainstreamweekly.net/article2142.html.

Bharti, Indu. "Bihar: Death in Coal Mafia's Den." *Economic and Political Weekly* 26, no. 17 (27 April 1991): 1091.

Bhatkhande, V. N. *Music Systems in India: A Comparative Study of Some of the Leading Music Systems of the 15th, 16th, 17th, and 18th Centuries*. New Delhi: S. Lal, 1984.

Blood, Peter R., ed. *Pakistan: A Country Study*. Washington, DC: Federal Research Division, Library of Congress, 1995. https://www.loc.gov/item/95017247/.

Bor, Joep, Françoise "Nalini" Delvoye, Jane Harvey, and Emmie te Nijenhuis, eds. *Hindustani Music: Thirteenth to Twentieth Centuries*. New Delhi: Manohar Publishers, 2010.

Brecher, Michael. *India and World Politics: Krishna Menon's View of the World*. New York: Frederick A. Praeger, 1968.

Brown, Judith M. "Gandhi, Mohandas Karamchand [Mahatma Gandhi] (1869–1948)." *Oxford Dictionary of National Biography*. Oxford: Oxford University Press, 2004.

Brown, Judith M., and Anthony Parel, eds. *The Cambridge Companion to Gandhi*. Cambridge: Cambridge University Press, 2011.

Carroll, Lucy. "Caste, Community, and Caste Association(s): A Note on the Organization of the Kayastha Conference and the Definition of a Kayastha Community." In *Contributions to Asian Studies,* edited by K. Ishwaran and Bardwell Smith, 10:3–24. Leiden: E. J. Brill, 1977.

Chakrabarty, Bidyut. *Social and Political Thought of Mahatma Gandhi*. London: Routledge, 2006.

Chakravorty, B. C. "Rajasthan Sector: 11 Inf Div Operations." Chap. 8 in *History of the Indo-Pak War, 1965*. S. N. Prasad, chief editor. New Delhi: History Division, Ministry of Defence, Government of India, 1992. https://www.bharat-rakshak.com/archives/OfficialHistory/1965War/1965Chapter08.pdf.

Chatterjee, Manini. "1930: Turning Point in the Participation of Women in the Freedom Struggle." *Social Scientist* 29, no. 7/8 (July–August 2001): 39–47. https://doi.org/10.2307/3518124.

Chatterjee, Partha. *The Nation and Its Fragments: Colonial and Post-Colonial Histories*. Princeton, NJ: Princeton University Press, 1993.

Childs, Sarah. *Women and British Party Politics: Descriptive, Substantive, and Symbolic Representation*. London: Routledge, 2008.

Dalton, Dennis. *Mahatma Gandhi: Nonviolent Power in Action*. New York: Columbia University Press, 1993.

Da'ud, Mulla. *Chandayan: Daud-viracit pratham Hindi Sufi prem-kavya* [The first Sufi love poem composed in Hindi, by Da'ud]. Edited and with an introduction by Mataprasad Gupta. Agra: Pramanik Prakashan, 1967.

Derichs, Claudia, and Mark R. Thompson. *Dynasties and Female Political Leaders in Asia: Gender, Power and Pedigree.* Münster: Lit Verlag, 2013.

Desai, Mahadev H. "Preface." In *Day-to-Day with Gandhi: Secretary's Diary,* edited by Narahari D. Parikh and translated by Hemantkumar G. Nilkanth, vol. 1. Varanasi: Sarva Seva Sangh Prakashan, 1968.

Desai, Miki, and Madhavi Desai. "The Colonial Bungalow in India." *The Newsletter* (International Institute for Asian Studies), no. 57 (Summer 2011): 26–27. https://iias.asia/sites/default/files/IIAS_NL57_2627.pdf.

Desai, Neera, and Usha Thakkar. *Women in Indian Society.* New Delhi: National Book Trust, 2001.

Deshpande, Vamanrao H. *Between Two Tanpuras.* Translated by Ram Deshmukh and B. R. Dhekney. Bombay: Popular Prakashan, 1989.

Devi, Meera. "Role of Women in the National Movement in U.P., 1919–47." PhD diss., University of Allahabad, 1982.

———. *Swatantrya sangram ki uttar pradeshiya veerangnayen* [The heroic women of Uttar Pradesh in the struggle for independence]. Lucknow: Bharat Prakashan, 2011.

Django. "The Mining Industry and Miners' Struggles in India." *Libcom.org,* 2001. https://libcom.org/library/mining-industry-miners-struggles-india.

"Dumraon (Zamindari)." *Indian Princely States.* 13 December 2016. http://members.iinet.net.au/~royalty/ips/d/dumraon.html.

Fischer-Tiné, Harald. "'White Women Degrading Themselves to the Lowest Depths': European Networks of Prostitution and Colonial Anxieties in British India and Ceylon ca. 1880–1914." *Indian Economic and Social History Review* 40, no. 2 (June 2003): 163–90.

Forbes, Geraldine. "The Politics of Respectability: Indian Women and the Indian National Congress." In *The Indian National Congress: Centenary Hindsights,* edited by D. A. Low, 54–97. New Delhi: Oxford University Press, 1988.

———. *Women in Modern India.* Vol. 4, pt. 2, of *The New Cambridge History of India.* Cambridge: Cambridge University Press, 1996.

Gandhi, Mohandas Karamchand [Mahatma Gandhi]. *An Autobiography: or, The Story of My Experiments with Truth.* Translated by Mahadev Desai. 2nd ed. Ahmedabad: Navajivan Publishing House, 1948.

———. *The Essential Gandhi: An Anthology of His Writings on His Life, Work, and Ideas.* Edited by Louis Fischer. New York: Vintage Books, 2002.

———. *Women and Social Injustice*. Ahmedabad: Navajivan Publishing House, 1942.

Gandhi, Rajmohan. *Gandhi: The Man, His People, and the Empire*. Berkeley: University of California Press, 2008.

Ghosh, S. K. *The Indian Mafia*. New Delhi: Ashish Publishing House, 1991.

Gonsalves, Peter. *Khadi: Gandhi's Mega Symbol of Subversion*. New Delhi: Sage Publications, 2012.

Grover, Verinder, ed. *Dr. Rajendra Prasad: A Biography of His Vision and Ideas*. New Delhi: Deep and Deep Publications, 1993.

Habib, Irfan. *Essays in Indian History: Towards a Marxist Perception*. New Delhi: Tulika, 1995.

Handa, Rajendra Lal. *Rajendra Prasad: Twelve Years of Triumph and Despair*. New Delhi: Sterling Publishers, 1979.

Jack, Homer A., ed. *The Gandhi Reader: A Source Book of His Life and Writings*. New York: Grove Press, 1994.

Jena, Indira. *Her Story: A Narration of Women in the National Freedom Struggle in Orissa and Bihar*. New Delhi: Pustak Mandir, 1999.

Karve, Irawati. *Kinship Organisation in India*. 3rd ed. London: Asia Publishing House, 1968.

Kaur, Manmohan. *Role of Women in the National Movement*. New Delhi: Sterling Publishers, 1968.

Kripalani, Sucheta. *Sucheta: An Unfinished Autobiography*. Edited by K. N. Vaswani. Ahmedabad: Navajivan Publishing House, 1978.

Kumar, Nirmal. *Rajendra Prasad and the Indian Freedom Struggle, 1917–1947*. New Delhi: Patriot Publishers, 1991.

Kumar, Radha. *The History of Doing: An Illustrated Account of Movements for Women's Rights and Feminism in India, 1800–1990*. London: Verso, 1993.

Lamb, Sarah. *White Saris and Sweet Mangoes: Aging, Gender, and Body in North India*. Berkeley: University of California Press, 2000.

Legg, Stephen. "Gendered Politics and Nationalised Homes: Women and the Anti-colonial Struggle in Delhi, 1930–47." *Gender, Place and Culture: A Journal of Feminist Geography* 10, no. 1 (2003): 7–27.

Madan, G. R. *Indian Social Problems*. Vol. 2, *Social Disorganization and Reconstruction*. New Delhi: Allied Publishers, 1967.

Malaviya, Madan Mohan. "The Congress Women-Volunteer Case of Benaras: A Criticism of the District Magistrate's Judgement." 1932. 267/216–276/POL. National Archives of India.

Marlay, Ross, and Clark Neher. *Patriots and Tyrants: Ten Asian Leaders.* Lanham, MD: Rowman and Littlefield, 1999.

Mohanty, Chandra Talpade, Ann Russo, and Lourdes Torres, eds. *Cartographies of Struggle: Third World Women and the Politics of Feminism.* Bloomington: Indiana University Press, 1991.

Moraes, Frank. *Jawaharlal Nehru—a Biography.* Mumbai: Jaico Publishing House, 2007.

Mundargi, Tirumal. "Congress and Zamindars: Collaboration and Consultation in Bihar, 1915–36." *Economic and Political Weekly* 25, no. 22 (2 June 1990): 1217–22.

Nauriya, Anil. *English Anti-imperialism and the Varied Lights of Willie Pearson.* NMML Occasional Paper, History and Society, New Series, no. 57. New Delhi: Nehru Memorial Museum and Library, 2014. http://www.nehrumemorial.nic.in/images/pdf/Anil_Nauriya_web_final_8_August.pdf.

———. "Some Did Not Seek Clemency: Pandit Parmanand of Jhansi." *Indian Express,* 1 March 2001. http://www.scribd.com/doc/93896220/Pandit-Parmanand-of-Jhansi.

Norvell, Lyn. "Gandhi and the Indian Women's Movement." *British Library Journal* 23, no. 1 (1997): 12–27.

Parekh, Bhikhu. *Gandhi: A Very Short Introduction.* Oxford: Oxford University Press, 2001.

Pratap, Mahendra. *Afghanistan: The Heart of Aryan.* Peping, China: World Federation, 1919. http://www.saadigitalarchive.org/item/20121213-1150.

Pritchett, Frances W. "The History of Indian Publishing: A Note on Sources." *India International Centre Quarterly* 10, no. 4 (December 1983): 467–71.

Pudaruth, Santosh Kumar. "A Reflection on the Aesthetics of Indian Music, with Special Reference to *Hindustani Raga-Sangita*." *SAGE Open* 6, no. 4 (October 2016). https://doi.org/10.1177/2158244016674512.

Ramaswamy, Vijaya. "Gender and the Writing of South Indian History." In *Approaches to History: Essays in Indian Historiography,* edited by Sabyasachi Bhattacharya, 199–224. New Delhi: Primus Books, in association with the Indian Council of Historical Research, 2011.

Rathore, Sharad. *Royalty in Transition: The Changing Face of the Rajput Woman in Rajasthan.* New Delhi: Rupa Publications, 2010.

Roy, A. K. "Fighting the Dhanbad Mafia: Life and Death of Gurudas Chatterjee." *Economic and Political Weekly* 35, no. 20 (13 May 2000): 1701–3.

Rudolph, Susanne Hoeber, and Lloyd I. Rudolph. *Gandhi: The Traditional Roots of Charisma*. Chicago: University of Chicago Press, 1983.

Ryder, Arthur William, ed. and trans. *The Little Clay Cart (Mṛchhakaṭika): A Hindu Drama Attributed to King Shūdraka*. Cambridge, MA: Harvard University Press, 1905. https://ia801401.us.archive.org/16/items/littleclaycartm01rydegoog/littleclaycartm01rydegoog.pdf.

Sachdev, Vibhuti, and Giles Tillotson. *Building Jaipur: The Making of an Indian City*. London: Reaktion Books, 2004.

Sangari, Kumkum. "Mirabai and the Spiritual Economy of Bhakti." *Economic and Political Weekly* 25, no. 28 (14 July 1990): 1537–52.

Sangari, Kumkum, and Sudesh Vaid, eds. *Recasting Women: Essays in Indian Colonial History*. New Brunswick, NJ: Rutgers University Press, 1990.

Sarkar, Jadunath. *A History of Jaipur, c. 1503 to 1938*. Revised and edited by Raghubir Sinh. Hyderabad: Orient Longman, 1994.

Sarkar, Sumit. *Beyond Nationalist Frames: Relocating Postmodernism, Hindutva, History*. New Delhi: Permanent Black, 2002.

———. *Modern India, 1885–1947*. New Delhi: Macmillan India, 1983.

———. *"Popular Movements" and "Middle Class" Leadership in Late Colonial India: Perspectives and Problems of a "History from Below."* Calcutta: K. P. Bagchi, for the Centre for Studies in Social Sciences, 1983.

———. "Post-Modernism and the Writing of History." *Studies in History* 15, no. 2 (1 August 1999): 293–322. https://doi.org/10.1177/025764309901500205.

———. *Writing Social History*. New Delhi: Oxford University Press, 1998.

Sen, Amartya. "India's Women: The Mixed Truth." *New York Review of Books,* 10 October 2013. http://www.nybooks.com/articles/archives/2013/oct/10/indias-women-mixed-truth/?pagination=false.

———. "Missing Women." *British Medical Journal* 304, no. 6827 (7 March 1992): 587–88. https://www.bmj.com/content/bmj/304/6827/587.full.pdf.

———. "Missing Women—Revisited: Reduction in Female Mortality Has Been Counterbalanced by Sex Selective Abortions." *British Medical Journal* 327, no. 7427 (6 December 2003): 1297–98. https://www.ncbi.nlm.nih.gov/pmc/articles/PMC286281/.

———. *Poverty and Famines: An Essay on Entitlement and Deprivation.* Oxford: Clarendon Press, 1981.

Sharma, Jai Narain. *Satyagraha: Gandhi's Approach to Conflict Resolution.* New Delhi: Concept Publishing, 2008.

Sharma, Sadhna. *State Politics in India.* New Delhi: Mittal Publications, 1995.

Shrivastava, Meenal. "Invisible Women in History and Global Studies: Reflections from an Archival Research Project." *Globalizations* 14, no. 2 (16 March 2016).

Singh, Thakur Jaidev. *Bharatiya sangeet ka itihas* [A history of Indian music]. Calcutta: ITC Sangeet Research Academy, 1994.

Singh, Vir. *The Life and Times of Raja Mahendra Pratap.* New Delhi: Low Price Publications, 2005.

Sinha, Mrinalini. "Gender in the Critiques of Colonialism and Nationalism: Locating the 'Indian Woman.'" In *Women and Social Reform in Modern India: A Reader,* edited by Sumit Sarkar and Tanika Sarkar, 452–72. Bloomington: Indiana University Press, 2008.

Sinha, Prakashwati. *Smriti ki shrinkhalayen* [A chain of memories]. Jaipur: Vaishali Press, 1963.

Sinha, Surekha. *Bharatiya raag peeyush* [The ragas of India—a fountain of nectar]. Jaipur: Vaishali Press, 1988.

———. *Bharatiya raagankur* [Flowering buds from India's ragas]. Jaipur: Shyaam Prakashan.

———. *Madhyayugin shastriya sangeet ke aadhar stambh-ashtasakha* [The eight essential poet-devotees who stand at the foundations of medieval classical music]. Jaipur: Panchsheel Prakashan, 1997.

———. *Man ki pukaar* [A cry of the spirit]. Jaipur: Sahityagar Prakashan, 2008.

———. *Man veena* [Melodies from the lute of the soul]. Jaipur: Sahityagar Prakashan, 2008.

———. *Pahari Baba.* Jaipur: Sahityagar Prakashan, 2008.

———. *Sailaab* [Outpourings]. Jaipur: Sahityagar Prakashan, 2007.

———. *Sangeet chintan* [Musical meditations]. Jaipur: Panchsheel Prakashan, 2008.

———. *Us dhoop ki chhaanh* [Some shade from that burning sun]. Jaipur: Sahityagar Prakashan, 2011.

Sofri, Gianni. *Gandhi and India: A Century in Focus.* Translated by Janet Sethre Paxia. Moreton-in-Marsh, UK: Windrush Press, 1999.

Spear, Percival. *A History of India, Volume 2: From the Sixteenth Century to the Twentieth Century.* Rev. ed. London: Penguin, 1990.

———. *Master of Bengal: Clive and His India.* London: Thames and Hudson, 1975.

Stille, Alexander. "The Body Under the Rug." *New York Times,* 10 February 2013. https://opinionator.blogs.nytimes.com/2013/02/09/the-body-under-the-rug/.

"Suggestions for Dealing with Women Who Take Part in the Civil Disobedience Campaign" and "Suggestions for Amendment of Section 28 of the Emergency Powers Ordinance." Documents dated 30 December 1931 to 22 January 1932. Government of India, Home Department, Political Branch, file no. 14/4. India Office: Public and Judicial Department Records, 1795–1950. L/P&J/4727. India Office Records and Private Papers, British Library.

Thapar, Romila. *The Penguin History of Early India: From the Origins to AD 1300.* London: Penguin, 2003.

Thapar-Björkert, Suruchi. *Women in the Indian National Movement: Unseen Faces and Unheard Voices, 1930–42.* New Delhi: Sage Publications, 2006.

Tharoor, Shashi. *Nehru: The Invention of India.* New York: Arcade Publishing, 2003.

Tharu, Susie, and K. Lalita, eds. *Women Writing in India: 600 B.C. to the Present.* Vol. 1, *600 B.C to the Early 20th Century.* New York: Feminist Press at CUNY, 1991.

Theilemann, Selina. *Divine Service and the Performing Arts in India.* New Delhi: APH Publishing, 2002.

Thomas, Paul. *Indian Women Through the Ages: A Historical Survey of the Position of Women and the Institutions of Marriage and Family in India from Remote Antiquity to the Present Day.* Bombay: Asia Publishing, 1964.

Thorat, Ashok. "Cultural Reflections in Address Terms and Greetings: An Indian Example." In *Language in Life and a Life in Language: Jacob Mey—a Festschrift,* edited by Bruce Fraser and Ken Turner, 393–98. Leiden: E. J. Brill, 2009.

Tillotson, Giles. *Jaipur Nama: Tales from the Pink City.* New Delhi: Penguin, 2006.

Wolpert, Stanley. *India.* 4th ed. Berkeley: University of California Press, 2009.